NATIONAL GEOGRAPHIC

TRAVELER

Amsterdam

NATIONAL GEOGRAPHIC
TRAVELER
Amsterdam

Christopher Catling

Contents

How to use this guide 6–7 About the author 8
Amsterdam areas 45–234 Travelwise 235–265
Index 266–269 Credits 270–71

Page 1: On the go in
Amsterdam
Pages 2–3: Canalside café and
glass-topped tour boat
Left: Boats and bikes—the best
way to navigate the city

How to use this guide

See back flap for keys to text and map symbols

The *National Geographic Traveler* brings you the best of Amsterdam in text, pictures, and maps. Divided into three main sections, the guide begins with an overview of history and culture. Following are six area chapters with featured sites selected by the author for their particular interest and treated in depth. A final chapter suggests possible excursions from Amsterdam.

The selected areas within the city and the surrounding regions are arranged geographically. A map introduces each chapter, highlighting the featured sites. Walks, drives, cycle, and boat rides, plotted on their own maps, suggest routes for discovering an area. Features and sidebars give intriguing detail on history, culture, or contemporary life.

The final section, Travelwise, lists essential information for the traveler—pretrip planning, special events, getting around, emergencies, and a glossary—together with a selection of hotels, restaurants, shops, and entertainment.

To the best of our knowledge, all information is accurate as of the press date. However, it's always advisable to call ahead when possible.

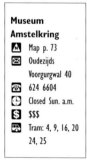

Color coding

130

Each area of the city is color coded for easy reference. Find the area you want on the map on the front flap, and look for the color flash at the top of the pages of the relevant chapter. Information in **Travelwise** is also color coded to each area.

Visitor information

Museum Amstelkring

- Map p. 73
- Oudezijds Voorgurgwal 40
- 624 6604
- Closed Sun. a.m.
- $$$
- Tram: 4, 9, 16, 20 24, 25

Practical information for most sites is given in the side column (see key to symbols on back flap). The map reference gives the page number of the map and grid reference. Other details are address, telephone number, days closed, entrance charge in a range from $ (under $4) to $$$$$ (over $25), and nearest public transportation in Amsterdam. Other sites have information in italics and parentheses in the text.

TRAVELWISE

THE NORTHERN CANALS

Color-coded area name

RENAISSANCE
$$$$ – $$$$$

Hotel name & price range

KATTENGAT 1.
TEL 621 2223
FAX 627 5245

Address, telephone, & fax numbers

A short step from the station and the buzzing commercial center, the Renaissance enjoys a quiet and scenic location at the start of the canal circle.

Brief description of hotel

405
All major cards

Hotel facilities & credit card details

SAMBO SECO
$$$

Restaurant name & price range

P.C. HOOFTSTRAAT 27
TEL 662 8146

Address, & telephone number

Smart Indonesian restaurant set in the trendiest street in Amsterdam. Wonderful traditional *rijsstaffel*.

Brief description of restaurant

40 Closed Sun
2, 3, 5, 20
All major cards

Restaurant closures & credit card details

Hotel & restaurant prices

An explanation of the price bands used in entries is given in the Hotels & Restaurants section (on p. 244).

AREA MAPS

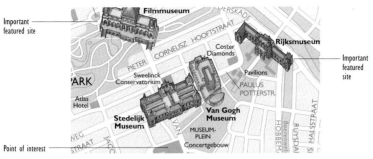

Important featured site

Important featured site

Point of interest

- A locator map accompanies each regional map and shows the location of that region in the city.
- Adjacent regions are shown, each with a page reference.

WALKING TOURS

Building outline

Walk route

Red numbered bullets link site on map to descriptions in the text

Direction of walk route

Featured site (in bold) on walk route

Alternative walk route

Point of interest not on walk route

- An information box gives the starting and ending points, time and length of walk, and places not to be missed along the route.
- Where two walks are marked on the map, the second route is shown in orange.

EXCURSION MAPS

Map reference

Point of interest

Important featured town

Road number

- An information box provides details including starting and finishing points, time and length of drive, and places not to be missed along the route, or tips on terrain.

NATIONAL GEOGRAPHIC
TRAVELER
Amsterdam

About the author

Christopher Catling, a member of the British Guild of Travel Writers, has worked as an author for 21 years. He has written more than 40 guidebooks, including top-selling titles on Venice and the Veneto, Florence and Tuscany. He is also a major contributor to websites and multimedia products such as *Expedia*, *Encarta*, and *AutoRoute Express*.

Catling fell in love with Amsterdam and its easygoing ways in 1987, when he was sent there to write a city guide for business travelers. He has since returned numerous times, allowing him to indulge his passions for art, architecture, and archaeology. Catling's mission in life is to encourage others to view the cultural environment as a resource equally worth preserving as the natural world. When not traveling or writing, Catling can be found walking with his family, playing the violin, or perfecting his surfing.

History & culture

Detail from Jan Vermeer's "The Kitchen Maid," in the Rijksmuseum

Amsterdam today

GEERT MAK, THE DUTCH JOURNALIST AND HISTORIAN, ARGUES THAT THE Netherlands has two types of people: the dike diggers and farmers who focus their lives around one small plot of ground, and the sailors and colonialists who look to the horizon and beyond. Amsterdammers are very definitely of the second type. They have never been afraid of sticking their necks out, of going out on a limb. This is what makes Amsterdam on the one hand such a maddening city, and on the other such an inspiration.

THE BIG VILLAGE

Despite the millions who visit the city every year, Amsterdam manages to retain the feel of a big village, and that is an important part of its charm. Big-town bustle is to be expected on the main shopping drag, from Centraal Station down Damrak and along Kalverstraat to Rembrandtplein. But step aside from this pulsating artery and you suddenly find yourself lost in the maze of Amsterdam's Grachtengordel (Canal Circle), exploring quiet leafy streets or cloistered courtyards of almost medieval charm. These are streets where people still live—the city center hasn't been totally colonized by offices and shops. Even the mayor travels about by bicycle and on public transportation so that he can listen to people's conversations, and find out what issues they really care about.

If you stay more than a few days in the city, you, too, will become part of this village community. Settling in is made so much easier by the sociability and linguistic dexterity of many Amsterdammers, who learn English, German, and French from an early age, and seem to have equal fluency in all three (not to mention their own language, Dutch). English, the language of pop music, movies, TV, and the Internet, is the one that Amsterdammers use most naturally and, unlike the French, whose language academy fiercely guards the purity of their native tongue, the Dutch seem pretty relaxed about mixing Dutch and English in the same sentence.

AMSTERDAM'S ETHNIC COMMUNITIES

If Amsterdam is a village in atmosphere rather than a colorless metropolis, it is a village with world dimensions. The diversity of faces on the street and the sheer range of restaurants in Amsterdam testifies to the fact that the city has a large ethnic population. Some 24.3 percent of the city's residents come from Turkey, Morocco, Surinam, Guyana, the Caribbean, China, and Indonesia. Bijlmermeer, in the city's southern suburbs, is jokingly referred to as the second biggest city in Surinam, because of its 35,000 Surinamese inhabitants.

Amsterdam's ethnic population is close-knit and inward looking. The Muslim community, in particular, finds itself at odds with a city that is so open-minded about drugs, alcohol, and sex, even though that same tolerance is responsible for a positive respect for minority rights, from which Muslims benefit greatly. The city's ethnic communities make their most visible contribution to the city's culture through food—Albert Cuypstraat's market stalls are piled high with exotic fruits and vegetables, and the spicy and varied cuisine of the Indonesian islands is a popular choice in a city whose native culinary staples are pea soup and mashed vegetables. By taking over and rejuvenating the Nieuwmarkt area of central Amsterdam, the Chinese community has made a much more emphatic contribution to the city's culture, and the opening of the He Wa Buddhist Temple in Zeedijk is certainly an optimistic sign of things to come.

AMSTERDAM'S UNIQUE STYLE

Despite all this cosmopolitanism, Amsterdammers retain a sentimental affection for those features of the city that are truly Dutch: The jaunty sound of barrel organs, the pealing carillons that play hymns or snatches from Beethoven to mark the passing of the hours, the comforting taste and vanilla scent of pancakes or waffles, or the cheerful sight of a well-

Almost everyone gets around by bike in this city of level streets and environmentally conscious citizens.

arranged bunch of flowers. This sentimental-
ity goes by the name of *gezelligheid,* which is
almost impossible to translate in any mean-
ingful way. Ask Amsterdammers to explain it
and they are more likely to give you examples
of gezelligheid, rather than a direct translation, because the English word coziness
sounds far too corny.

For a resident of the Jordaan, gezelligheid
might be singing songs around a piano in a
crowded brown café on a Saturday night. To a

university lecturer living in the Plantage, by
contrast, it could be listening to the music of
Sweelinck on a 17th-century organ in the
Oude Kerk. To others it is simply letting their
hair down with friends, losing track of time
in reminiscence, or gossiping over coffee in
a waterside café.

Wander the canal circle at night, staring
into the brightly lit, book-lined interiors of the
houses, and you may conclude—correctly—
that Amsterdammers are avid readers. The fact

that you can glimpse such intimate detail at all is another endearing feature of the city—the habit of leaving curtains and blinds open at night, to reveal chic spotlit interiors, striking works of art, and carefully chosen pieces of furniture.

Some say that this habit of showcasing one's interior derives from a moralistic desire to prove that you are a clean-living citizen—in effect saying, "Look through my windows; I have nothing to hide." In reality, it may

Leidseplein is the meeting place between visitors and native Amsterdammers looking for a relaxed ambience.

just be showing off—more a case of people advertising to friends and passersby what good taste they have. Whatever the reason, it adds pleasure to the experience of walking the streets of Amsterdam—almost like strolling through the pages of an interior design magazine.

LIBERAL ATTITUDES

The immaculate decor and preference for gleaming white that characterizes so many Amsterdam homes contrasts ironically with the often squalid state of the city's streets. Annoying aspects of the city include the graffiti that scars so many beautiful historic buildings, the drug addicts who hang around Centraal Station, and the prostitutes of the Red Light District. Dutch visitors from the provinces are often shocked by what they find in their capital. Amsterdam is very different from their own neat towns and villages, where it is a social crime not to keep your house immaculately painted, your windows gleaming and curtained with lace, your garden planted with a tasteful display of colorful plants.

Many people have tried to explain this apparent contradiction—how friendly, sociable, and moralistic Amsterdam, so endearing in many ways, can also be a byword for some of

humankind's worst excesses. What is it about the city and its people that allows the squalid and the cultured to coexist?

Perhaps it's the city's famous "tolerance," which dates back at least to the 17th century, when religious free-thinkers were welcomed, Jewish refugees given a home, printing presses encouraged, and brothels licensed and managed by civil servants responsible to the city council.

The people themselves say that it results from a love of individual freedom and a hatred

Easygoing Amsterdam has always encouraged the expression of eccentricity in its many different forms.

of hypocrisy. That in turn leads to the Amsterdam state of mind that says, "I don't like what you are doing, but I recognize that I have no right to interfere with your rights if I don't want you to interfere with mine." There is a logic here that acknowledges that personal freedoms are only available to those who, in

turn, seek to impose no constraints on their neighbors.

It is an attitude that has much in common with the ideals of such Enlightenment philosophers as Thomas Paine (1737–1809), whose treatise on *The Rights of Man* (1792) had a considerable impact on the contents of the United States Constitution. But Amsterdam has gone further in terms of radical public policy than many an American state would tolerate. Here cannabis dealers and prostitutes are not locked up; they are respected, tax-paying citizens whose views count and who are valued members of the local chamber of commerce.

Everyone in Amsterdam agrees that social experiments are worth making, but there is also much talk about how to deal with the unexpected consequences. There is no doubt that Amsterdam's popularity as Europe's number-one weekend destination has much to do with the easy availability of drugs and

sex. Even the most liberal-minded citizens have begun to wonder whether things haven't gotten out of hand.

All this begs the question of just how far personal freedoms should go—and this is where logic fails to provide an answer. There is no obvious line to be drawn between what is acceptable and what is not. When not discussing the performance of Ajax, the local soccer team, people spend hours arguing over this topic, turning the city's brown cafés (so

The view from Westerkerk overlooks the Jordaan, where refugees have found a new home throughout the centuries.

called because of the mellow patina of their tobacco-stained, wood-paneled walls) into mini debating chambers. Newspapers and TV programs contribute to the discussion, and somehow a broad consensus is reached between the extremes of conservatism and liberality.

Squatters seize empty houses to protest against the high cost of housing and lack of less expensive homes for first-time buyers in the city.

RECLAIMING THE STREETS

Every so often, Amsterdammers get the chance to make their views known via the ballot box. In recent years, they have backed mayors who have promised more conservative policies, and in particular the need to reclaim parts of the city that have become no-go areas for ordinary people.

One conspicuously successful example of social experiment is the cleaning up of the Zeedijk area, once the notorious haunt of heroin pushers. In a model of cooperation between the city council and property owners, Zeedijk's shored-up and rat-infested buildings were comprehensively restored during the 1990s. The district is now home to streets rich in character, lined by a mix of small bars, restaurants, and antique shops, and the bustling carryouts and grocery stores of Chinatown. The He Wa Buddhist Temple, which opened here in 2001, is a sign of the optimism of the local community, although the junkies and dealers have not left the city, just moved to a different area.

Zeedijk's success has encouraged the city council to embark on other restoration schemes. In 2000, the wind- and rain-swept parking lot for buses that lay behind the Van Gogh Museum was comprehensively re-landscaped, with expensive stone paving and swaths of green, dotted with modernist pavilions serving as cafés and museum shops. During 2001, the cobbles and tram tracks of Dam Square were ripped up to transform this windy wasteland into a more attractive Italian-style piazza.

Amsterdam's pedestrian shopping streets, which run into Dam Square, are cleaned every morning. If you get up early enough, you will see the cleaners making their way down the streets, removing graffiti from buildings and chewing gum from the pavements. Perhaps this is an exercise in futility, given that the next day the streets will be littered with discarded gum again, but it does indicate a refreshingly new attitude of intolerance to urban debris—as do plans to issue on-the-spot fines to people who urinate in the streets, to dog owners who do not clean up after their pets, and to cyclists who stray onto the sidewalk or disobey traffic lights.

THE SQUATTER MOVEMENT

This would not be Amsterdam, of course, if everyone agreed that the clean-up was entirely a good thing. There are others who like the city to be gritty, not prissy, and they say that too much pandering to middle-class values takes the spirit out of the place. Amsterdammers subscribing to this view protested furiously at the construction of the Stadhuis-Muziektheater complex on the edge of the Jodenbuurt district in the 1980s. To clear the site so that construction work could begin, the police had to wage urban warfare, battling with squatters building by building to evict protesters who demanded cheap homes, not elitist opera and ballet.

Because it is no longer in the news, many people mistakenly believe that the squatter movement died out in the 1980s. In reality, it is still alive and as well-organized as the business empires that it exists to challenge. Known as *Krakers,* the squatters have their own Internet site, magazine, and TV program. As recently as 2001, squatters occupied the former Planet Hollywood restaurant in a former movie theater on Reguliersbreestraat, refusing to move on the grounds that the plan to build luxury apartments was immoral. Eventually they were evicted by police using tear gas and water cannon.

CITY OF ARTISTIC ENDEAVOR

The squatters wanted to turn the Planet Hollywood building into an arts center. Some would argue that Amsterdam has more than enough homes for art already. In this city, alternative culture is the mainstream, and this is recognized in generous state subsidies to help artists in the difficult years at the start of their careers. State-funded, interest-free loans, repayable over many years, also encourage ordinary people to become art patrons and invest in modern art. Art is interpreted liberally, covering photography and video, dance and drama, as well as painting and sculpture.

Some argue that even this isn't enough. A particular concern is the high cost of city-center property. Even in the formerly working-class Jordaan district, the haunt of artists and artisans a decade ago, it is hard to find affordable space suitable for use as a studio. Critics argue that the city lacks *broedplaatsen,*

Storming the barricades

The metal pillars that separate pavements from road space in Amsterdam—nearly as much a part of the city scene as the battered bicycle—are to be abolished. Standing about 2 feet (60 cm) high and bearing the triple cross of the city's coat of arms, the pillars serve to cordon off from the road the generous amount of space allotted to pedestrians in the canal circle.

Most of the pillars display a history of battering; they have been knocked askew by heedless motorists or by harried truck drivers delivering goods to city-center stores. Because maintaining the pillars costs too much, they are scheduled for replacement by decade's end with raised curb stones, painted yellow. ■

breeding spaces, where young artists can find their métier through experimentation and involvement with a community of fellow artists at different stages of their careers.

The big new arts complex being built in the Oosterdok (Eastern Docks), opening in 2002, may go some way to answering this need. The fact that it is being built at all is some recognition of the important role that the arts play in the city's overall economic mix, for Amsterdam is a city of artistic and intellectual endeavor. As well as being one of the world's biggest markets for books, it is a major publishing center in its own right, with global businesses based here producing textbooks, directories, art and reference books, and magazines. The city has more than its fair share of architects, composers, moviemakers, and journalists, inspired by the freedom to be just what they wish.

WEALTH & STATUS

Per capita income in Amsterdam is very high—toward the top of the European league. All this prosperity adds up to a lot of people wanting to live in the heart of the old city. A stylish canal house is the ultimate status symbol, and desperate measures are sometimes employed to get to the head of the line

when houses become available. Househunters have even been known to read newspaper obituaries to identify houses that might become available because of the death of their owners. Such interest in living in a historic home explains why, even now, formerly run-down areas of the city center are being transformed into the spacious luxury apartments that are so in demand.

One area of the city remains unclaimed. Wander down the leafy canals of the Red Light District and look up, above the neon-lit windows and sex shops, to see just how beautiful and varied the canalside houses are. Such charming buildings would make very desirable apartments, but the owners can make so much money at present from renting to prostitutes that they can afford to leave the upper rooms unoccupied. Will Amsterdam's Red Light District some day turn into a property speculator's dream or a polite bourgeois district full of wealthy professionals

working in banking, financial services, or in-formation technology?

The very thought is enough to evoke a wave of public antipathy. Most Amsterdam-mers are adventurers at heart, people who eschew the safe and comfortable solutions to the dilemmas of life, who prefer the city to be a challenging, refuge from conventionality.

The appeal of Amsterdam in this respect has been well summed up by Geert Mak, a journalist and a professor of urban studies at

Prostitution in Amsterdam—legal, profitable, and well-organized—is as old as the city.

the University of Amsterdam. In a newspaper article published in 1995, Mak observed that "Amsterdam remains the refuge of all those striving to free themselves from the stifling atmosphere of small communities, and that too forms part of the city's strength and vitality." ■

History of Amsterdam

ONE QUESTION FASCINATES EVERYONE WHO STUDIES AMSTERDAM'S history: How did a bog-ridden, one-street town, founded as a squatter community by a bunch of lawless fishermen, grow to become the dynamic hub of one of Europe's most powerful mercantile nations?

ORIGINS

Archaeologists date the origins of the city to around 1175, when the first settlers put down roots, living in a huddle of fishing huts built on the low marshy banks of the Amstel River. This land formed part of the vast estates of the wealthy Bishops of Utrecht, but nobody had previously made any attempts to colonize it because the whole region was subject to catastrophic floods. These early inhabitants lived a difficult life, but at least they were free—owing no taxes or feudal duties to any landlord, whether religious or secular.

THE AMSTEL GETS ITS DAM

Over the next 200 years, the squatter settlement turned into a thriving and cosmopolitan commercial center, whose original shape can still be traced as you walk the streets of the modern city.

Amsterdam stands at the point where the Amstel River joins the IJ, then a shallow, fish-filled inland sea. Just before it joins the IJ, the Amstel River splits into several branches. One of these is now paved over to form Damrak, the city's main street, but originally it was a waterway, which the first settlers sealed off by building a dam. Using sluices to control the level of the water on the river side, and a lock gate to allow boats in and out, Damrak thus became a natural harbor where boats could unload their goods onto the bank side. This dam is what gave the city its rather prosaic name: Amsterdam (originally Amstellredamme) simply means "the Amstel dam."

Several of the long streets running parallel to the Damrak include the place-name elements *voorburgwal* and *achterburgwal*, meaning "before the wall" and "behind the wall." They mark the line of the town's first defensive ramparts and palisade. The area within these walls is still known locally as Wallen (Walls).

This area was depicted in the earliest map of Amsterdam, a bird's-eye view drawn by Cornelius Anthoniszoon in 1534, now in the Amsterdam Historical Museum (see pp. 64–67).

FROM FISHING VILLAGE TO COSMOPOLITAN PORT

The first documentary reference to the new settlement appears in a parchment preserved in the city archives and dated October 27, 1275. Bearing the seal of Floris V, Count of Holland, this grants "the people abiding near the Amsteldam" the right to travel freely within the County of Holland without paying tolls when using bridges and locks.

Floris no doubt bestowed this privilege on Amsterdam in order to gain the town's support in his bid to wrest territorial control from the Bishop of Utrecht. Floris wanted to extend the border of Holland northward to incorporate Amsterdam, but he was thwarted by the powerful bishop, who sent in one of his henchmen to assassinate him. This sparked a war in which Amsterdam unexpectedly took the bishop's side by giving refuge to the Count's assassin. William II, son and successor to Floris V, took revenge by laying siege to Amsterdam, which surrendered after two weeks. William vented his anger by tearing down the walls and revoking the town's privileges. Later, magnanimous in victory, he relented and in 1300 the town received a new charter, granting the residents the right to elect their own council, pass their own laws, police their own streets, and try miscreants in their own courts.

These were very substantial freedoms and privileges in a feudal age, and the charter was certainly one of the factors instrumental in Amsterdam's transformation from a fishing

The Dutch cog ship in this Oude Kerk window brought riches to many an Amsterdam merchant.

village to one of the most powerful cities in northern Europe. Here, traders, merchants, bankers, craftsmen, and other members of the emergent urban middle class could live and prosper; they could take control of their own lives, free of the feudal obligations that enslaved so many of their country-dwelling contemporaries.

THE SHIP OF TRADE

One other crucial factor that helped Amsterdam flourish was the invention in the 14th century of the cog—a sturdy, broad-beamed, seagoing cargo ship with a capacity ten times greater than that of existing vessels. It opened up a new era in European trade by making it cheap and safe to transport basic commodities over long distances by sea, so much so that historians have likened the impact of the cog to that of the jumbo jet in our own age.

Until the invention of the cog, most goods in Europe had traveled by coastal vessel or by packhorse and riverboat, attracting tolls and taxes en route that greatly added to their cost. Safe, cheap, and efficient sea transport changed all that. Wool, grain, salt, and timber could now be transported much more cheaply by sea from northern Europe, where they were in abundant supply, to southern Europe, where they were in demand. These ships returned laden with luxury goods from the Mediterranean, from Arabia, and from the Orient—silks, spices, perfumes, wines, and dried fruits.

Amsterdam's entrepreneurial shipbuilders and merchants were quick to latch onto the opportunities presented by this new seaborne

trade. At first, Amsterdam was simply one of several port towns located around the Baltic and the North Sea to enjoy growing commercial prosperity. Soon enough, however, it began to compete with the others by offering lower import duties and customs levies, thus eclipsing much bigger and far longer-established places such as Antwerp and Bruges (Brugge).

The Dutch cog symbolizes Amsterdam's success as a city of trade. The triple cross was stamped on goods leaving Amsterdam as a mark of high quality.

AMSTERDAM MIRACLE

In addition to being a city of entrepreneurs, Amsterdam was a deeply religious city, with numerous churches, chapels, and convents. In 1345, the first of a series of miracles occurred that was to turn it into a pilgrimage center important enough to attract prestigious visitors, including a succession of Holy Roman Emperors and their entourages.

The miracle happened when a dying man was given Communion as part of the last rites. He vomited and the mess was thrown into the fire. The next day, the Communion host was found pristine and intact, having survived mastication, ingestion, and burning. Visitors to the site of the miracle soon began reporting other miraculous occurrences: The sick and dying were healed and when word spread, pilgrims began to flock.

Devout Catholics still celebrate the miracle with a silent candlelit procession (the Stille Omgang) on the anniversary of the occasion, March 17. Apart from this, the only reminder of the miracle in the modern city is a pillar set in the sidewalk of the busy street, Rokin. All that survives of a chapel built on the site of the miracle is this gray granite column.

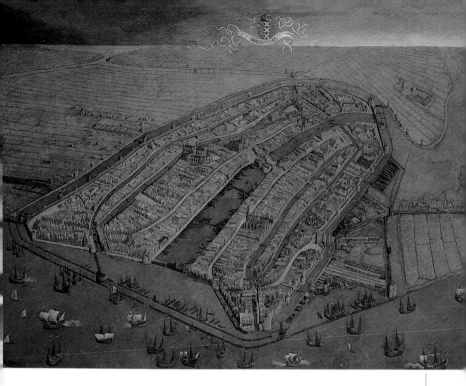

This detailed view of Amsterdam by Cornelius Anthoniszoon, showing the city in 1534, is on display in the Amsterdams Historisch Museum.

PROTESTANT REVOLUTION

In the city there were many others, however, who saw Catholicism as a corrupt force, and who deeply resented the power that Catholics wielded over business as well as religious affairs. Calvinism, based on the teachings of the French Protestant reformer, John Calvin (1509–1564), became the banner under which many of the city's middle-class merchants, bankers, shipowners, and shopkeepers decided to fight for greater self-determination. Calvinism appealed to the citizens of Amsterdam because it reflected their values of sobriety, hard work, and discipline. It was a very well organized religion, which enjoined strict obedience to the teachings of the Calvinistic church. Music was an important part of worship, and Calvinists sang psalms and hymns to the tunes of the popular music of the day, adding enormously to the religion's appeal.

When the Catholic authorities tried to prevent people from attending meetings, worshipers first held their assemblies in secret. Eventually the sheer numbers involved made this impossible, and huge open-air meetings often turned into riots as the authorities tried to prevent them from taking place. In many cases, however, the militiamen simply refused to carry out their orders, believing that the punishments demanded for open worship were out of proportion to the crime.

DUTCH REVOLT

In 1555, the Habsburg Holy Roman Emperor, Charles V, decided to put his son, the Spanish king, Philip II, in charge of the Low Countries. At that time, the Low Countries included modern Belgium and parts of northern France, as well as the Netherlands. The Habsburgs, one of Europe's most powerful ruling families, had acquired control of the Low Countries in 1482, adding it to a vast empire that also took in parts of Spain, Italy, Switzerland, Austria, and Germany, won by a combination of conquest, marriage, and inheritance.

Philip was a fanatical, almost monk-like Catholic, who made it his life's mission to stamp out Protestantism within the borders of the Habsburg colonies. In order to accomplish this goal, he appointed Spanish noblemen to powerful positions in the Netherlands, including the so-called Iron Duke, Fernando Alvarez de Toledo.

Opponents of the Habsburgs rallied around the Protestant Prince Willem of Orange, and in 1572 he led an army of volunteers in the first battle of the Dutch Revolt. Bitter battles were fought between the two armies, but the desire for freedom inspired the people of the northern Netherlands to great feats of selflessness. The town of Leiden, in particular, earned Prince Willem's praise and gratitude for withstanding a year-long siege in 1574 that left many of its citizens near death from disease and starvation. Their heroism proved to be the turning point of the war. By refusing to bow to repression, they exhausted the Spanish will to fight and gave Willem the time he needed to gather reinforcements and inflict a decisive defeat on the Spanish.

THE ALTERATION

Matters in Amsterdam came to a head in May 1578, by which time the Spanish were demoralized and in retreat. Calvinists loyal to Prince Willem entered the city and arrested the Catholic administrators, who were put on a ship and made to leave. The event has gone down in Dutch history as the Alteratie, the Alteration, a neutral term that gives no hint of its enormous consequences. Catholicism, not Calvinism, was now banned in the city, and the Calvinists, not the Catholics, occupied all the key positions of power. But more importantly, the city was at peace, and everyone was free again to pursue the business of creating wealth.

It took another year before the Spanish at last accepted defeat. The final peace was signaled by the signing of the Treaty of Utrecht in 1579, whereby the seven northern provinces of the Netherlands effectively declared independence from the Catholic south (modern Belgium), and formed a new Republic of the United Provinces. They agreed to pool resources for mutual defense in the event of external threat, but otherwise each province had a large degree of self-determination.

Having lost their grip on the Protestant north, the Spanish instituted harsh measures in the Catholic south that further boosted Amsterdam's fortunes. A flood of Jewish and Protestant refugees fled Antwerp and other southern cities, ending up in Amsterdam. This created appalling problems of overcrowding, squalor, and anti-immigrant feeling, but ultimately it was to the city's benefit. The newcomers brought with them the skills that laid the foundations for the city's preeminence in banking and in the diamond-processing industry. With nothing left to lose, they simply threw themselves into clawing their way back to prosperity, working hard, and contributing to what rapidly became a booming economy.

GOLDEN AGE

The Treaty of Utrecht ushered in an era of peace, prosperity, and achievement known as the Dutch Golden Age. The major landmarks of the Golden Age read like an astonishing catalog of achievement. By 1597, Dutch explorers had sailed to Indonesia and produced the necessary charts and maps to allow their fellow countrymen to follow in their wake. In 1602, the highly organized Dutch set up the East India Company (Verenigde Oost-Indisch Compagnie or VOC) to manage and coordinate trade with the Far East. The VOC established trading ports at strategic points along the route and all the way up to China and Japan and down to Tasmania, gaining a strategic foothold in southern Africa, too. By 1611, Amsterdam had usurped the position of the Spanish, Portuguese, and Venetians to become Europe's biggest importer of spices and other exotic commodities from the Far East.

In 1613 work began on the canal circle, part of a well-thought-out plan to control the growth of the city and to accommodate the demand for more warehousing and more berths for ships. At the same time it provided an opportunity for merchants to plow their earnings back into the local economy, encouraging them to build prestigious canalside houses. These they decorated with works of art that kept the city's artists busy and threw up some of the greatest talents of the age such as Rembrandt, Frans Hals, Vermeer, and Ferdinand Bol.

In 1616, Willem Schouten of Hoorn, the harbor town to the north of Amsterdam, rounded the tip of South America (which he named Cape Horn after his birthplace). That same year, Jan Pieterszoon Coen, another Hoorn native, founded the city of Batavia (modern Jakarta) in Indonesia.

Amsterdam saw the formation of the Dutch West India Company (West Indische Compagnie or WIC) in 1621, modeled on the to Amsterdam sent letters home expressing their astonishment at the sheer scale and excitement of a city entirely dedicated to making money.

NAVAL WARS

Such preeminence was not to last for long. The English were quick to copy any new ideas

The English warship _Royal James_ fires on Dutch vessels during a 1666 sea battle. Having colonized much of the Americas and East Indies, the Dutch had a constant battle to keep them.

VOC, and in 1626, Peter Minuit explored the Hudson River, where he purchased the island of Manhattan as a base for the company's operations.

Dutch entrepreneurs were everywhere, and Amsterdam was the place to which they brought back their exotic trade goods and their wealth. Shiploads of Ming-dynasty porcelain imported from China set first Amsterdam—and then all Europe—alight with demand for the new and exotic vases, jars, and bowls. This led to the creation of an industry based just south of Amsterdam, in Delft, that was devoted to producing imitation Chinese porcelain—Delftware. Contemporary visitors

that gave the Dutch a competitive advantage, whether it was advances in ship design, the idea of trading shares on a stock exchange, or the creation of low-cost marine insurance.

Amsterdammers scarcely had time to enjoy their prosperity before English privateers were attacking their ships. In 1664, the English seized Manhattan from the Dutch, took control of the island's New Amsterdam colony, and renamed it New York. This typified the state of warfare that was to exist on and off between the two nations for the next 100 years, and it didn't even stop after the Dutch prince, William of Orange, was crowned King of England in 1689.

DECLINE & REVOLUTION

Despite the Anglo-Dutch wars, many Amsterdammers continued to prosper and some became extremely wealthy, building the palatial mansions that earned the southernmost part of the canal circle the nickname of the Golden Bend. But, as so often happens when one entrepreneurial generation hands on its wealth to the next, the upper echelons of Amsterdam society were full of people living on wealth rather than creating it: the shareholders, property owners, and bankers who enjoyed enormous privileges.

The scene was set for another Alteration as those who didn't share in this wealth suffered from a slow but steady decline in the economy, worsened by high taxation and a series of very harsh winters. Present-day Dutch galleries contain numerous pictures of snowy landscapes and skaters on the frozen canals of Dutch cities—evidence of the mini Ice Age of the latter half of the 18th century. The harsh reality

behind these Christmas-card scenes is that many people died of starvation or hypothermia.

Also displayed are group portraits showing the dour trustees of the various charitable institutions that existed to provide for the poor. Such charity came at a price, and many people preferred to starve on the streets rather than be subjected to the degrading almshouse.

When Revolutionary French soldiers marched into Amsterdam in the snowy winter of 1795, many residents went out to greet the

Idyllic winter scenes are important historic evidence of Europe's mini Ice Age. They belie the hardship that must have resulted.

invaders rather than defend the city. The old regime in Amsterdam scarcely put up any resistance when relieved of its duties as councillors and regents. In what has gone down in Dutch history as the Velvet Revolution, Amsterdam and the Netherlands simply became part of the French Empire.

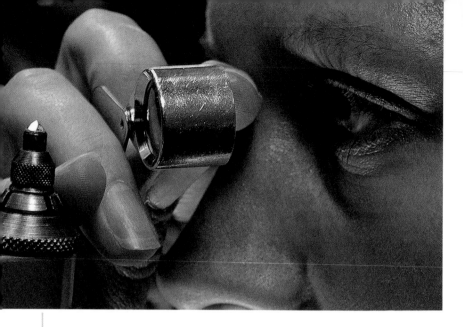

Jewish refugees from Antwerp settled in Amsterdam, establishing the city as the center of Europe's diamond-processing industry.

CONSTITUTIONAL REFORM

If Dutch intellectuals believed that France would lead them into a new and more enlightened age, they were mistaken. After the Revolution came Napoleon, who installed his brother, Louis Bonaparte, on the newly created throne of the Netherlands. As king, Louis threw the citizens out of their town hall, which he turned into his palace. He ordered the demolition of the Waag, the public weigh house, in Dam Square, because he didn't like merchants and traders spoiling his view. The relegation of the city council to subservient status was symbolized by its move to a much smaller building (now the Grand Hotel, see p. 247) on Oudezijds Voorburgwal.

After the defeat of Napoleon, European leaders met at the Congress of Vienna to redefine the territorial map of Europe and the Dutch regained their independence and sovereignty. Still hungry for democratic reform, Amsterdammers took to the streets in a series of riots in the 1840s. The government of the day responded by putting Johan Rudolf Thorbecke in charge of drawing up a plan for constitutional reform, and the new Constitution, with provisions for the first directly elected Dutch parliament, came into force in 1848.

ECONOMIC REVIVAL

At the same time as a measure of democracy was introduced, Amsterdam experienced economic rejuvenation as a reward for infrastructural modernization. In 1876 the 15-mile (24 km) Noordzeekanaal (North Sea Canal) was opened to shipping, providing a fast route from the city to the open sea. The traditional route, through the shallow Zuider Zee, had silted up to the extent that big ships had stopped calling at Amsterdam's harbor. Now large modern vessels bearing tin, timber, tea, coffee, rubber, quinine, and other commodities from the Indonesian colonies were able to dock at new quays built on the western side of the city.

These ships, in turn, were able to complete their journey faster and more cheaply as a direct result of the opening of the Suez Canal. In addition, the discovery of major new diamond fields in South Africa gave a great boost to the city's diamond processing industry, to the benefit of the city as a whole but especially to the Jewish community, who made up the bulk of Amsterdam's diamond-industry work force. From being among the city's poorest inhabitants, they now began to enjoy better working conditions in modern factories, and higher wages.

The Concertgebouw music theater (above) and other major public buildings are among the many civic benefits that resulted from the city's 19th-century rejuvenation.

In 1847, Amsterdam gained a rail link to Rotterdam, but only a temporary station. The city had to wait until 1889 before today's grand Centraal Station was completed, just one of several imposing buildings that were being constructed at the time. Others included the huge art-filled Rijksmuseum, the Concertgebouw concert hall, and the new commodities exchange—the Beurs van Berlage. Serious consideration was given to a plan to fill in the city's major canals to create wide, Parisian-style avenues. Amsterdam owes a great debt to those conservationists who fought against such plans, ensuring the city survived with its beautiful 17th-century canal circle intact.

EARLY 20TH CENTURY

Amsterdam's rejuvenation led to a period of short-lived prosperity that was fractured by World War I. The Netherlands adopted a position of neutrality, but nevertheless suffered from food shortages as a result of the grim war taking place almost on its doorstep, in the fields of Flanders and in Germany. In the interwar period, Amsterdam hosted the 1928 Olympics, building a stadium for the purpose in the south of the city in an area now full of factories. During the Great Depression of the 1930s, many thousands of unemployed Amsterdammers were given work on job creation schemes, including the construction of the Amsterdam Bos, a much-valued recreation park and green lung in the southern suburbs. It was at this time, too, that the city council produced a far-sighted document, called the General Development Plan, that made provision for the controlled growth of the city over the remainder of the 20th century, including the establishment of Schipol airport, which grew from a tiny airfield on the reclaimed land of Haarlemmermeer to the fourth-busiest airport in Europe.

NAZI OCCUPATION

The Netherlands tried once again to remain neutral at the start of World War II, but Hitler simply ordered the country to surrender to his will. He demonstrated the consequences of refusal by sending bombers to destroy the city of Rotterdam and threatened that the same treatment would be meted out to every city in the Netherlands, one by one, until the Dutch gave in. The cruelty of this inhuman act, which left 8,000 dead, 80,000 homeless, and Rotterdam a smoldering ruin was compounded by the fact that the Dutch had already surrendered by the time of the bombing, which continued anyway.

**High-spirited revelers celebrate Queens'
Day wearing the colors of the royal House
of Orange.**

Amsterdammers watched in stunned disbelief as the tanks and troops rolled into their city. A year later, when 400 Jews were rounded up in the city, dockworkers led a general strike, but the protest only lasted two days as the Nazis caught and shot the strike leaders. In 1942, Anne Frank and her family went into hiding and very nearly survived the war (see pp.146–47), which ended with mass starvation during the bitterly cold winter of 1945.

By this stage, some parts of northern Europe had already been liberated, and the Netherlands effectively became a buffer between the Allies and Hitler's Germany. Rail, sea, river, and road blockades designed to prevent food and supplies reaching Germany also left the Netherlands starving, and there was no gas or electricity to help Amsterdammers survive one of the coldest winters of modern times. Buildings were ransacked for timber to feed fires, and anything edible—including rats and flower bulbs—ended up inside the stomachs of people at risk from typhoid, diphtheria, and cholera.

LIBERATION

That is one reason why Liberation Day (May 5) is still celebrated in Amsterdam with such fervor, and why the city's flea markets are full of people mulling over bent and broken odds

city's *Provos* added a raft of novel demands to the political agenda.

These anarchists, who adopted the name Provos after one newspaper branded them *provocateurs*, were a small group of radical thinkers who decided to influence Amsterdam politics through the use of humor and street theater. The wide sidewalks of Spui Square, in front of the statue called Het Amsterdamse Lieverdje—The Amsterdam Rascal—became the Saturday night meeting place for young radicals who would try to stir up public feeling about grievances both real and imagined. Perhaps the most visible anti-establishment protest took place in 1966, when smoke bombs were let off in an attempt to disrupt the marriage of Princess Beatrix and Claus von Amsberg.

AHEAD OF THEIR TIME

Members of one splinter group, the *Kabouters,* or Gnomes, succeeded in being elected to the city council, where some of their bolder experiments have gone down in city mythology. One was the idea of providing a free bicycle for anyone who needed one. Painted white (symbolic of peace), the bikes were to be placed at strategic points around the city. If you needed a bike, you just grabbed the nearest and then left it out for the next person who needed a ride. The idea lacked nothing in terms of simplicity or logic, and it foundered only because meaner spirits stole the bikes, repainted them, and sold them for drug money.

That other cities, including Copenhagen, have introduced white bikes with much more success—computerized tracking devices deter theft—proves that such ideas were not impractical but simply ahead of their time. In many respects, that has been Amsterdam's role in the late 20th century—a city at the heart of Europe daring to be different and to challenge old thinking. From tolerating European integration, gay marriage, euthanasia, and all forms of consensual sexual activity, to the decriminalization of drugs and the rehabilitation rather than imprisonment of criminals and drug addicts, Amsterdam is a thoroughly modern city. It sees itself as a catalyst for change not just in the Netherlands, but across Europe as a whole. ∎

and ends. Nobody who lived through the war years in Amsterdam can break the habit of hoarding and trading anything that might be of possible use. Neither will the war generation ever forget the sight of American and Canadian B-17s dropping food crates from the sky in early May 1945, or their first blissful taste of bread, tea, Spam, and American chocolate.

The children of that generation, those born in the 1940s and '50s, seem not to have been cowed by their parents' experiences, but rather inspired to create a new and better world. The 1960s and '70s saw the triumph of radicalism all over Europe, but nowhere more so than in Amsterdam. Here, in addition to fighting for the cause of nuclear disarmament and calling for an end to all forms of discrimination, the

Architecture & arts

AMSTERDAM HAS ITS OWN UNIQUE AND PARTICULAR CHARM. WITH THE possible exception of Venice, with which Amsterdam is often likened, no other city can match its architectural homogeneity. Unlike Venice, however, Amsterdam is a city not of grand effects but of small and intimate details.

ARCHITECTURE

Like the music of Bach or Mozart, Amsterdam is a city of repeated patterns, in which each slight departure from the main theme has the power to thrill. Spotting the endless variations is one of the great pleasures of strolling around this most elegant of cities.

The basic pattern is provided by the way that each building in the canal circle is of similar width and height, the result of deliberate and far-sighted town planning. The city council's decision to control building standards was born of necessity. Like many other cities in medieval Europe, Amsterdam was largely built of timber, with roofs of reed or straw, the only exception being the churches. Dedicated to God and symbols of the city's aspirations, they were considered special enough to warrant being built from expensive imported sandstone.

Combustible construction materials, combined with rudimentary chimneys and fireplaces, ensured that just about every town and city in Europe suffered a devastating fire at some stage in its early history. In the case of Amsterdam, fire struck twice in the 15th century, in 1421 and 1452, and on each occasion the city was all but destroyed.

Building standards

The city fathers responded to the problems by issuing instructions that all buildings must in future be built of non-flammable materials, and, in typical Amsterdam fashion, they offered householders a subsidy to help underwrite the costs. In typical Amsterdam fashion as well, some people ignored or found a way around the rules. The two oldest surviving buildings in Amsterdam (in the Begijnhof, see p. 70, and on Zeedijk, see p. 90) are both built of timber—yet the first was built in 1477 and the second in 1550, well after the date when city ordinances demanded the use of brick for the walls and ceramic tiles for the roof.

Grachtengordel

The medieval city became increasingly crowded as the population of Amsterdam grew in the 15th and 16th centuries. When refugees from Antwerp began to flood the city in 1585, the city council decided to expand Amsterdam by digging the Singel (Belt) canal. The canal wrapped around the city, allowing for new buildings on both banks, with a mix of commercial, residential, and state-owned property, such as the city arsenal, as well as berths for ships and even shipyards for their construction and repair. The period between 1585 and 1593 saw military and industrial activity shift to the Oostelijke Eilanden, artificial islands constructed in the harbor to the east of the city, where the Maritime Museum now stands. This paved the way for the city to develop in a more genteel way, with residential areas explicitly designed for gentlemen, and a special district set aside for artisans.

The man entrusted with working out how this should be done was a humble carpenter by the name of Hendrick Staets (1575–1649). Although he lacked paper qualifications in town planning, Staets came up with an elegant and logical plan: He would wrap three canals around the core of the old city, then use the soil removed during the canal excavation to create building plots.

Staets calculated everything with a surveyor's precision. Each canal was to be precisely 82 feet (25 m) wide, broad enough to accommodate four lanes of barges, and 7 feet (2.1 m) deep. Housing plots were to have precisely 98 feet (30 m) of frontage. The maximum height was stipulated to ensure that properties backing onto each other did not steal each other's light. Back annexes (such as the one in which Anne Frank and her family hid) were permit-

Appropriately, Jacob van Campen's relief of Icarus falling from the sky decorates the Bankruptcy Court in the Koninklijk Paleis.

ted for accommodating servants. Shops and commercial activity were strictly relegated to the short radial canals, so that anyone looking down the length of the canals would see an unbroken vista of palatial residences. Industrial activity was only permitted in the ironically named Jordaan (Garden), which explains why housing plots cost least on the Prinsengracht, facing the Jordaan, and most on the Herengracht, closest to the city and farthest from the smoke and smell. Altogether the canal circle would stretch for a length (including both canal banks) of 7.5 miles (12 km). Combined with the Jordaan, this would treble the city's capacity for growth.

Striking a blow for individuality

If the Canal Circle (Grachtengordel in Dutch) had been built in strict military fashion according to these formulae, Amsterdam would now be a curiosity—but a deeply dull one. From the start, variations began to creep

in. Wealthy merchants bought more than one plot and built very wide houses. Speculators and builders subdivided their plots into smaller properties. Most of the houses were built with their main roof ridge at right angles to the canal. To finish off the ridge with a simple triangle would make the house indistinguishable from a common warehouse, so architects began to design ornate gables. The earliest ones took the form of stepped brickwork, but Philip Vingboons (1608–1675)

Amsterdam's distinctive architectural style is just one of the successful ingredients that have made it a paragon of town planning.

introduced the more curvaceous design known as a neck gable (resembling the neck of a wine bottle) in 1638 (see p. 144) and this was widely copied. Other designs soon followed, each consisting of a square or rectangular brick core, flanked by decorative scrollstones—the name given to the carved sandstone side pieces that give the gable its individual character.

If you were wealthy enough, you would commission your own designs, carved with motifs that advertised to the world that you were a successful merchant by depicting ships, bales of silk, dolphins, and flying fish—even slaves. Otherwise you would take whatever the

This neck gable, though typical, boasts an elaborate sandstone crest and side pieces.

stone mason supplied from stock, ready-carved—which explains why the same designs and motifs appear again and again all over the city.

Even if you couldn't afford a unique gable, you could commission a simple *gevelsteen* (gable stone). As the name suggests, these were initially set in the gable, but later they appeared lower down on the house front, typically above or beside the front door. The small rectangular stone was carved with images that identified your name, house, or profession in a variety of different (and sometimes humorous) ways. Other ways to make your house look a little bit special included enormous windows of sparkling glass, ornate fanlights, heavily embossed front doors, and stoops, or staircases, leading to the front door and decorated with cast-iron balustrades.

Warehouses & hoist beams

People couldn't afford any of these stylistic flourishes without an income, and despite the aim of making the canal circle purely residential, warehousing was integral to many designs. In the oldest stretches of the canal circle, in the northern sector, you can see fine warehouses, now converted to apartments.

The Renaissance step gable was one of Amsterdam's earliest architectural styles.

They are easy to spot because of their sail-shaped shutters, often painted in distinctive colors to contrast with the surrounding brickwork. The heavy wooden shutters could be opened to let in light or to allow goods in or out on the end of a hoist.

Residential houses often had offices on the ground floor and warehouse space in the attic. Goods were winched up by means of the hoist beams that still project from many canalside houses and in some cases are still used to lift large items of furniture into the houses through the windows. In order to stop goods from bumping against the brickwork and windows, many houses were built with a facade leaning forward at an angle from the perpendicular. There were several additional advantages to building house fronts "in flight," as this was called. Rainwater was kept clear of the facade, so the exterior timberwork did not rot and damp was reduced; soot and other airborne pollution was less likely to cling to the brickwork, so the building remained relatively clean. For those who were houseproud and wanted to show off their facade, a leaning house front was easier to admire looking up from street level.

Some house fronts leaned to an exaggerated degree, posing the real danger of the

incorporate such classical features as cornices, balustrades, and pediments. After the lively and sometimes quirky design of the 17th century, these 18th-century buildings seem conventional and dull.

The same cannot be said for the style that swept Amsterdam in the early 20th century, when, after a 200-year period of relative

French-style pediments came into fashion during the 18th century.

A lifting beam and hoist betray the mercantile origin of this gable.

house collapsing, or of bricks falling away if the mortar rotted. Building regulations limited the tilt to a maximum of one inch in every three feet (25 mm in every meter), but this rule was widely ignored, as you can see by looking at the picturesque buildings on Reguliersgracht, at the spot known as the Seven Bridges. To reduce the risk of the gable falling down, iron clamps were used, attached to tie rods connecting the gable to the roof ridge. These can often be seen if you look behind the gable.

French style & modernism
Later buildings in the canal circle broke radically with the Dutch tradition. Instead of end-on gables, it became the fashion among wealthy families to build houses with wide frontages and ridges running parallel to the canal. These facades, often of sandstone,

stagnation, the city regained its place in international trade and began to suffer from major overcrowding. H.P. Berlage, the innovative designer of Amsterdam's new stock exchange (see pp. 52–53) was asked to draw up a plan for the city's expansion, and he came up with a scheme that allowed for large houses for the city's wealthy in the garden suburbs of Amsterdam South, with working class accommodations to the west and east. Although the sumptuous villas of the Museum Quarter and Amsterdam South are beautifully designed and still very desirable properties, Berlage and his followers—members of the so-called Amsterdam school—poured their creativity into producing innovative low-cost housing. Built around a series of courtyards, with bulbous corner towers and eye-catching spires, the estate complexes of Spaarndammerbuurt (west) (see pp. 136–37) and De Dageraad (see

p. 210) are inspiring examples of the belief that cheap housing need not be dull.

Because it maintains a huge legacy of historic buildings, central Amsterdam offers few opportunities for new architecture to occur—with the exception of Renzo Piano's NEMO museum, an elegant building that fills an empty part of the city skyline with a bold

Renzo Piano's striking NEMO building is the latest addition to the cityscape.

sculptural form that alludes to Amsterdam's maritime heritage. You have to travel to the suburbs to see other examples of what contemporary architects have done. In Bijlmermeer, for instance, you can see stark and dehumanizing 1970s tower blocks of the kind that nobody would want to build any more alongside the far more inspiring ING Bank complex of 1987, built without right angles in rejection of the boxlike form of most office buildings.

ART & COMMERCE

Having built themselves such handsome town houses, the merchants and bankers of Amsterdam now sought to furnish them in similar style. Their voracious appetite for art to hang on their walls created Europe's first commercial art market; astonished visitors to Amster-

dam, encountering paintings for sale everywhere—in stores, street markets, and galleries— never failed to comment upon this fact. Elsewhere in Europe, art was the prerogative of wealthy patrons—the Church, guilds, charitable institutions, monarchs, and powerful aristocrats—while in Amsterdam, everyone could, and did, own a work of art.

Vermeer's "Woman Reading a Letter" is a lovingly rendered domestic scene.

Those who could afford it commissioned their own portraits, treating art as a form of photography, making a record of themselves at the height of their career or at a significant moment, such as marriage. Others banded together to commission group portraits: It was common practice for guilds, civic guards, militia companies, and charitable institutions to hire one of the leading painters of the day to make a record of their membership, preserving their portraits for posterity.

Rembrandt and Frans Hals excelled in both group and individual portraiture, raising this rather static form to the heights of great art, but neither was fully appreciated in his own lifetime. Both died in poverty—Frans Hals in a home for the old and destitute in Haarlem, and Rembrandt in the Jordaan, to be buried in an anonymous grave, in the Westerkerk—

leaving it to future generations to judge just how far these two artists towered above their contemporaries.

Off-the-shelf morality

Contemporary taste was not for Hals' and Rembrandt's bold monumental and expressive works of genius, but for minutely observed

Still life paintings celebrate nature's abundance but remind viewers that all will pass.

landscapes, cityscapes, interiors, and morality tales. Dutch art of the Golden Age is characterized by an almost fanatical devotion to clarity of draftsmanship and line, rendering in paint as close as possible a representation of the real world.

Some patrons purchased art for its sheer technical bravado. Amsterdam's art galleries were (and still are) full of wintry scenes with snow on eaves and skaters on ponds, or the interiors of churches, showing the artist's skill in using that most difficult of all colors, white.

Many paintings bought off the shelf from the city's art dealers (including Rembrandt) promote a specific morality. Amsterdam's art patrons seem to have liked paintings that either depicted virtuous behavior, or its opposite. Vermeer was the master of domestic scenes in which patient and modestly dressed

women carry out their household duties with resignation and almost religious devotion, turning simple tasks, like pouring milk or sweeping a cobbled alley, into sacramental acts.

Deliberate ambiguities

Vermeer's poignant portrait of the "Woman Reading a Letter" in the Rijksmusuem, depict-

Adriaen van Ostade's "The Fishwife" shows how Amsterdam artists loved to paint real life.

ing an apparently pregnant woman reading a letter, is perhaps the most explicitly moral; a sea chart in the background suggests that the master of the house is abroad. This portrait of a faithful wife—keeping her love for her absent seafaring husband alive in her heart—could almost be Penelope waiting for her Odyseus to return from the Trojan Wars.

Jan Steen's morality tales depict the opposite of virtue. His paintings, which show children drinking and smoking and adults neglecting their tasks, appear to be a warning against self-indulgence, but his rogues and wastrels are painted so lovingly that you cannot help but to wonder whether licentiousness is being condemned or celebrated. The fact that Amsterdam burghers bought these paintings in such quan-

tities suggests they enjoyed the deliberate ambiguity.

Still lifes

No such ambiguity surrounds the many still-life paintings in Amsterdam's museums. Typical of a Dutch still life is an assemblage of gorgeous and exotic objects: flowers and butterflies, imported fruits and spices, beautifully bound books, richly patterned oriental rugs. Nearly always, there is a worm or caterpillar slowly nibbling away at the pretty scalloped petal of a scented carnation to remind us of our mortality and of the transience of worldly luxuries—an apt moral for a city awash with exotic luxuries. Some objects have symbolic meanings: a watch for time, a musical instrument for order and harmony (though they can also symbolize indolence and idleness). Patrons would also have been privy to the pre-Freudian language of visual and linguistic puns deployed by artists to amuse their patrons. Jewelry boxes, vases, and

candlesticks could stand for the male and female genitals; feathers, mirrors, and cut-glass decanters betokened vanity; dogs symbolized licentiousness; eggshells the frailty of the human condition. Reading a still life could be a stimulating puzzle and a perfect conversation piece, as well as an aesthetic experience.

Tulip mania

Tulips feature prominently in many still-life pictures, because, of all the exotic imports that

Today's thriving Dutch bulb industry, reflected in city parks and gardens, is a legacy of the 17th-century tulip craze.

Amsterdam merchants brought back to the city, few were as costly, or as transient, as the Turkish tulip bulb. Amsterdammers built up collections of tulips in the way that other people acquire coins or postage stamps. Delft factories turned out specially designed tulip vases, like elongated pyramids, standing in pairs, some three feet (one meter) or more from the ground, with a series of cup-shaped bowls up each of the four sides, in which to display tulip blooms.

The most highly prized blooms were those that suffered from an unusual viral condition in which the pigment in the petals broke into flame- or feather-like striations. Such was the desire among collectors to own the finest specimens that the bulbs were traded on the Amsterdam commodities exchange. At the height of the tulip fever that gripped the city in the 1630s, bulbs were fetching higher prices than emeralds, Ming vases, or Arab stallions.

Flower power

The tulip was symbolic in many ways of the desire of nouveau riche Amsterdammers to flaunt their wealth. Though family fortunes were blown away in what was known as "the wind trade" (so-called because speculation in

Amsterdam is one of the best places in Europe to hear top-notch blues and jazz.

bulbs was as insubstantial and elusive as the wind), the tulip came to have a permanent and honorable place in Dutch culture. It remains the fourth best-selling flower (after roses, chrysanthemums, and carnations, all of which feature in still-life paintings) in the enormously successful Dutch horticultural industry.

PERFORMING ARTS

Amsterdam is synonymous with the Royal Concertgebouw Orchestra, one of the world's great ensembles displaying professional polish and interpretative flair. Tickets are hotly sought after, so you need to reserve well in advance of a visit to the city. If you can't obtain them, there are many other ways to experience top-class music, including the Netherlands Opera and its orchestra at the Muziektheater, and the Netherlands Philharmonic and the Netherlands Chamber Orchestra at the Beurs van Berlage (see p. 52).

Amsterdam doesn't have any home-grown pop, rock, roots, or jazz bands of note, but appreciative audiences for all forms of contemporary music ensure that it is a favorite venue for touring musicians. In the world of jazz and blues, such Amsterdam venues as Maloe Melo (see p. 265) and BIMHuis (see p. 265) are legendary—no matter who is playing when you pay a visit, the quality will be consistently outstanding.

In Amsterdam's hippie heyday, the nightclubs Melkweg and Paradiso (see p. 265) were bywords for alternative avant garde and progressive rock; today they have settled into the mainstream. Melkweg, housed in a converted dairy, offers a varied daily performance program that ranges across reggae and roots, Latin and dance, video, circus, and puppetry. A similar mix—though with more emphasis on mainstream dance music, rock, and Europop—characterizes the live performances at Paradiso, which is now housed in a converted church.

Some of the city's smaller clubs are renowned not so much for the acts on stage as they are for the stylish dress of the clubbers who attend theme-party nights. People come to Amsterdam from all over Europe to party in an atmosphere of hedonistic eroticism. Gay Amsterdam has greatly influenced the inventiveness and outrageousness of some of the costumes and the displays of physique that you will see at these events. If you are not brave enough to take part yourself, you can always look at the photographs displayed outside the clubs in Rembrandtplein and Amstelstraat to get an explicit idea of just what an eye-opening experience a visit to a city club can be. ∎

Amsterdam's commercial heart is a chaotic mass of trams, bicycles, buskers, and barrel organs. The contrasts come thick and fast—from grand churches and palaces to condom shops and a sex museum.

Nieuwe Zijde

Wind-direction indicator at Centraal Station

Nieuwe Zijde

FROM THEIR NAMES, YOU MIGHT BE tempted to think that Amsterdam's Nieuwe Zijde (New Side) district is younger than its neighbor, the Oude Zijde (Old Side, see p. 71). In reality, the two parishes are named after their respective churches.

Old Side's Oude Kerk (Old Church) was founded around 1250, and is therefore almost as old as the city itself.

New Side got its name from the far grander Nieuwe Kerk (New Church), a relative newcomer, founded in 1408 when it was built in the Flamboyant Gothic style to symbolize the city's growing status and prosperity.

The New Church stands on one side of Dam, the city's main square and the site of the historic dam from which Amsterdam got its name (see p. 22). The church is partnered by the Royal Palace, originally built to serve as a prestigious town hall for the city in 1648–1665. Both look across to the National Monument, a moving memorial to the dead of World War II and the central focus of the city's annual Remembrance Day ceremony, when Queen Beatrix lays a wreath at the foot of this obelisk. From this main square, Damrak cuts down through the middle of the historic city center dividing Nieuwe Zijde (to the west) from Oude Zijde (to the east). Now the city's main street, Damrak was originally a branch of the Amstel River , used as a harbor for fishing boats, lighters, and sea-going cargo ships.

For centuries, the New Side district was open to the sea. Anyone strolling around the area up to the end of the 19th century would have seen a forest of masts and rigging, felt the sea breeze, smelt the salt-laden air, and heard the cry of gulls. Today Amsterdam's main railroad station cuts the city off from its harbor. The construction of the station between 1882 and 1889 signaled the decline of Amsterdam as a major center of maritime trade. Despite this, there are still ancient streets, buildings, and waterways redolent of that bustling mercantile city of old, hidden just beneath the brash surface of the modern city. ■

Symbols of Dutch trade: Atlas supporting the globe and a Dutch cog atop the Koninklijk Paleis

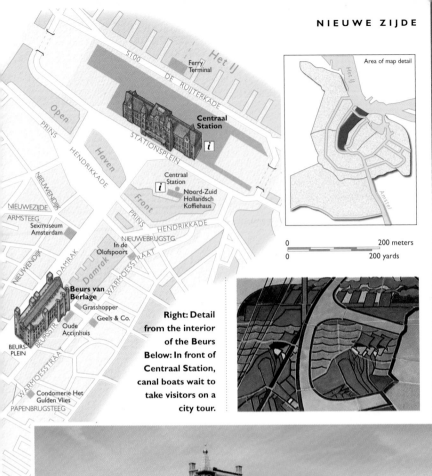

Right: Detail from the interior of the Beurs
Below: In front of Centraal Station, canal boats wait to take visitors on a city tour.

The palatial
Centraal Station
was built as a
grand entrance to
the city.

Centraal Station

WHERE SAILING SHIPS FROM INDONESIA AND JAPAN,
Tasmania, and the Americas once unloaded their precious cargoes,
commuters now pour through the imposing portals of Amsterdam's
Centraal Station. As a visitor to Amsterdam, this is probably the first
building you will see when you arrive.

When the railroad age came to
Amsterdam in the 1870s, several
sites were considered for the
station. The decision to build here
was controversial because the
harbor, though now in decline, was
still a potent symbol of the city's
maritime origins. The construction
of the station would separate the
city once and for all from its harbor
on the IJ River. To compensate for
the loss of the seaward view, the
authorities hired P. J. H. Cuypers

(1827–1921), the leading architect
of the day, to design a station that
would serve as a monumental
gateway to the city.

Completed in 1889, the station
was built on a massive artificial
island, resting on some 8,700
wooden piles driven into the
ground for support. It bears a
strong resemblance to the Rijksmuseum, Cuypers' other great public building, which was constructed
simultaneously on the city's south-

ern edge (see pp. 192–97). Two massive **towers** flank the **central portal** of red brick with sandstone detailing. The western tower displays a clock, while the constantly wavering hand of the dial in the eastern tower indicates the direction of the wind. In between are **reliefs** decorated with heroic scenes in which merchants from all over the world offer their goods in homage to the Maid of Amsterdam, a symbolic personification of the city.

TO THE HARBOR

The station underpass leads beneath the platforms to the waters of the modern **harbor.** From here the view stretches westward to the modern docks lining the North Sea Canal. This wide canal, opened in 1876, links Amsterdam with the Noordzee (North Sea). To the east, new artificial islands are being constructed to provide offices, hotels, conference centers, and much-needed housing for some 20,000 families.

At the rear of the station, reached via the main hall, a **ferry terminal** offers free rides across the IJ, worth taking just for the views of the busy harbor, and for a glimpse of the relatively rural north bank of the IJ. The ferries run all day nonstop from jetties 40 and 42. It takes just two minutes to cross the river and the ferry returns after a two-minute interval. ■

Visitor information
- Map p. 47
- Platform 2, Centraal Station, & Stationsplein 10
- 0900 400 4040
- Centraal Station Metro, all buses & trams to Centraal Station
- Museumboot & Canal Bus to Centraal Station

Trams still offer a fast and convenient way to get around the city.

Getting picked up

You can indulge in the Amsterdam ritual of midmorning coffee at two nearby atmospheric cafés. The station's first-class waiting room, on Platform 2b, is now a stylish café called **1e Klas** (see p. 247); its art deco fittings, wood paneling, and lions flanking the entrance remind travelers of the golden age of steam trains and cloche hats. On the same platform you will find a branch of the VVV tourist office (see p. 242), but be forewarned that the lines here can move at a snail's pace.

Leave the station and veer left across Stationsplein (the paved area in front of the station) for another branch of the VVV, this one located in the cream-painted timber building on the waterfront. Built in 1911 as the **Noord-Zuid Hollandsch Koffiehuis,** the tourist office has a delightful café downstairs where you can sip your java with a waterside view. ■

Geels & Co. Koffie- en Thee-museum
Map pp. 46–47
✉ Warmoesstraat 67
☎ 624 0683
🕐 Open Tues., Fri., & Sat. 2 p.m.–4 p.m.

🚇 Centraal Station Metro, all buses & trams to Centraal Station
🚢 Canal Bus, Museumboot, & Artis Express to Centraal Station

Damrak & Warmoesstraat

AS YOU EMERGE FROM CENTRAAL STATION, THE MAIN street of Amsterdam, called Damrak, lies straight ahead. Over to the left, glass-topped boats wait to carry visitors on canal-boat tours, mooring in the insignificant little pool also known as Damrak, once the busiest spot in Amsterdam. Warmoesstraat (Vegetable Garden Street), Amsterdam's oldest thoroughfare, runs parallel to Damrak. At one time a prestigious address, it now lies on the fringes of the Red Light District.

GOT ANY I.D.?
When selling tickets for concerts given by his brilliant children —8-year-old son Wolfgang and 14-year-old daughter Nannerl—Leopold Mozart lied about their ages, deducting a year from each to make them seem even more gifted. ∎

Samuel Pepys (1633–1703), the London diarist, visited Amsterdam several times in the 1660s and was astonished by the hustle, bustle, and noise of its boat-filled harbor. One or two buildings remain from his time, including a beguiling old tavern called **In de Olofspoort,** located at the end of Nieuwe-brugsteeg (New Bridge Alley), to the left of Damrak. Strictly speaking, this is a *proeflokaal,* one of the tasting bars where you can sample different kinds of spirits, notably *jenever* (gin)—though today they also sell beer and other drinks. The building, with its step gable and wooden window shutters, dates from 1619, though it looks much older.

A great leap of the imagination is required to picture Warmoesstraat as a once respectable street. In the 17th century, Sir Thomas Nugent recommended it to English travelers on the grounds that its innkeepers were the only honest ones in town, and the Mozart family lodged here in 1766.

Today a few pockets of gentility remain: There are some good-value restaurants at the northern end of Nieuwebrugsteeg, and at No. 63 stands the fine old-fashioned shop of **Geels & Co.,** tea and coffee merchants, with its original decor. The small **Koffie- en Thee-museum** (Coffee and Tea Museum) above the shop displays tea and coffee antiques.

Opposite the shop is Oude-brugsteeg, an alley that brings you out on to the southern end of Damrak beside the **Grasshopper** café. Written in bold letters around the eaves of the café is this legend: *De Cost Gaet Vor de Baet Uyt.*

Colloquially translated, it means "Nothing Ventured, Nothing Gained"—an appropriate motto for such a spot, for this was the heart of mercantile Amsterdam in the 17th century.

Opposite the café lies the **Oude Accijnhuis,** an incongruously sedate classical building, built in 1683 to house the tax collector's office. Merchants came here to pay duty on their goods before they were taken to be sold in the Beurs van Berlage, the commodities market (see pp. 52–53) that stands alongside the Oude Accijnhuis.

Retrace your steps up Oudebrugsteeg, and back on Warmoesstraat, at No. 141, you will find the kind of shop that only Amsterdam could produce: the **Condomerie Het Gulden Vlies** (Golden Fleece Condom Shop). This thoroughly respectable establishment sells gift-wrapped condoms in more forms than you can imagine.

Opposite the shop, Papenbrugsteeg takes you out on to Damrak, with the Beurs to the right and the city's biggest department store (built 1911–13) to the left. Called **De Bijenkorf** (The Beehive), this is Amsterdam's answer to Macy's or Bloomingdales and is the place to shop for fashion, toys, household goods, and designer furniture (see p. 261). ■

Attention-grabbing signs advertise cheap hotels and snack bars along Damrak.

ALS VOORHOOFD STREKT DE STEEN OP DE INGANGSBOGEN.
'T VERSTAND DES HANDELS BREKE IN HELDRE LYN

DAAR UIT : TUSSCHE
VEEL OMGANGSDAG

"Adam and Eve and the Fruits of Human Labor" marks the entrance to the Beurs.

Beurs van Berlage

AT LEAST A QUARTER OF THE LENGTH OF DAMRAK IS taken up by the great bulk of the Koopmansbeurs (Merchants' Exchange), now known as the Beurs van Berlage, after H.P. Berlage, the building's architect. Merchants from all over the world came here to make their fortunes, haggling noisily over the price of tobacco, sugar, silks, Chinese porcelain, spices, and even tulip bulbs when tulip mania hit the country in 1636.

Beurs van Berlage Museum

www.beursvanberlage.nl

- Map p. 47
- Beursplein 1
- 530 4113
- Closed Mon.
- $$$
- Tram: 4, 9, 14, 16, 20, 24, 25

The first exchange building was erected in 1607. Until then, merchants simply carried out their business on the quayside or in the surrounding streets. Berlage's building, constructed between 1898 and 1903, is the third on the site, and it established a new landmark in Dutch architectural history. The architects of most buildings of this era (including the railroad station and the Rijksmuseum) looked backward for their inspiration to the Gothic and Renaissance eras. By contrast, the design of the Beurs is forward looking and modern, which is why it was derided when it was first unveiled. Even so, within a matter of months it was being studied eagerly by the young

architects of the Amsterdam school, who went on to build some of the city's most innovative, early 20th-century housing estates (see pp. 136 and 210).

The most prominent feature of the Beurs, the clock tower, bears the legends: *Duur Ur Uuur* (Await Your Hour) and *Beidt Uw Tyd* (Bide Your Tide), both of which demonstrate Berlage's basic antipathy to the fast-paced business that went on in the exchange. His political sympathies were well to the left of center, and many of the building's interior friezes glorify the concepts of cooperation and communal ownership of wealth, in direct challenge to the raw capitalism of the free market that once thrived inside.

MENSCH ALS DINGEN ZYN
'T BESTAAN BEOOGEN

Berlage's building no longer functions as an exchange: Electronic trading has killed off the lively transactions that once took place here. Instead it has been converted into a series of concert and exhibition halls, home to the Netherlands Philharmonic and Chamber orchestras. There is also a café and restaurant.

Attending a concert is one way to view the palatial interior. The other is to visit the **Beurs van Berlage Museum,** whose entrance on Beursplein is carved with a frieze depicting human labor—

Eve and her progeny on the left bear fruits, while Adam, on the right, carries timber for building. The **Toorop Hall** is a feast of Arts and Crafts design once used for Chamber of Commerce meetings. The rooms to either side provide the opportunity to study the tile pictures, murals, stairwells, textiles, and furniture that Berlage and his colleagues made for the building. You can also climb the narrow wooden staircase to the 130-foot (40 m) tower, for a view over the rooftops of Amsterdam, as part of the admission price. ■

Medieval in influence but modern in style, the former Beurs is now a concert hall and exhibition center.

Razing his allowance

The Dutch national poet Joost van den Vondel (1582–1674), a contemporary of Rembrandt and William Shakespeare, once labeled the merchants' exchange "bringer of misery; sunlight never penetrates your building."

Vondel had good reason to hate the place. After beginning his professional life as a hosier, he went bankrupt, then turned to writing epic poetry and drama to rebuild his fortunes. Though Vondel did well, his son squandered his hard-earned wealth in speculation at the exchange. Vondel was forced to seek employment again, this time as a clerk in the city pawnbrokerage (see p. 75). At the age of 80, he was fired for writing poetry on company time. His remains are stored in an urn in Nieuwe Kerk. ■

Dam Square & Koninklijk Paleis

DAM SQUARE IS AMSTERDAM'S PRINCIPAL PUBLIC SPACE, A pigeon-infested expanse of cobbles that completed a face-lifting in 2001 as part of an 8-million-dollar plan to make it more attractive. Dominating the eastern side of the square is the somber Koninklijk Paleis (Royal Palace), built between 1648 and 1665 as the city's Stadhuis (Town Hall).

The Stadhuis was built when Amsterdam was at the peak of its powers as a maritime trading nation, a fact celebrated in the decorations. The gilded weather vane is shaped like a Dutch *kogge*—cog—a small but sturdy ship that sailed the oceans, bringing back exotic commodities to make the city wealthy. The carved pediment shows the Maid of Amsterdam receiving homage from the oceans and continents of the world, symbolized by sea gods, fish, lions, and unicorns.

On the roof, the bronze figure of Peace holds an olive branch, a reference to the Treaty of Münster,

signed in 1648, which ended the Eighty Years' War against Spain and ushered in a period of growth and prosperity. Peace is flanked by Prudence and Justice, a reminder that this building served as a civil and criminal court, as well as being the home of Amsterdam's city government.

The Stadhuis's conversion to a palace took place in 1808 when Napoleon invaded the Netherlands and put his brother, Louis Bonaparte, on the Dutch throne. The massive structure, Amsterdam's most prestigious public building, was designed by Jacob van Campen in the classical style that was fashionable in the mid-17th century. Classicism demanded at least the appearance of marble; the nearest material available to van Campen was gray-white sandstone. Sadly this is now streaked with black and gray from airborne pollution, so the building looks less imposing than it once did.

VISITING THE PALACE

Built to impress: Amsterdam's Town Hall was later converted to a royal palace.

Right: A drum major conducts a regimental band outside the Koninklijk Paleis.

Finding your way into the building can present a challenge. The entrance (which is through the right-hand arch in the facade arcade) was deliberately kept small and inconspicuous to make the building easier to defend. The cellars served as the city's bank vault, and could be used for storing literally millions of gold florins.

The first room you come to on a tour of the splendid interior is the small **Tribunal.** It's the most highly decorated room in the whole palace, though the lack of any color hints at the chilling purpose to which it was put. Here the death sentence was pronounced, in full view of the crowds gathered in the square outside, on any poor citizen found guilty of a capital crime, such as murder, witchcraft, or treason. The sculptures, executed in clinical

white marble, were intended to remind the judges to exercise Justice and Prudence.

Opposite the entrance is the marble seat of the secretary who recorded the death sentence in the city annals, and over it a plaque commemorates the laying of the

first foundation stone when work on the Stadhuis began in 1648. A figure representing the city of Amsterdam stands above the plaque, flanked by the gods of the Amstel and IJ rivers.

THE UNIVERSE IN MINIATURE

Coming out of the Tribunal, turn right to reach the main staircase, which leads to the **Citizens' Hall,** a huge and colorful room whose rich decorative scheme represents the cosmos. The marble floor is inlaid with brass maps of the northern sky and the eastern and western hemispheres, while a huge figure of Atlas, supporting a celestial globe, looks down from above the entrance to the Magistrates' Court. The Maid of Amsterdam is

Brass and marble maps symbolize the global reach of Amsterdam's trade.

portrayed again, this time flanked by the gods of Wisdom (Pallas Athena) and Strength (Hercules).

Off this central room lie the smaller chambers that served as meeting rooms for the city council and various branches of the city's administration. Classical references abound, giving clues to the function of the different rooms.

Above the entrance to the **Magistrates' Court** stands a marble statue of blind Justice, holding an executioner's sword, and flanked by figures symbolizing Death and Retribution. Venus, goddess of love, looks across to the office where marriages were registered, while Icarus (who tried to fly but fell from the sky when the sun melted his wings of feathers and wax) plunges head first to the earth

in the relief atop the entrance to the office where citizens filed for bankruptcy. The decorative festoon above depicts poisonous plants, rats gnawing on unpaid bills, and an empty money chest.

Ceiling paintings and massive narrative paintings lend color to many of the rooms. Again, these tell stories from classical literature and the Bible. Solomon prays for wisdom, and Moses appoints a council of 70 wise men to advise him in the vast canvases that hang in the **City Council Chamber,** placed here to remind members that they were ultimately accountable to God.

FROM NAPOLEON TO TODAY

Here and there a few reminders survive from the era when the

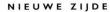

elegant furniture in the neoclassic style popular at the time.

Today, the palace is no longer the home of the Dutch monarch—Queen Beatrix has her official residence in Den Haag (The Hague)—but it continues to be used for state events, including the reception of foreign heads of state when they are invited on formal visits to the Netherlands.

NATIONAAL MONUMENT

One annual ceremony performed by the Queen is the laying of a wreath on the **Nationaal Monument** on Remembrance Day (May 4). The monument, renovated in 2000, lies on the opposite side of Dam Square from the palace, in front of the Grand Hotel Krasnapolsky (see p. 245).

This obelisk of creamy travertine was erected to preserve the memory of the World War II dead. It contains earth from each province in the Netherlands, as well as from Indonesia (the former Dutch East Indies). The victims are represented by naked chained figures beneath the outstretched arms of the crucified Christ. Today the monument serves as a popular meeting place for both locals and visitors to Amsterdam. ■

PILES

The construction of the palace involved sinking an extraordinary number of wooden piles, each 36 feet (12 m) long. The exact number is easily remembered by a formula taught to every Amsterdam schoolchild: Put a 1 before the number of days in the year and a 9 behind—the result is 13,659. ■

Stadhuis first served as a palace for the court of Napoleon (1808–1813). Empire-style chandeliers light several of the rooms, and the Bankruptcy Chamber has a suite of

Rendezvous and remembrance: The Nationaal Monument is both a meeting place and a memorial to those who died in World War II.

Nieuwe Kerk

MODELED ON THE SPLENDID GOTHIC CATHEDRAL AT Amiens, in northern France, the Nieuwe Kerk (New Church) on Dam Square dates back to 1408 and is only new in relation to the early 13th-century Oude Kerk (see p. 82). It was completed at the time when the medieval Gothic style was being eclipsed by the new Renaissance style.

The **Koninklijk Paleis and Nieuwe Kerk represent the twin poles of church and state.**

Opposite: The 1648 baroque pulpit in Nieuwe Kerk

Nieuwe Kerk
www.nieuwekerk.nl
- Map p. 46
- Dam Square
- 638 6909
- Occasionally closed for rearrangement of exhibitions
- $$$
- Tram: 1, 2, 4, 5, 9, 13, 14, 16, 17, 20, 24, 25

To see the precise point at which Gothic yielded to Renaissance, you need to walk around the outside of the church. As you circle it by heading to the right of the entrance (down an alley called Eggertstraat, then left onto Gravenstraat), you will pass several well-loved Amsterdam watering holes. **De Drie Fleschjes** (The Three Flasks) is a colorful old *proeflokaal* (tasting bar), and alongside is **Het Huys met de Gaeper** (The House with the Gaper), a *wijnlokaal* (wine-tasting bar). The "Gaper" in question is a wooden figure in a helmet, set above the door. He would once have adorned—and advertised—the premises of an apothecary, and he is opening wide so the apothecary can look inside his mouth and diagnose his complaint.

Continuing left brings you to the northern transept, the last part of the church to be completed. Looking up, you will see that the beautiful geometric Gothic tracery gives way to typical Renaissance shell hoods, niches, and columns. Note also a feature typical of Dutch churches: The attractive small shops built up against the church wall were deliberately constructed for the practical purpose of providing an income that was used for the upkeep of the church. Although it continues to be the national church of the Netherlands (and the place where the Dutch monarch is crowned), the Nieuwe Kerk is now mainly used as a concert hall and a venue for art exhibitions. If you

don't want to pay the entrance fee, go inside the south transept just to get a sense of the airy splendor of this magnificent building.

The present appearance of Protestant austerity is a result of the Alteration of 1578 (see p. 26), when this Catholic church was taken over by the Dutch Reformed Church and stripped of its medieval statues and frescoes. To emphasize the break with the Catholic past, the liturgical focus of the building was moved to the nave, with its immense baroque **pulpit** dating from 1648. Beside it is the gorgeous **organ case** of 1645, which only survived a devastating fire that gutted the church in the same year because it had been dismantled and removed to the organmaker's workshop for repair. Opposite is an imposing mid-17th-century baroque **choir screen,** with a marble base and exuberant barley sugar-twist columns of brass.

In place of the high altar, the ceremonial focal point of a Catholic church, the city fathers placed the splendid **tomb** of Admiral Michiel de Ruyter (1607–1676). De Ruyter won many sea battles in the Anglo-Dutch Wars of 1665–67 and 1672–74 before being killed fighting the French in the seas near Sicily. He was held up as a model citizen for his courageous service and given an elaborate state funeral. Allegorical figures of Power, Prudence, and Perseverance—reminders of his many sterling virtues—flank De Ruyter's massive monument. ■

A WALK THROUGH THE HEART OF AMSTERDAM

A walk through the heart of Amsterdam

Medieval and modern Amsterdam lie cheek by jowl in this walk, which passes through the historic core of the city, moving from the tempting window displays of Amsterdam's busiest shopping street to the quiet cloisters of the city's former orphanage and convent.

The walk starts on **Dam.** As its name suggests, this square was built on the site of the original dam across the Amstel River, after which the city is named. Old paintings in the Amsterdam Historical Museum (see pp. 64–67) show goods being carted across the cobbles in wheelbarrows and on sleds, and an arcaded building in the middle of the square—the 1565 Waag (Weighhouse). It was demolished in 1808 because King Louis Napoleon thought it interrupted his view from the Royal Palace.

Above: Madame Tussaud with a Dutch flavor
Opposite: The leafy court-yard of the Amsterdams Historisch Museum

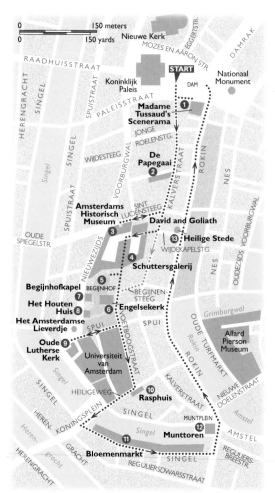

Ⓜ Also see area map pp. 46–47

► Dam

⟷ 1.6 miles (2.5 km)

🕒 3 hours

► Dam

NOT TO BE MISSED
- Begijnhof
- Bloemenmarkt

With the Royal Palace on your right, walk across Dam Square to Kalverstraat. To your right is the Peek & Cloppenburg department store, with **Madame Tussaud's Scenerama** ❶ on the top floor (see p. 70). Modern stores line pedestrian-only Kalverstraat, the city's main shopping street. On the right, just before Nos. 66–72, don't miss the tiny entrance to a splendid neo-Gothic church of 1848 that replaced a once-secret Catholic church. The church is known as **De Papegaai** ❷ (The Parrot), after the bird carved in stone to the left of the entrance, and served as a clandestine church when open Catholic worship was prohibited in Amsterdam (see p. 86).

Turn right down Sint Luciensteeg to the entrance, on the left, of the **Amsterdams Historisch Museum** ❸ (Amsterdam Historical Museum, see pp. 64–67). The entrance wall is decorated with *gevelstenen* (gable stones) rescued from demolished houses. These carved sandstone plaques were used to identify houses in the days before numbering was introduced, and usually gave a clue to the houseowner's occupation or name. Here you will see depictions of a milkmaid and a porter, and a plaque inscribed "de Swarte Molle" (the Black Mole)—perhaps marking the house of a furrier, or a pun on the owner's name.

Built as a secular convent, the Begijnhof represents a haven of peace and spiritual tranquility.

Rather than entering the museum here, go back to Kalverstraat and turn right. Look for another narrow entrance, set back on the right, with a leaning doorway dated 1581. The carvings on the doorway depict children, dressed in the red and blue uniforms of the city orphanage, seated around a table from which the Holy Ghost is rising in the guise of a dove. A bronze pillar topped by a moneybox, once used for collecting charitable donations, stands in front of the gate.

Passing through the arch, you come to the quiet tree-shaded courtyards where orphanage children once played, surrounded by a dignified group of buildings converted in 1580 from the former convent of St. Lucy. The city's foremost architects—Hendrick de Keyser and Jacob van Campen—were chosen to undertake this work, showing the high priority given to welfare projects by the city authorities in the Golden Age.

The courtyard is a pleasant spot for coffee; the museum café, on the right, is called **David and Goliath** after the colorful mid-17th-century figures carved in wood that stand guard near the entrance. These once formed part of a fairground attraction in the Jordaan district.

Just beyond the café, on the left, a set of glass doors leads into the **Schuttersgalerij** ❹ (Civic Guard Gallery). This is a public footpath that passes through the museum

(path only open 10–5); if it's closed, go back to Kalverstraat, turn right, and take the first right, Begijnensteeg, to continue with the walk. The gallery is lined with group portraits of members of the various city militias—volunteer police forces, responsible for maintaining law and order in Amsterdam from the 17th to early 19th century.

Leaving through the glass doors at the far side of the gallery, continue down the alley to a small door in the wall on the right that leads into the courtyard of the **Begijnhof** ❺ (see p. 70), a peaceful residential enclave where people come to absorb the spiritual atmosphere of this former convent. The convent church, rebuilt in 1727, is now known as the **Engelsekerk** ❻ (English Church) because it was used by the English community in Amsterdam. It is normally locked, but lunchtime concerts are often held inside (see the noticeboard by the door for details).

Opposite, at No. 30, is the **Begijnhofkapel** ❼ (see p. 70), built in 1671 as a clandestine church and disguised as a house. Beside it, at No. 34, is **Het Houten Huis** ❽ (The Wooden House), the oldest surviving house in Amsterdam, built in 1470, but not open to the public.

Leave the Begijnhof the way you came in and turn right onto the irregularly shaped square called **Spui**. Over to the right, in front of the Athenaeum bookstore, stands the 1960 bronze statue of a scruffy urchin called **Het Amsterdamse Lieverdje** (The Amsterdam Rascal). It became a symbol of alternative Amsterdam in the 1960s and '70s when anti-establishment demonstrators gathered here on Saturday nights for street theater and impromptu demonstrations.

Cross the road over to the **Oude Lutherse Kerk** ❾ (Old Lutheran Church), now part of the Amsterdam University Library, then turn left and second right, down Voetboogstraat. This leads to **Heiligeweg** (Holy Way), so called because medieval pilgrims used to process along here to the site of the Miracle of Amsterdam (see p. 24).

At the junction of the two roads you will see the preserved gatehouse of the **Rasphuis** ❿, the 17th-century prison where the inmates were set to work rasping brazil wood to make a powder used as dyestuff. The doorcase

How do you say that with flowers? The Dutch indulge their love of blooms at Bloemenmarkt, the floating Flower Market.

depicts naked chained men on either side of the allegorical Maid of Amsterdam, and a cart piled high with timber pulled by snarling hyenas, lions, and boars.

Turn right onto Heiligeweg, cross the next bridge, and turn left into **Bloemenmarkt** ⑪, also known as the floating Flower Market. You would hardly know that the flower-sellers' shops lining the left-hand side of this street were based on floating barges moored in the Singel canal. The sight of such a variety of flowers, topiary shrubs, and terra-cotta pots is colorful and absorbing. If you want to buy bulbs or plants, standholders will advise you on what customs regulations will allow and what will grow best.

At the end of the market, turn left to the **Munttoren** ⑫ (Mint Tower), so named because it briefly housed the city mint from 1672 to 1673. The lower part of the tower, with its gunports and "bacon-strip" courses of alternate brickwork and sandstone, belonged to the ancient city walls, built around 1480. Until this time, the city had been defended by an earthen rampart. To defray the cost of

rebuilding the defenses, petty criminals were given the choice of paying their fines either in money or bricks. City architect Hendrick de Keyser added the steeple in 1620. It contains a fine carillon, which plays a tune every quarter of an hour.

As you go, look across to the gray classical building on the opposite bank. This is the **Allard Pierson Museum** of archaeological antiquities (see pp. 78–79). Just beyond, at Rokin 99, is a striking post-modern version of a gabled canal house, jokingly called the **OudHof (Old Court)** built from pink granite and blue-tinted glass. Continuing down Rokin, you cannot miss the 30-foot-tall (9 m) granite column in the middle of the sidewalk, just by Wijdekapelsteeg. The **Heilige Stede** ⑬ (Miracle Column) is all that survives of a chapel built on the site of the Miracle of Amsterdam, which brought pilgrims in their thousands to the city from 1345. Devout Catholics still commemorate the event by coming here in silent candlelit procession (known as the Stille Omgang) on March 17, the anniversary of the Miracle of Amsterdam. ∎

Amsterdams
Historisch
Museum
www.ahm.nl

⚑	Map p. 46
✉	Kalverstraat 92
☎	523 1822
$	$$$
🚋	Tram: 1, 2, 4, 5, 9, 14, 16, 20, 24, 25

Amsterdams
Historisch Museum

AMSTERDAM'S FORMER ORPHANAGE PROVIDES THE atmospheric setting for the maze of rooms making up the Amsterdam Historical Museum. Displays cover the history of the city from its medieval origins to the present day, and there are one or two surprises, such as the carillon keyboard in the loft where you can try your hand at composing tunes on a set of church bells.

The city's former orphanage now houses a collection devoted to the history of Amsterdam.

The museum deserves at least two visits: First a quick familiarization tour to gain an overview of Amsterdam's history, and then a longer return visit once you know the city better. Half the fun is comparing present-day Amsterdam with the city depicted in the museum's many historic maps and paintings.

ORIGINS OF AMSTERDAM

Room 1 provides a basic introduction to the evolving shape of Amsterdam through an illuminated map. This section shows how the city grew from a fishing settlement on the Amstel River delta to a city of 750,000 inhabitants in the course of its 750-year history.

Displays beside the map illustrate graphically the boggy terrain that the first settlers encountered. Slow colonization of the marshy terrain of north Holland began in the 10th century, but was abruptly halted by devastating floods in the 12th century. The next wave of colonizers learned from this. They built ditches to drain excess water, and dikes, or embankments, to prevent newly acquired land from

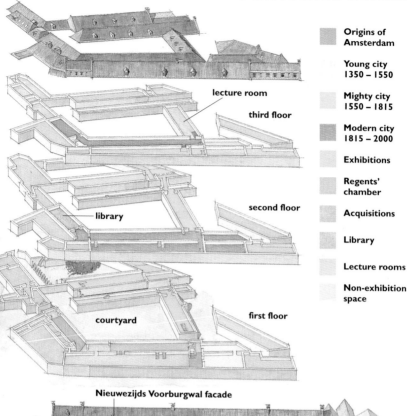

lecture room

third floor

second floor

library

courtyard

first floor

Nieuwezijds Voorburgwal facade

Origins of
Amsterdam

Young city
1350 – 1550

Mighty city
1550 – 1815

Modern city
1815 – 2000

Exhibitions

Regents'
chamber

Acquisitions

Library

Lecture rooms

Non-exhibition
space

flooding. The few artifacts that archaeologists have found from that era tell their own story: Fish spears, cauldron hooks, clogs, and saws suggest a settlement of fishermen and boatbuilders subsisting among the reeds.

YOUNG CITY

Room 2 leaps forward a century to the now-bustling medieval city, where cesspits full of discarded rubbish provide archaeologists with a picture of growing prosperity. Bones indicate a diet that had become more varied; meat was now widely eaten as well as fish. Pottery from all over Europe points to extensive trade connections, while broken shears and scraps of cloth show a town where people pursued specialist trades as weavers, tailors, shoemakers, and carpenters. The large quantity of pilgrims' souvenirs demonstrates Amsterdam's popularity as a pilgrimage center, and delicately shaped leather shoes suggest that people were not just surviving—they had the time and money to indulge in dressing fashionably.

Room 3 explains the basis of this

The café in which Amsterdam's Gay Rights Movement began is now an exhibit in the history museum.

growing prosperity, with exhibits on trade and the sturdy Dutch *kogge*— or cog—the ship used by Amsterdam merchants to carry grain, timber, salt, and wine. The huge iron cauldron in the middle of the room came from the city's medieval dockyard and was used to boil tar for making ships watertight.

MIGHTY CITY

In Room 4 you can see the extraordinarily detailed and accurate bird's-eye view of Amsterdam drawn by Cornelis Anthoniszoon in 1538. It was shortly after this that Amsterdam joined the mounting resistance to Spanish rule. The city's growth from adolescence to adulthood can perhaps be dated to 1578, when Amsterdam declared itself independent and forced the Catholic city government to give way to Protestant reformers.

The museum sets the scene for Amsterdam's Golden Age, characterized by sea voyages to distant shores (charted in Room 5 onward) in search of a new route to the East Indies and the rapid establishment of Dutch trading settlements in the Americas, Africa, the East Indies, Australia, and Tasmania. Untold wealth poured into the city, but the citizens seem to have responded with calmness and sobriety—at least, that is the picture given by the many paintings and displays in Rooms 6 through 12, where charitable works and the care of the less fortunate is a recurring theme. Among the many moralistic pictures and group portraits of charity trustees, one painting stands out: Rembrandt's painting of the "Anatomy Lesson of Dr. Jan Deijman" in Room 11, painted in 1656. Most of it was destroyed by fire in 1723, and what survives is the deathly white corpse, viewed in shortened perspective, which Dr. Deijman is about to dissect at the beginning of a public lecture on anatomy, sponsored by the Guild of Surgeons.

MODERN CITY

The last section of the museum contains new displays that bring the story right up to date. These are among the most entertaining ones in the museum, though the early part—dealing with the Napoleonic era and the 19th-century decline of the city—may seem dull unless you are interested in portraits of worthy Amsterdammers or 19th-century furniture. Things lighten up when the displays start to deal with the General Expansion Plan of 1935, the far-sighted blueprint for the controlled expansion of the city. Room 19 contains a typical 1930s kitchen from the Landlust suburb of western Amsterdam, where the city's first apartments were built to cope with the acute and worrying housing shortage. War intervened, and the museum documents the nightmare of the Holocaust and the so-called Hunger Winter of 1945, when thousands died of starvation and disease in the final winter of the Occupation (see p. 31).

By contrast with these horrors, the museum takes an affectionate look at the postwar era and the progenitors of today's coffee shops, gay bars, and anarchistic political movements. Room 23 has a White Car, an eco-friendly, electric two-seater vehicle, which symbolizes the idealism of the 1960s. The thinking was that people need not buy their own cars, but use communally owned vehicles instead, which they

could pick up from various points in the city—a kind of taxi service without a driver. The scheme foundered because there simply weren't enough vehicles or pick-up points. Nearby, in Room 24, is a reconstruction of the legendary Café 't Mandje (see p. 91), run by Bet van Beeren from 1927 to 1967, and one of the first public places in Amsterdam where gays and lesbians could meet socially.

This is the last room devoted to permanent displays, but there are often temporary exhibitions focusing on some aspect of Amsterdam and its people, so check what is on at the time of your visit. ■

This historic gable stone came from a house on Oude Schans, or Old Moat.

Legacy of 1960s radicalism: Free cars like this were to be placed on every street.

A city of keels & wheels

Number one on the list of most popular tourist attractions in Amsterdam is a guided boat tour around the city's canals. Millions of visitors hop on a Canal Bus or glass-topped boat every year. Amsterdammers themselves, by contrast, rarely use the canals to get about the city; for them, cycling is the only way to go. It's almost a religion. If you want to truly understand the Dutch mind-set, take to a bike—and then to the streets—yourself.

A lovingly maintained antique craft

On the water

Although Amsterdam is built around a 15-mile (24 km) network of canals, these waterways are underutilized. Speed restrictions are enforced so that the wash from speeding boats does not erode the canal banks. Watercraft that ply the wide canals must therefore travel at a leisurely pace—fine for tourists with plenty of time to take in the splendors of the city's Golden Age architecture, but hardly a practical option for harried commuters.

As a result, most canal transportation is geared toward visitors. Several firms offer hour-long guided tours (with commentaries in various languages) operating from the canal basin in front of the Centraal Station, or from piers along Damrak, Rokin, and near the Rijksmuseum. Taking one of these tours is a great way to see Amsterdam from a different perspective. It's also ideal for gaining a basic sense of direction in a city whose radial layout that can make things confusing.

In addition, boats offer a practical transportation option for visiting the major museums. Depending on your route, you can take the Canal Bus, the Museumboot, or the Artis Express from Centraal Station, getting on or off whenever you like (see pp. 238–39); boat tickets also allow discounts on museum admissions.

Among the leading canal-boat tour operators are **Rederij Lovers**, whose tours depart from the canal basin in front of Centraal Station (*Prins Hendrikkade 25–27, tel 530 1090, www.lovers.nl*) and **Rederij P. Kooij**, departing from Rokin, opposite Spui (*Rokin bij het Spui, tel 623 3810*).

On your bike

Amsterdam residents have been using bikes to get around the city since the 19th century. The flat terrain is ideal for cycling. Amsterdam's sidewalks—minefields of potholes and loose cobbles—tend to discourage scooters and in-line skating.

You will encounter an astonishing variety of bikes. Some have gaily painted frames, child seats, dog seats, shopping baskets, or trailers; others are designed for two or more riders; and still others have big flat-bed trailers sticking out in front, indicating their role as household movers.

Cyclists have their own lanes, junctions, and traffic lights. These often run against the flow of motorized traffic, and they frequently deliver you to your destination by a different route from the one you would take as a pedestrian. Cycling around the city liberates you to discover points farther afield, and rental bikes are available at low cost from a number of places around they city (see p. 239).

One final point to remember: Thousands of bikes get stolen every week. The thieves (mostly junkies) are everywhere, which is why Amsterdammers will triple-lock their bike frame to an immovable object before leaving it. If you make it easy for the bike thieves, they will help themselves. ∎

Above: Single bikes are often pressed into service as tandems.
Below: Approximately 5,000 people live in floating domiciles.

More places to visit in Nieuwe Zijde

BEGIJNHOF

Separated from Spui, one of Amsterdam's shopping streets, by no more than a high wall, the Begijnhof (see p. 62) is a place of spiritual calm amid the bustle of the city. Beguins were lay nuns who led a religious life without taking vows of chastity and poverty, living in convents like this one (founded in 1346) and devoting themselves to educating the poor and nursing the sick. So renowned were the Beguins of Amsterdam for their charitable work and industrious way of life that they were exempted from the laws that prohibited Catholic worship and institutions when Amsterdam became a Protestant city at the Alteration of 1578 (see p. 26). The last member of the order died in 1976. Today, the houses are rented at a nominal price to Catholic women—elderly widows and students from the city's university.

Kama Sutra in bronze: Historic art in the Sexmuseum

Among several buildings of note around the courtyard, the **Begijnhofkapel**, at No. 30, is especially interesting. From the outside it looks just like a house, but beyond the small front door lies a clandestine church whose interior is crammed with tier upon tier of wooden galleries, added as the Catholic congregation grew over the centuries since the church was first built in 1671. Hung around the walls are medieval painted panels depicting the Miracle of Amsterdam (see p. 24), and some of the subsequent miracles experienced by pilgrims who came to the shrine in the city in search of a cure for their ailments.
🗺 Map p. 46 ✉ Enter from Gedempte Begijnensloot ☎ No telephone 🕐 Chapel closed Mon. a.m. 🚊 Tram: 1, 2, 5

MADAME TUSSAUD'S SCENERAMA

This attraction mixes waxworks of international personalities—actors, pop stars, and politicians—with local content. For children, this can be an interesting way to discover the highlights of the Dutch Golden Age, through animatronic tableaus featuring the soldier and statesman Prince William of Orange, and the Golden Age artists Rembrandt and Vermeer. There is also a reconstruction of a typical merchant's house, and a beautifully crafted model of Amsterdam in the 17th century.
🗺 Map p. 46 ✉ Dam 20 ☎ 522 1010
💲 $$$ 🚊 Tram: 4, 9, 14, 16, 20, 24, 25

SEXMUSEUM AMSTERDAM "VENUSTEMPEL"

Only in Amsterdam would you find a museum devoted to sex on the city's main street. Although some would dismiss this as an excuse to display pornography, the museum has many displays that throw a humorous light on attitudes toward sex in historical times. Examples of historic pornography include delicate Japanese netsuke and fine art deco bronzes. There are etchings produced by the Imperial Court Designer for the titillation of aristocratic members of the Austrian Court of the Habsburgs, and tinder boxes and clay pipes carried by foot-soldiers in the Napoleonic Wars and 19th-century ladies' fans, with erotic scenes painted on them. The museum also has displays illustrating the more extreme manifestations of human sexuality, but they are clearly signposted if you wish to avoid them.
🗺 Map p. 47 ✉ Damrak 18 ☎ 622 8376
💲 $ 🚊 Centraal Station Metro, all buses and trams to Centraal Station ⛴ Canal Bus, Museumboot, & Artis Express to Centraal Station. ∎

Packed into Amsterdam's Oude Zijde district are the University Quarter, the Red Light District, Chinatown, the Diamond District, and the city's earliest dockyards and warehouses—an area of fascinating contrasts.

Oude Zijde

Stained glass artwork in the Oude Kerk (1555)

Oude Zijde

THE OUDE ZIJDE, OR OLD SIDE, IS AMSTERDAM'S OLDEST RESIDENTIAL quarter. The area is also known as the Wallen (The Walls): Its two principal canals— Oudezijds Voorburgwal and Oudezijds Achterburgwal—were dug just within and outside the city's medieval ramparts.

Most of the streets and canals of the Oude Zijde run parallel to these walls, but one street cuts right across them, pursuing its own wayward path. This is Zeedijk, and its name (Sea Dike) indicates that it follows the line of the original embankment built to protect medieval Amsterdam from flooding.

Zeedijk was, for many centuries, the rough end of Amsterdam—the abode of sailors and poor migrants. As recently as the 1980s it was a byword for squalor, the notorious haunt of heroin pushers and addicts. Today it has been transformed into the focal point of a reinvigorated shopping and restaurant district, thanks in part to the gradual takeover of the district by Amsterdam's Cantonese community, whose splendid new temple lends its own exotic character to this vibrant area. Alas, there are still pushers and addicts who remain.

Oude Waal has a colorful mix of merchants' houses and floating homes.

Farther south another change takes place in the University Quarter. Quiet and peaceful as this is, you are never more than a street away from the core of Amsterdam's Red Light District. It is perfectly safe to visit, though it is best not to carry valuables that would attract the attention of a potential mugger. ■

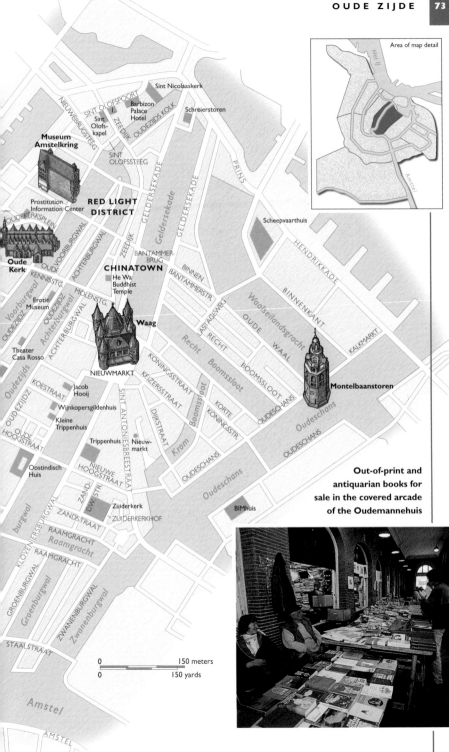

Area of map detail

Sint Nicolaaskerk

Sint Olofspoort
Barbizon
Palace
Hotel
Schreierstoren
Sint
Olofs-
kapel

Museum
Amstelkring

SINT
OLOFSSTEEG

Scheepvaarthuis

HENDRIKKADE

Prostitution
Information Center

RED LIGHT
DISTRICT

BINNENKANT

Oude
Kerk

BANTAMMER-
BRUG

CHINATOWN

BINNEN
BANTAMMERSTR

He Wa
Buddhist
Temple

Erotic
Museum

Waag

Montelbaanstoren

Theater
Casa Rosso

NIEUWMARKT

Jacob
Hooij

Wijnkopersgildenhuis

Kleine
Trippenhuis

Trippenhuis

Nieuw-
markt

Oostindisch
Huis

Out-of-print and
antiquarian books for
sale in the covered arcade
of the Oudemannehuis

Zuiderkerk

ZUIDERKERKHOF

BIMhuis

RAAMGRACHT
Raamgracht

Raamgracht

STAALSTRAAT

0   150 meters
0   150 yards

Amstel

AMSTEL

One of Amsterdam's most spectacular gables—at Oudezijds Voorburgwal No. 187—suggests that the owner traded in Africa.

Universiteits-museum de Agnietenkapel
www.uba.uva.nl

Map p. 72

Oudezijds Voorburgwal 231

525 3339

Closed Sat. & Sun.

Tram: 4, 9, 14, 16, 20, 24, 25

University Quarter

AMSTERDAM IS NOT NOTED FOR ITS SCHOLARS AND thinkers—Leiden was the main center of learning in the Netherlands. Instead, Amsterdam preferred its young to acquire practical skills, as surgeons, architects, artists, or soldiers, by joining a guild. Nevertheless, those with an intellectual bent formed the Athenaeum Illustre (Illustrious School) in 1632, a degree-granting body from which Amsterdam's university evolved.

Today's University Quarter lies to the east of Dam Square and is reached by walking along Damstraat to the first bridge and turning right down the far bank of Oudezijds Voorburgwal. As you cross the bridge, look right to No. 187, dated 1663. The gable is flanked by the carved figures of an Indian and an African, seated on bales of tobacco. Was the owner a tobacco merchant, or did he trade in slaves? It's difficult to tell, because merchants often used the figures of Africans, Turks, or Indians to symbolize the exotic origins of their stock.

AROUND THE FORMER CITY HALL

Two blocks down on the left is the entrance to the courtyard of the

Grand Hotel. This noble building, converted to a hotel in 1993, was originally built in 1647 as the headquarters of the Admiralty and has symbols of war and justice carved in the pediment. In 1808, when King Louis Napoleon took the Stadhuis (Town Hall) on Dam Square as his palace, the city council moved to this building, where it remained until 1988, when the new Stadhuis and Muziektheater complex (see p. 106) was completed. Not all of the majestic Grand Hotel is in the 17th-century classical style: Coming out of the courtyard, the former City Hall to the left was built in the 1920s in the restrained art deco style of the Amsterdam school.

On the opposite bank of the canal stands the **Oude Vleeshuis** (Old Meat Market), an 18th-century building whose gable is decorated with the heads of horned cattle. Farther along, heading south, across the next bridge and to the right, is a classical doorcase, carved with lion masks and cherubs, dated 1624. This once led to a tavern known as De Brakke Grond (The Brackish Ground), a name that indicates the quality of the terrain in the 17th century. Today **De Brakke Grond** is a cultural complex with a small theater renowned for its dynamic and experimental productions (entered from Nes, the street that runs parallel to Oudezijds Voorburgwal).

UNCLE JOHN THE PAWNBROKER

The next building along to the left is the huge **Bank van Lening.** In this case, "bank" is a euphemism for pawnbroker, and the big building provided warehousing for goods offered as security against loans. The inscription over the door tells those who already have gold to pass on by—this bank is for those who

are in need. Established in 1578, the Bank van Lening provided an alternative to commercial pawnbrokers who charged extortionate interest rates. The loan rates here were set in accordance with the borrower's means, at a rate that took into account the individual's ability to repay. To Amsterdam's needy citizens, the institution was known affectionately as Ome Jan (Uncle John).

Crossing the next bridge, look left to Nos. 215–217, with its ornate Renaissance-style stucco cornice dating from the late 18th century. On the right, at No. 231, stands the Agnietenkapel, fronted by its lively gateway of baroque strap-work, with the words "Athenaeum Illustre" worked in wrought iron across the top, referring to the body that evolved into today's university. Once part of the convent of St. Agnes, this simple but graceful chapel of 1470 was taken over by the Athenaeum Illustre in 1632. Members created the fine Renaissance lecture theater, which now forms part of the **Universiteits-museum de Agnietenkapel** (University Museum Chapel of St. Agnes), covering the history of education and student life in the city.

Students at Amsterdam's university take a break between lectures.

De Brakke Grond
- Map p. 72
- Nes 43
- 622 9014
- Tram: 4, 9, 14, 16, 24, 25

The House on the Three Canals stands on the site of the demolished city wall.

THE MEETING OF THREE WATERWAYS

Continuing down the canal, look across to the elegant classical facade of No. 316, designed by Philip Vingboons in 1655 and featuring a stucco panel of a sleeping pilgrim guarded by angels. At the bottom end of Oudezijds Voorburgwal stands the intriguing **Huis op de Drie Grachten** (The House on Three Canals) of 1609, with step-gabled facades facing each of the three waterways—Oudezijds Voorburgwal, Grimburgwal, and Oudezijds Achterburgwal. To the south it looks across the graphically named Grimburgwal (Muddy Ditch Wall). Heading right at this point will take you to Oude Turfmarkt, where you will find the interesting **Allard Pierson Museum** (see pp. 78–79), the university's museum of antiquities. The museum is part of the gray-brick complex on the opposite bank of the Grimburgwal canal that houses the main university campus, built on the site of the city Gasthuis (Hospital). Over to the left, on the eastern side of Oudezijds Achterburgwal, you will see the original hospital gate, carved with elderly male and female figures flanking the city's coat of arms.

A short way up on the right is another old gateway, carved with a pair of ancient pince-nez spectacles. This leads through to the **Oudemannehuis,** founded in the early 17th century as a home for elderly paupers, rebuilt in 1754. Now part of the university, you can go through the glass doors into a corridor lined with booksellers'

fishing nets—as shown in the 1645 carving above the door. One of the women in the frieze is being whipped and the inscription, translated, means "My hand punishes but my intention is good." If only this had been true—in fact, the warders ran the Spinhuis like a brothel, selling the sexual services of the inmates. Some of these were certainly prostitutes, but others were ordinary women who had committed no crime, condemned to incarceration by their own families for petty misdemeanors.

As you emerge from Spinhuissteeg, look left at No. 187, which has a plaque dated 1727 carved with a rebus; the picture of the house and the man are a visual pun on the name of the owner, a Mr. Huysman. Turning right up Oudezijds Achterburgwal takes you past various faculty buildings to Oude Hoogstraat, with its shops selling new and antiquarian books, textiles, crafts, and clothing.

DUTCH EAST INDIA COMPANY

Heading right, from the exit to Oudemanhuispoort, look for a narrow gateway at No. 24, on the right. The highly ornate facade of the **Oostindisch Huis** (East India House), now part of the University of Amsterdam, faces you as you pass through into the courtyard. Though not large, it was the headquarters and nerve center of the Dutch East India Company whose vast trading empire stretched halfway around the world (see p. 26). Nobody knows who designed the building, which dates from 1605, but the playful strapwork in the gable and above the windows, combined with the effective use of contrasting red brick and creamy sandstone, are all the notable trademarks of Hendrick de Keyser (1565–1621). ∎

The former headquarters of the Dutch East India Company now serve as a university department.

stands specializing in second-hand and antiquarian books. The fine gateway at the other end of the corridor, on Kloveniersburgwal, was carved by Anthonie Ziesenis in 1786 and shows two elderly men supported by the youthful female figure of Charity, holding a fruit-filled cornucopia.

THE WOMEN'S PRISON

Kloveniersburgwal is named after the *kloveniers*, the militiamen of the Guild of St. Adrian, who policed this district in the 17th and 18th centuries. If you turn left here, then take the third left, on Spinhuissteeg, you will find the preserved doorway of the **Spinhuis** up on the right. Here, women who had been convicted of petty crimes were put to work spinning flax and making

Allard Pierson Museum

THE ALLARD PIERSON MUSEUM IS DEVOTED TO THE archaeology of ancient Egypt, Greece, Rome, and western Asia. Difficult as it is to bring these subjects to life, this small museum does it very well, making the most of a rich collection of ancient artifacts found during excavations in the early decades of the 20th century.

Allard Pierson Museum

www.uba.uva.nl/apm

- Map p. 72
- Oude Turfmarkt 127
- 525 2556
- Closed Mon., Sat., & Sun. a.m.
- $$$
- Tram: 4, 9, 14, 16, 20, 24, 25
- Museumboot

The collection, owned by the University of Amsterdam, is one of the biggest university museums in the world. The displays on the ground floor provide a chronological journey through ancient **Egypt,** from the earliest prehistoric pottery (5000 B.C.) to the beautiful and colorful textiles of the Coptic era (5th to 11th centuries A.D.). In between there are models of the pyramids of Giza, cases full of stunning jewelry, and carved reliefs of grand Egyptian rulers in polished sandstone, not to mention mummies of crocodiles and monkeys, cats and birds, and a full explanation of the mummification process. The Coptic textiles are among the most enjoyable displays. Preserved against rot by the dry nature of the Egyptian desert climate, these delicate, colorful rags and fragments of garments woven in linen and wool are decorated with an eclectic amalgam of

Roman sarcophagus dating from the 2nd century B.C. and decorated with men and women dancing in a naked drunken frenzy, in honor of Bacchus, god of wine. Scholars have speculated that the destruction of the grape in order to give birth to wine is a metaphor for human death and resurrection. Much of this part of the collection is displayed thematically to illustrate everyday life in Roman times. One outstanding exhibit—a graceful couch used for reclining at banquets—suggests that life was very comfortable, at least for wealthy Romans.

The ancient **Greek** section consists largely of ceramics decorated with scenes from Greek epics and mythology. Right at the very end, though, you will find a delightful case devoted to animals in antiquity—terra-cotta frogs, bronze lions, stone cockerels, and a ferocious wild boar, not to mention sundry cats, goats, pigs, and a solitary grasshopper. Some are toys, others were made as offerings to the gods and represent some of the disguises these deities adopted when visiting earth-bound mortals. ■

Egyptian, Christian, and Roman motifs.

On the opposite side of the corridor is a small but select collection of material from **western Asia** (principally from Iran), with some fine examples of prehistoric ceramics, including elegant water jugs with long spouts shaped like an ibis beak, used for ceremonial libations.

Upstairs, you can see the star of the comprehensive collection of material from **Cyprus,** the reconstruction of a two-seater funerary chariot, whose remains were discovered in 8th-century B.C. tombs at Salamis.

From Italy there are reconstructions of **Etruscan** temples and houses based on models found in tombs, as well as a bathtub-size

Despite its sober exterior, the Allard Pierson Museum overflows with splendid antiquities.

De Leuuwenburg, a fine Dutch Renaissance house, stands guard on the fringes of the city's sex-shop district.

Red Light District

A FEW BLOCKS FROM AMSTERDAM'S MAIN STREET LIES THE city's infamous Red Light District. During the day it has the air of a fairly ordinary part of Amsterdam, but in the evening the facades are lit up by neon lights advertising sex shops and "live" shows. Unfortunately, the sex industry has taken over some of Amsterdam's most beautiful canal houses, many of which are being sadly neglected by their owners.

Hash Marihuana Hemp Museum

- 🅰 Map p. 72
- ✉ Oudezijds Achterburgwal 148
- ☎ 623 5961
- 💲 $$$
- 🚊 Tram: 4, 9, 16, 20, 24, 25

To sample the area, you only have to walk from Dam Square down Damstraat and turn left at the second bridge, onto Oudezijds Achterburgwal. Four doors down on the left you will find the **Hash Marihuana Hemp Museum,** which answers any questions you might have about the weed and its cultivation. A few doors farther down is the **Amsterdam Tattoo Museum and Library,** a semi-serious venture that puts body art in the Western world into a wider anthropological context.

A left turn in seedy Stoofsteeg takes you to a bridge with vistas up and down Oudezijds Voorburgwal. On the other side of the bridge, to the right, No. 136 was the home of Admiral Maarten Harpertzoon Tromp (1598–1653), who scored

many victories in naval battles against the English. The admiral is depicted here resting on a cannon with a sunken ship in the background. On the opposite bank, note the fine run of bell gables (Nos. 101–107), so called for their shape.

Next on the left you will come to the magnificent **Oude Kerk** (Old Church; see pp. 82–83), a beacon of religion and culture incongruously ringed by red-light windows. Enjoyment of its fine exterior is made somewhat challenging by prostitutes who solicit visitors by calling from doorways or rapping their knuckles on the windows.

If you are curious to know more about the red-light phenomenon, the **Prostitution Information Center,** to the north of the church, is the place to go. The center was set up in 1994 to inform the public on all aspects of prostitution.

The next stretch of Oudezijds Voorburgwal contains some of Amsterdam's oldest surviving houses, although the area is tainted by drug pushers who hang around the bridges and adjacent side streets. Across the canal lies No. 57, which greatly resembles the Oostindisch Huis (see p. 76). At No. 40 you will find the delightful **Museum Amstelkring** (see pp. 86–89).

On the opposite bank, No. 19 is a splendid sandstone house with a very tall neck gable and scroll stones carved in the shape of giant fish. On this side, No. 18, attributed to Hendrick de Keyser, has a plaque on its facade showing Egmond Castle, which is on the coast just west of Alkmaar. Next comes No. 14, called **De Leeuwenburg** (The Lion City) after the sandstone carvings of lion masks set into the brickwork separating the first and second floors. These in turn refer to the coat of arms of the Baltic port city of Riga, the original home of the first owner of this house. Built in 1600, the house retains several rare features, including the cellar shop, whose entrance protrudes from the facade into the street; the wooden window shutters on the ground floor, which could also be opened up to create an awning above and a shop counter below; and the tiny leaded windows filled with green-tinted glass.

Several carved gable stones have been reset in the wall that terminates the canal. To the right of the wall stands the sluice gate that controls the flow of fresh water from the canals to the IJ River beyond. Turning left into Nieuwebrugsteeg takes you past the engaging In de Olofspoort *proeflokaal* (see p. 50) and out onto Damrak and Centraal Station. ∎

Despite its apparent impact on spelling skills, marijuana cultivation is promoted openly in this city of liberal drug laws.

Amsterdam Tattoo Museum & Library
www.tattoomusuem.nl

⬛ Map p. 73

✉ Oudezijds Achterburgwal 130

☎ 625 1565

🕐 Closed a.m. & all day Mon.

💲 $$$

🚊 Tram: 4, 9, 16, 20, 24, 25

Prostitution Information Center

⬛ Map p. 73

✉ Enge Kerksteeg 3

☎ 420 7328

🕐 Closed Mon., Thurs., & Sun.

🚊 Tram: 4, 9, 16, 20, 24, 25

Oude Kerk

Oude Kerk
www.oudekerk.nl

- Map p. 73
- Oudekerksplein 23
- 625 8284
- Closed Sun. a.m.
- $$$
- Tram: 4, 9, 16 20

THE CITY'S OLDEST CHURCH WAS FOUNDED IN THE EARLY 13th century, but most of the surviving structure dates from the rebuilding of 1306. Dedicated to St. Nicholas, patron saint of seafarers, it contains the tombs of several admirals, as well as those of some of Amsterdam's most illustrious citizens.

You can climb the Oude Kerk spire or stay at street level and listen to its bells.

Opposite: The sonorous tones of this spectacular 1724 organ bathe modern visitors in music from three centuries ago.

It is often said of Protestant churches that their white walls and vast windows symbolize the clear light of reason, but the beautiful Oude Kerk (Old Church) did not start out this way. Today's light-filled interior was the result of iconoclasm—Calvinists attacked this church in 1566, destroying statues, images, and works of art in a protest against laws that kept them from worshiping freely.

The iconoclasts did not destroy everything, however. As you enter the church you can see paintings in the timber vaults that survived because they were out of reach. Over to the right, on either side of the high altar, **medieval choir stalls** with carved seats (misericords) show scenes from popular moral tales, including *Reynard the Fox*, as well as peasants in the midst of some very basic bodily functions. Perhaps these examples of medieval humor survived because they appealed to the somewhat cynical Amsterdam frame of mind, which is also in evidence in the room off the south transept where marriages took place: The legend above the entrance reads "Marry in haste; repent at leisure."

Dating from the Protestant era are the **box pews** of city dignitaries in the nave. The **organ,** built in 1724, is the most ornate object in the church. It sounds as magnificent as it looks. A schedule of organ recitals and choral evensong can be found posted in the church porch. These events are well worth attending, for that is when the building really comes to life as a place of worship rather than as a curious relic from the past.

BONES & BELLS

Every inch of the floor is covered with **grave slabs,** carved with names, symbols, and coats of arms of those buried beneath. The grave of Saskia van Uylenburg, Rembrandt's first wife, lies in the north aisle. Rembrandt painted many tender portraits of her and was devastated when she died on June 14, 1642.

A memorial to the Amsterdam-born composer Sweelinck (1562–1621) rests in the opposite aisle. Sweelinck was the Oude Kerk's official organist, and the Sweelinck-canotorij—Sweelinck Singers—perform here regularly and help to keep his music alive.

As you leave the church it's worth circling to the right for a look at the massive **bell tower** of brick and sandstone. Rising high above the church, this intricate tower is topped by the imperial crown of the Holy Roman Emperor Maximilian I. (In 1489 the Habsburg Holy Roman Emperor granted Amsterdam the right to display the imperial crown in its coat of arms in return for loans granted by the city bankers on rather generous terms.) The tower can be climbed as part of a guided tour (book at least a week in advance). If you are here at the quarter hour you will hear a tune played on the carillon of 47 bells, installed in 1658. ∎

Sex & drugs in Amsterdam

The open—and legal—consumption of soft drugs in Amsterdam is a result of recent liberal legislation. Open prostitution, by contrast, is almost as old as the city itself. Unscrupulous local officials made small fortunes from the industry in the 17th century, when keeping a brothel was seen as one of the perks of office.

Today the Red Light District is an undeniable part of Amsterdam's tourist appeal. The city has acknowledged the sex industry, choosing to bring it into the mainstream rather than pretend it doesn't exist. Prostitutes are licensed and receive regular health checkups; their earnings are audited; and they pay income tax. They even have representatives in the local Chamber of Commerce. If you visit this area, the local police distribute leaflets explaining how to avoid trouble. Urinating in the street, shouting or disturbing the peace, and parking without paying for a ticket are all subject to heavy on-the-spot fines. Using soft drugs or visiting a prostitute, by contrast, are considered above board.

Tolerance for tricks and treats

Amsterdam's permissiveness in matters of sex and drugs attracts a substantial amount of tourism to the city, but it upsets politicians in many neighboring nations. Their own attempts to stamp out drug use, they argue, are being undermined by the cavalier attitude of the Dutch. Drug use is commonplace all across Europe, Amsterdammers reply; the only difference here is its degree of openness. They also contend that cannabis is no different from alcohol—just another form of recreational drug—and point to the greater impairment of faculties from tippling than toking.

Former Amsterdam mayor Schelto Patijn introduced a new cooling-down law—the *afkoeluurtje*—whereby bars around Rembrandtplein and Leidseplein can sell nothing stronger than coffee and soft drinks in the last hour before they close. The idea is to combat the drunken vandalism that has been a regular side effect of weekend nightlife in the area. Dope smokers have been quick to point out that violence is not a documented behavior of the stoned.

Even the most tolerant Amsterdammers, however, are beginning to question where the fun limit lies. Decorum and good manners once dictated that you smoked dope only in a "coffeeshop," that you indulged neither in public nor in front of children. Nowadays the air is clogged with the cloyingly sweet smell of cannabis in many places around the city—notably the train station, where your first impression of Amsterdam is likely to be colored by the sight of open drug use and by the addicts who beg from newly arrived visitors. Any establishment with the word "coffeeshop" in its title sells various types of pot and hash, as well as coffee, beer, and fruit juice. (The place to go just for coffee or a beer is a café or a brown café.)

Brothels, sex shops, and a few windows have spread well beyond the historic confines of the Red Light District. So-called "smart drug" shops—selling herbal ecstasy, magic mushrooms, and sex-enhancing chemicals— have sprung up all over the place, including along Amsterdam's main shopping streets.

The government has not yet decided how to deal with this latest phenomenon. It will probably continue to turn a blind eye—as it has always done—in the interests of that famous Dutch virtue: If you tolerate the peculiarities of others, they in turn will be unlikely to interfere with your own. ∎

Left: If the sign says "coffeeshop," you can be sure to find much more than caffeine on the menu.

Above: In Amsterdam's (in)famous Red Light District, even the bulbs lighting the canal bridges glow a rosy pink at night.

Right: Sex shops abound throughout the Red Light District.

Erotic Museum

The Erotic Museum *(Oudezijds Achterburgwaal 54, tel 624 7303; www.eroticmuseum.com, $$)* is packed from floor to ceiling with erotic pictures, from late-19th-century sepia-tint photographs to a series of self portraits by the late John Lennon, sketched during his "lie-in" peace protest at the Amsterdam Hilton Hotel in 1969. ■

Two museums in one: The Amstelkring is both an early merchant's house and a secret church.

Museum Amstelkring

 Map p. 73

✉ Oudezijds Voorburgwal 40

☎ 624 6604

🕐 Closed Sun. a.m.

$ $$$

🚋 Tram: 4, 9, 16, 20, 24, 25

Museum Amstelkring

BEHIND THE ORDINARY FACADE OF THIS 17TH-CENTURY merchant's house in the Red Light District lies an extraordinary secret. From the very functional downstairs rooms, narrow stairs lead up to a clandestine church, where Catholics worshiped in secret for centuries. Now beautifully preserved in its original state, the Museum Amstelkring, also known as Ons' Lieve Heer op Solder (Our Dear Lord in the Attic), is a fascinating monument to Catholic history.

The first owner of the house, hosiery merchant Jan Hartman, was not himself a Catholic. He built the house in 1661–63 for his own use, and constructed another two houses at the back to rent out to tenants. With an eye to greater income, he then rented out the whole of the roof space running across all three houses to the local Catholic community.

At that time, Catholics were not allowed to practice their religion in public. The Protestant city council that resulted from the Alteration of 1578 (see p. 26) voted to allow Catholic worship to continue in the city only on condition that the churches did not look like churches. Neither could they be accessible from public roads. At first, Catholics worshiped in living rooms and

makeshift churches. Later they built fully furnished churches, privately owned and entered (like this one) from a side alley.

A PRIESTLY HOME

Jan Hartman's heirs and successors allowed the church to flourish here until 1793, when local Catholics bought all three houses and turned them into a home for the parish priest. Few significant changes have been made to the house, with the result that it has preserved its 17th-century appearance. The functional downstairs rooms served as office and warehouse. The main living room, the **Sael,** on the second floor, is decorated along classical Dutch lines with strict regard for geometry: Only one of the two doors opposite the fireplace is functional—the

other leads nowhere and was added purely for symmetry.

The front room, the **Bovenkamer,** overlooks the canal and served as a living room and bedroom. The bed, built in an alcove over the stairs, could be closed by day, disguised as a cupboard—an ingenious space-saving device. As you climb the staircase, you can glimpse another room that resembles a cupboard. This **Kapelaanskamer** was a secret room where the priest could hide if necessary.

Next comes the airy and spacious church. As the small congregation continued to grow throughout the 17th and 18th centuries, two **galleries** were added, suspended above the main body of the church by iron rods

Galleries were added to the clandestine church in the 18th century to accommodate the growing congregation.

Right: "The Baptism of Christ" (1716) hanging above the mock marble altar is by Jacob de Wit (1695–1754).

Amstelkring facade – simple spout gable

The front house is furnished as it was in the 1660s. attached to the roof timbers. The house continued to be used as the parish church for the area until 1887. By this time the law had been reformed, allowing Dutch Catholics to build conventional churches once again. The new parish church of St. Nicholas, or Sint Nicolaaskerk (see p. 96), was built on the waterfront in 1887. If you look out from the windows of the clandestine church you can see the twin spires of the new church over the rooftops.

Behind the altar, stairs lead down to the ground floor via a series of rooms once used by the priest and now housing pictures, objects, and documents explaining the history of Catholic worship in the city. The 17th-century kitchen survives in the basement, along with a few "modern" innovations from the mid-19th century (including an indoor toilet).

Fortunately, all this has been kept intact, thanks to prompt action by a group of local amateur historians who realized the importance of the church in 1888 when it was faced with demolition. They bought it and opened it as a museum in that same year—a pioneering example of heritage conservation in action. ∎

main entrance

wooden viewing gallery of church

clandestine church

priest's bedroom

rear house

kitchen

the Sael, or main living room

middle house

the Kapelaanskamer, the priest's secret hiding place

house on the canal

A painting of the Nativity decorates a room used by the priests.

Zeedijk

IF AMSTERDAM'S STREETS OCCASIONALLY LEAVE YOU appalled by the squalor of graffiti-scarred buildings, sex shops, drug dealers, addicts, and dog feces, take heart from the story of Zeedijk. Once the haunt of muggers and drug pushers, the street has been reclaimed progressively for the enjoyment of everyone, through a program of building restoration and renewal begun in the early 1990s. Today nobody need fear strolling down this street of antique shops and jazz cafés, tapas bars, and Chinese supermarkets.

He Wa Buddhist Temple
- Map p. 73
- Zeedijk 106–118
- Closed Mon.

THE SAILORS' QUARTER

Zeedijk begins to the east of Centraal Station, behind the Barbizon Palace Hotel and the huge twin-towered Sint Nicolaaskerk. The first section of Zeedijk is particularly attractive, especially at the junction with Sint Olofspoort, where the buildings lean in all directions. They were deliberately built like this so that goods could be winched up to the warehouse space in the gable without bumping against the front of the house.

Zeedijk follows the line of the medieval city walls (hence its serpentine shape on the map). Sint Olofspoort was the site of one of the main city gates. The gate has now gone but one of the city's oldest houses has survived. **Zeedijk No. 1** dates from 1550 and is one of only two medieval timber buildings left in the city (see p. 62). It is now a colorful café, **Int Aepjen** (In the Apes)—so named because an earlier owner kept monkeys (*aapjes*), given to him by sailors in payment for their lodgings.

Opposite, at No. 2A, is the entrance to **Sint Olofskapel,** whose sculptures show a grim life-sized skeleton and garlanded skulls. The chapel was built in 1425 and restored in 1992 and now serves as a conference and banqueting center for the **Barbizon Palace Hotel.**

Several buildings in the vicinity have gable stones (plaques). On the right, on Sint Olofsteeg, a plaque on the side wall of No. 3 shows a spotted leopard (perhaps indicating this was once a furrier's). At the next bridge, on the right, another plaque shows the medieval St. Olof's gate and another opposite depicts a cooper at work. The wind-

ing gear below the bridge belongs to the locks that were once used to hold back the tidal waters of the IJ River, before it was closed off from the open sea. From this bridge there is a good view southward to the Oude Kerk's spire (see pp. 82–83).

GAY AMSTERDAM & CHINATOWN

The next stretch of Zeedijk is lined with upscale antique shops whose windows offer glimpses of rare and tempting treasures. At No. 63, on the left, the shopfront survives from Bet van Beeren's café, **Café 't Mandje,** now immortalized in the Amsterdams Historisch Museum (see pp. 64–67). Bet ran the café from 1927 to 1967 as a haven for lesbians and gays when they had nowhere else to go in the city.

Beyond lies Amsterdam's **Chinatown,** a miniature Hong Kong, complete with authentic smells, restaurants, and stores selling rice cookers and coromandel screens. Here you can shop for temple dogs and giant gilded Buddhas, consult an acupuncturist or a Chinese herbalist, buy gold and jade, or eat in one of the restaurants specializing in Cantonese seafood. You can also seek spiritual help at the **He Wa Buddhist Temple,** which opened in September 2000, built and funded by the thriving local Chinese community. ■

Symbol of renewal: The He Wa Buddhist Temple stands in an area once blighted by neglect.

Nieuwmarkt

Zuiderkerk

- 🗺 Map p. 73
- ✉ Zuiderkerkhof 72
- ☎ 689 2565
- 🕐 Closed Sat. & Sun.
  (tower open
  June–Sept.
  Wed.–Sat., with
  tours at 2 p.m., 3
  p.m., & 4 p.m.)
- 🚋 Tram: 4, 9, 14, 16,
  20, 24, 25

Once a city gate, the Waag is now a stylish café.

NARROW AND INTIMATE ZEEDIJK LEADS OUT ONTO THE windswept open space of Nieuwmarkt (New Market), which has cafés, restaurants, and a daily market selling flowers, cheeses, fruits, and vegetables. The area has gone upscale in recent years, with the once-desolate and graffiti-scarred Waag (Weighhouse) now converted into a popular café and restaurant, with summer terrace.

The **Waag** started out life as Sint Anthoniespoort—St. Anthony's Gate—built in 1488 to control the road into the city from the south. Almost as soon as the building's brick walls were completed, the city began to expand beyond the walls, and this building became redundant as a gate. It was transformed instead into a public weighhouse where local merchants and manufacturers (especially those making cannons and anchors) could check the weight of their goods.

MEETINGS OF THE GUILDS

The upper rooms of the Waag were used by the city's medieval guilds,

each of which had a separate entrance. Facing Zeedijk (on the northwestern corner) is the entrance used by members of the masons' guild. The relief above the door, carved by Hendrick de Keyser in the early 17th century, shows various tools of the trade: In the central roundel above the door is a bearded figure holding a bricklayer's trowel, while there are roofers' tools to the left, plumbers' tools to the right, and more bricklayers' and masons' tools below.

Circling around to the right, the door of the painters', glaziers', and sculptors' guild shows their patron saint—the evangelist St. Luke—seated on his symbol, an ox.

Farther around, beside the entrance to the Café in de Waag, the words "Theatrum Anotomicum" (Anatomy Theater) carved above the door signal the entrance to the surgeons' guild.

Rembrandt's first important public commission—one that helped establish his reputation as an artist—is entitled the "Anatomy Lesson of Dr. Tulp" (1632). This depicts Dr. Tulp, the renowned surgeon (he was also the mayor of Amsterdam), lecturing to members of the guild in this theater (the painting now hangs in the Mauritshuis Museum in Den Haag—see p. 226).

CANNON & WINE COOPERS

This part of Amsterdam, in addition to being the immigrant quarter, formed the city's first industrial district—one that resounded to the noise of metal- and wood-working in the 17th and 18th centuries. Two local manufacturers who dealt in iron, copper, lead, and armaments were the wealthy Trip brothers; their elegant house can be seen to the south of Nieuwmarkt.

To get there, turn your back on the Waag and cross to the right-hand (western) bank of the Kloveniersburgwal canal. As you make your way across, take note of the varied gables on the buildings on this side of Nieuwmarkt; **Nos. 34–36** boast a gable stone carved with knights on horseback.

It is also worth diverting down the second alley to the right, Koestraat, to see the **Wijnkopersgildenhuis** (Wine Coopers' Guild House) on the left (No. 10). This fine building of 1633 has the guild's patron, St. Urban, carved above the entrance, plucking grapes from a vine.

Walking back up Koestraat, turn right and look across Kloveniers-

St. Luke the Evangelist, patron saint of sculptors, is a relief to see above the entrance to the guild meeting rooms.

A brooding sky silhouettes the crown-topped spire of the Zuiderkerk.

gable over which two sphinxes are draped—their precise significance has never been established. The diminutive house resulted from the coachman's complaint that his masters were extravagant in building such a palatial mansion for their home, and that he himself would be content with a house no wider than the Trip brothers' front door. Whether he really meant this or not, the Trip brothers took him at his word.

ZUIDERKERK

The next bridge left down Klove-niersburgwal leads to Nieuwe Hoogstraat, with its shops specializing in antique clothes, and African and Indonesian tribal art. The first right, Zanddwarsstraat, leads to the **Zuiderkerk** (Southern Church). There are wonderful views over the heart of Amsterdam to the city's harbor and to the open countryside beyond from the church's magnificent tower. Built between 1603 and 1611 to the designs of Hendrick de Keyser, it was the first large church in the Netherlands constructed specifically for Protestant worship, as opposed to being converted from an existing Catholic church. English architect Christopher Wren came to study it when he was faced with a similar task—the building of the great Protestant cathedral of St. Paul's in London—following the 1666 fire.

No services have been held here since 1929. After years of neglect, the church has been turned into an information center with exhibitions on development plans for Amsterdam and its environs—far more interesting than it sounds, especially if you have an interest in modern architecture and planning issues. The church now sits at the center of an area that has been comprehensively redeveloped since the war. The Nazis attempted to eradicate

burgwal canal to the huge gray sandstone **Trippenhuis** on the opposite bank. Built in a classical style, its facade is broken up by Corinthian pilasters, and the chimneys are carved in the shape of huge mortars, symbolizing the armaments industry, the source of the Trip brothers' wealth. Justus Vingboons (1612–1672), architect and brother of Philip Vingboons, designed this house in 1660, observing the brothers' request for one facade but two separate houses. Look carefully at the middle windows and you will see the dividing wall behind the glass.

On this side of the canal is No. 26, known as the **Kleine Trippenhuis,** built in 1696 for the Trip brothers' coachman. The facade is a mere 10 feet (3 m) wide, but it has an ornate semicircular the Jewish quarter during their occupation of the Netherlands (see p. 31), and city planners finished the job in the early 1980s when the Metro was built, along with the new Stadhuis-Muziektheater complex. The church is now surrounded by the Pentagon housing development (so called for the shape of the site), designed by Theo Bosch in 1983–84.

One route back to the city center lies down Zanddwarsstraat. Bridges force you to turn right onto Raamgracht, left over the canal, left again, and right down Groenburgwal, a street with an interesting mixture of old and new canal houses, warehouses, and houseboats. Halfway down, at No. 42, is the simple 18th-century Gothic **English Episcopal Church,** built for, and still used by, the English community in Amsterdam. The next right, Staalstraat, has antique shops and the very attractive **Saaihal** (Cloth Hall) on the right. Completed in 1641 to the design of Pieter de Keyser (1590–1657), the son of Hendrick, the gables are draped in theatrical bunches of linen, carved in sandstone, in a witty reference to the building's use as the guild house of the Cloth Merchants. From here the massive bulk of the Stadhuis-Muziektheater complex, the home

of the Nationale Ballet and the Nederlands Opera, lies to the left (see p. 106), while turning right takes you via Nieuwe Doelenstraat to Rokin and the Allard Pierson Museum (see pp. 78–79). ∎

A busy street-side scene in Zuiderkerk

Jacob Hooij

At Kloveniersburgwal 10–12, don't miss Jacob Hooij (see p. 263), the highly photogenic herbalist shop. Founded here more than 200 years ago, it still sells about 400 different herbs and spices—some for cooking, others for medicinal use. One of their best-selling lines is licorice. Once sold as a remedy for sore throats, today it comes in all shapes and sizes, from button-shaped dropjes to shoelaces and cartoon characters. ∎

A waterside stroll

Amsterdam's first dockyards and warehouses were located just beyond the city walls, which are traced in this walk around the city's original waterfront. The route passes through an area of Amsterdam still crowded with moored vessels of all types, from houseboats to sturdy seagoing sailing ships.

With your back to Centraal Station, head left for the Barbizon Palace Hotel. Next door to the hotel is the baroque **Sint Nicolaaskerk** ❶ (Church of St. Nicholas), built in 1887 as the successor to the secret attic church in the Museum Amstelkring (see pp. 86–87). Saint Nicholas, also known as Santa Claus, is the patron saint of seafarers, and the dedication of the church reflects the fact that this was the sailors' quarter of Amsterdam.

Turning left (as you face the church), it is a short walk to **Prins Hendrikkade 84–85** ❷, called Batavia, named for the capital of Indonesia (Jakarta was once known as Batavia). Several of the firms based in this fine art deco building continue to trade with

The drum-shaped Schreierstoren, or "Tower of Tears"

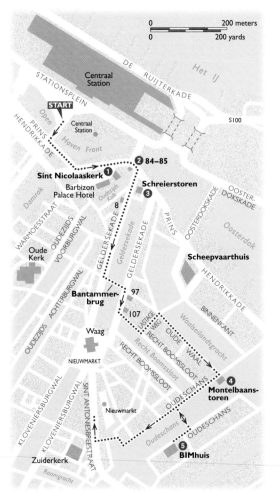

📖 Also see area map pp. 72–73

▶ Centraal Station

↔ 1.1 mile (1.8 km)

🕐 2 hours

▶ Oudeschans

NOT TO BE MISSED

- Sint Nicolaaskerk
- Prins Hendrikkade
- Schreierstoren
- Montelbaanstoren
- BIMHuis

Indonesia (formerly the Dutch East Indies).

Continue past this building, following the curve of the road to reach the **Schreierstoren ❸**, an attractive drum-shaped tower built in 1482. The name is said to mean "Weepers' Tower" or "Tower of Tears," and it is from here that sailors' wives watched their menfolk depart on hazardous voyages. A plaque on the tower records that one such voyage began on April 4, 1609, led by Henry Hudson, in search of the fabled westward passage to the Spice Islands. Instead, Hudson and his crew ended up stumbling across

Manhattan Island and the Hudson River.

Continue to the right of the tower, down Geldersekade, where fishermen once unloaded their catch for sale in the fish market on Nieuwmarkt. There are several elegant 18th-century houses to admire at the start of the street. Number 8 exhibits a splendid frieze above the door, showing tobacco leaves spilling out of bales and barrels, while No. 16 has an exotic plant forming the central rib of the tall window above its doorway.

Farther down on the left is the **Bantammerbrug**, one of several art deco

Catholic Sint Nicolaaskerk honors St. Nicholas, patron of seafarers.

bridges in the area with ornate wrought-iron lamp standards at each corner. Cross the bridge and turn right, noting No. 97, a fine step-gabled 17th-century house with a plaque indicating that its owner was involved in the cognac trade. Number 107, to the right, built in 1634, is known as the "House with Eight Entrances," because eight different chandlers and ships' suppliers had their premises here.

Turn left down leafy Recht Boomssloot, a canal named after the 16th-century ship-wright, Cornelis Boom. His shipyard, on the site of Amsterdam's oldest dockyard, once occupied Lastageweg, the first street to the left. A modern school and housing estate now stand on this historic spot.

On the other side of this precinct, you emerge onto Oude Waal (Old Wall). From here there are sweeping views across the boat-filled Waalseilandsgracht to the spiky outline of the **Scheepvaarthuis,** literally the "Ship Voyage House," on the opposite bank. Built by J.M. van der Mey for a shipping company in 1916, this

embankment and the variety of boats moored in the canal. At the end of the street is the **Montelbaanstoren ④,** a tower that leans rather perilously over the edge of the Oudeschans canal. The Oudeschans—meaning "Old Rampart"—formed part of the extended city defenses constructed in 1512. Hendrick de Keyser added the attractive spire that rises from the Montelbaanstoren in 1606.

Turning right to walk up Oudeschans, look across the canal to the opposite bank, lined with old **warehouses** converted into apartments. All have very simple and unadorned triangular gables and small windows (light was not such a priority in buildings used primarily for storage), with sail-shaped shutters painted in distinctive colors.

One of the warehouses (No. 73) contains the legendary **BIMHuis ⑤** (see p. 265), famous among jazz lovers the world over as a venue for improvised music. Posters outside give details of forthcoming performances.

Montelbaanstoren, once a defensive tower, now houses pumps that help clean city canals.

decorative office block is one of the earliest and finest examples of the distinctive Amsterdam school style of architecture (see p. 52). The maritime theme is worked into all the building's decorative details, from the rippling railings that surround it to the carvings of a bearded Triton breasting the surf over the entrance.

Turn right along Oude Waal, noting the attractive houses and warehouses lining the

Beyond are the converted warehouses called the Grote Zwaan, Kleine Zwaan, Grote Pauw, and Kleine Pauw (Great and Little Swan and Peacock, respectively).

At the end of the canal, the bridge to the right will lead you back to the Nieuwmarkt district (see pp. 92–95), but this is a good spot to stop for a moment and enjoy the various views before returning to the city center. ∎

Rembrandt made his home in this quarter of Amsterdam because he loved its color and vitality. Today, from the area's flea markets to its state-of-the-art museums, the artist's judgment is still justified.

Jodenbuurt, Plantage, & Oosterdok

Rembrandt self-portrait outside his former home

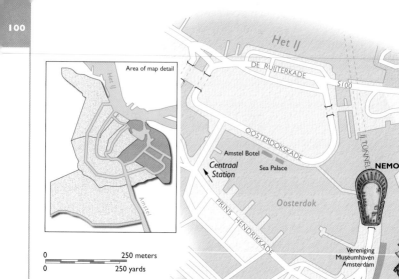

Area of map detail

Het IJ

Amstel

DE RUIJTERKADE

S100

OOSTERDOKSKADE

Amstel Botel

Centraal
Station

Sea Palace

IJ TUNNEL

NEMO

Oosterdok

Amsterdam

PRINS HENDRIKKADE

Rapenburgwal

Vereniging
Museumhaven
Amsterdam

0   250 meters
0   250 yards

Oosterdok

**Nederlands
Scheepvaart
Museum**

Oude-schans
OUDESCHANS

NIEUWE

UILENBURGERSTRAATEL

VALKENBURGERSTRAAT

KATTENBURGER-
PLEIN

NIEUWEVAART

De
Slyswacht

Gassan
Diamond
Works

RAPENBURGER
PLEIN

Entrepotdok

LAAGTE

**Museum het
Rembrandthuis**

Holland Experience

JODENBUURT

ANNE FRANK STR.

Entrepotdok

SINT
ANTONIESSLUIS

JODENBREESTR.

Flea Market

WATERLOOPLEIN

NIEUWE HERENGRACHT

Nationaal
Vakbonds-
museum

Verzetsmuseum

**Stadhuis-
Muziektheater**

Zwanenburgwal

Mozes en Aäronkerk

MR. VISSERPLEIN

Portugees-
Israëlitische
Synagoge

WERTHEIM-
PARK

HENRI
POLAKLAAN

PLANTAGE KERKLAAN

Planetarium

Arsenal

Holocaust
Memorial

WATERLOO
PLEIN

De Dokwerker
JONAS DANIEL
MEIJERPLEIN

PLANTAGE

Geologisch
Museum

Amstel

**Joods Historisch
Museum**

Waterlooplein

HORTUS

**Hortus
Botanicus**

PLANTAGE

MIDDENLAAN

BLAUW-
BRUG

PLANTSOEN

Hollandse
Schouwburg

PLANTAGE

PLANTAGE MUIDERGRACHT

Plantage

Muider-

Renzo Piano's
NEMO stands on
the edge of the
rejuvenated
docklands.

Jodenbuurt, Plantage, & Oosterdok

AMSTERDAM, UNDER PROTESTANT RULE FROM 1578, offered a safe haven for refugees fleeing persecution in other parts of Europe. Although they received no credit for it at the time, the Jews and Protestant dissenters who found a new home in this area brought with them skills and a work ethic that would allow the city to blossom economically, laying the foundation for the Golden Age.

They settled to the east of the city, in what was then a slum area beyond the medieval city walls. Still known to this day as the Jodenbuurt—the Jewish District—it bears the scars of the Nazi Holocaust, and the story of the almost total eradication of Amsterdam's Jews is poignantly told at the Joods Historische Museum (Jewish Historical Museum; see pp. 108–109). Nearby is the house where Rembrandt painted most of his masterpieces, drawing inspiration for his bearded Old Testament prophets from the ordinary people of the Jodenbuurt's streets. Close by are the factory chimneys of the Gassan Diamond Works. Excluded from many established professions and trades, the Jews of Amsterdam took to diamond cutting and polishing and established Amsterdam as the world center for trading in diamonds.

Side by side with the slums of the Jodenbuurt is the leafy suburb of Plantage (meaning "the Plantation"), originally an area of parks and gardens, with tea gardens, theaters, and public promenades. Though the area was built up in the 19th century, the pleasure gardens survive in the form of Amsterdam's huge zoo, and in the ponds, palm houses, and flower beds of the Hortus Botanicus (Botanical Gardens; see p. 110).

Immediately north, in Oosterdok, the scene shifts again. One block from the zoo, you can taste the salt in the air and feel sea winds in your hair. Right beside the harbor, a former naval depot has been turned into a maritime museum, while alongside is the ultramodern science museum newMetropolis (known more commonly as NEMO, see pp.122–23). ∎

DIJKSGRACHT

OOSTELIJKE EILANDEN

KATTENBURGERSTRAAT

Kattenburgervaart

GROTE KLEIN WITTENBURGERSTRAAT

WITTENBURGERSTRAAT

Wittenburgervaart

WITTENBURGER-GRACHT

Oosterkerk

Nieuwevaart

OOSTENBURGERGRACHT

OOSTENBURGER-PARK

KADIJK

Museumwerf 't Kromhout

HOOGTE KADIJK

ZEEBURGERSTRAAT

African savanna

Entrepotdok

ARTIS

Manatee and Hippo House

Insect House

Aquarium

SARPHATISTRAAT

Singelgracht

MAURITSKADE

Muiderpoort

gracht

ALEXANDER PLEIN

Singelgracht

MAURITSKADE

Tropenmuseum, Kindermuseum

LINNAEUSSTRAAT

OOSTERPARK

Rembrandt bought this house at the height of his fame. A later bankruptcy forced him to sell it.

Museum het Rembrandthuis
www.rembrandthuis.nl

 Map p. 100
✉ Jodenbreestraat 4
☎ 520 0400
💲 $$$
🚋 Tram: 9, 14, 20

Museum het Rembrandthuis

REMBRANDT LIVED AND WORKED IN THIS HANDSOME house from 1639 to 1656. It was the birthplace of his son, Titus, and where his wife Saskia died, and it was here that he created his masterpieces, including "The Night Watch" (1642). Ultimately, the house was to ruin him. Living well beyond his means, Rembrandt was declared bankrupt. Everything was sold, and he moved to cheap rented accommodations in the Jordaan.

The inventory compiled by the Secretary of the Chamber of Insolvency listed every one of Rembrandt's possessions prior to their sale, and has provided a wealth of information about the artist, his house, and his work. From it, we know exactly what was where in the house, room by room. This information proved invaluable in 1998 when the Rembrandt

House was comprehensively gutted and rebuilt. All the 19th- and 20th-century clutter was removed, and the house was returned to the way Rembrandt himself would have known it.

EXPENSIVE HABITS
The house was completed in 1606, though Rembrandt didn't move in until January 1639. He borrowed

the sum of 13,000 guilders to buy it (a huge amount, but he was a celebrated artist with good earning prospects). Unfortunately, Rembrandt had expensive tastes. He was a dealer as well as an artist, and he bought numerous paintings and engravings from his contemporaries, intending to resell them at a profit. Some of these works (mainly dramatically painted scenes from the Bible and classical mythology) have been loaned back to the Rembrandt House Museum and now hang on the walls of the downstairs rooms, which Rembrandt used as an art gallery.

CABINET OF CURIOSITIES

Rembrandt also kept a collection of rare and exotic objects, which has been re-created in the upstairs **Cabinet Room.** Such acquisitions of curiosities, forerunners of modern museums, were common enough among the very wealthy, but Rembrandt was a mere artist, and his collecting habits added to his financial burden. To try and make ends meet, he converted the attic into a big studio space and took in scores of pupils. The artist was not beyond passing off his pupils' work as his own, in order to drive up the price (one reason why so many of his paintings in public and private collections have now been demoted to "School of Rembrandt"). All this was to no avail. Far from paying off his debts, he actually borrowed more, until his creditors grew impatient and called in the bailiff.

THE MASTER ENGRAVER

Rembrandt often used the objects he collected as props in his paintings, and he frequently copied the work of artists he admired, such as Dürer, not as deliberate plagiarism, but more as a tribute from one great artist to another. He would also drag people in off the streets to serve as

his models, as you can see if you visit the comprehensive collection of engravings displayed in the gallery built beside Rembrandt's house, a lasting memorial to his essential earthiness. For all his high spending, he was most at home depicting ordinary people—beggars, workmen, street characters—even farm animals, with a realism and a spontaneity that were rare in his day. ∎

Rembrandt drew his biblical characters from those he encountered in the streets of Amsterdam.

Are You Experienced?

Beside the Rembrandt House is an attraction called the Holland Experience. This 30-minute multimedia show covers the highlights of Holland's eventful history, complete with smells and realistic soundtrack (Jodenbreestraat 17, tel 422 2233; www.holland-experience.nl, $$$, tram: 9, 14, 20). ∎

The genius of Rembrandt

O f all the great artists to come out of the Netherlands during the Golden Age, Rembrandt remains one of the most enigmatic—and, at the same time, one of the most human.

Rembrandt van Rijn was born in 1606 in Leiden, where his wealthy father owned and operated a mill on the Rhine River. (The family name "van Rijn" means "of the Rhine.") Though pushed toward a career in law, he gave up his university studies to concentrate on art. Amsterdam was the place where artists could best make a living, so Rembrandt moved here in 1631.

The city's guilds and civic guards were in the habit of commissioning group portraits to hang on their clubroom walls. Rembrandt's first commission was to paint the renowned Dr. Tulp giving an anatomy lesson, observed by a group of distinguished guild surgeons. "The Anatomy Lesson of Dr. Tulp" (1632), a somewhat stilted composition, now hangs in the Mauritshuis Museum in Den Haag (see p. 226). The surgeons who commissioned the work wanted to be shown in a flattering light —preferably in full profile—so their poses are awkward. But the sponsors were happy, the painting was well received, and fame and fortune followed. Rembrandt, however, rapidly grew restless, chafing against the restraints and conventions of the time.

Rembrandt's etchings

Even as he continued to produce portraits and large oil paintings of biblical subjects for public consumption, Rembrandt turned to engraving as a more private activity. His combination of hard line (achieved by etching the printing plate with acid) and of softer lines and shading (produced by cutting the plate directly with etching tools) marked him as a technical innovator. The Jewish quarter where he lived

provided him with a constant source of subjects. He would approach passersby and ask them to model for him as he sketched out his Old Testament prophets with lined faces and flowing beards. He also loved to draw neighborhood characters: rat-catchers, vagabonds, beggars, organ-grinders.

Personal tragedy

Rembrandt's engravings were eagerly sought by collectors. On canvas, too, he began to depart from convention—in ways that did not please his patrons. It's possible that events in his personal life made him less eager to please the self-important *burghermasters* (mayors) and *nouveau riche* merchants for whom he toiled. His wife, Saskia, and three of their four children died, leaving only the sickly Titus. In 1642, the year of Saskia's death, Rembrandt painted "The Night Watch" (see p. 196); now considered a masterpiece of realism, it was openly derided in its day. Among Rembrandt's transgressions, according to the critics, was letting the figures overlap so that some are partly hidden.

After this, Rembrandt received fewer commissions, prompting him to retreat into his own world. He moved to a modest house in Rozengracht, in the Jordaan, where he painted as much for his own satisfaction as for public consumption. In 1665 he produced the brilliant "Jewish Bride," with its impressionistic background, and its paint applied so lavishly as to be three-dimensional. These experiments in technique, 200 years ahead of their time, help to explain the luminescence of the portrait and its intense emotional quality.

"The Jewish Bride" would be one of Rembrandt's last works. Titus died in 1667 at the age of 27, and Rembrandt followed in less than a year. He was buried in an unmarked pauper's grave in Westerkerk (see p. 145)—an ignoble end for a towering artistic talent. ■

Left: Rembrandt's "Self Portrait as the Apostle St. Paul" (1666)
Above: The enigmatic "Jewish Bride"
Below: The "Anatomy Lesson of Dr. Tulp"—the painting that made Rembrandt's name

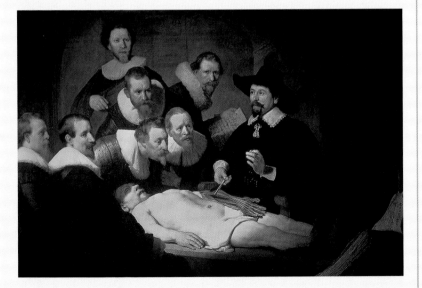

Gassan Diamond Works

- Map p. 100
- Nieuwe Uilenburgerstraatel 173–175
- ☎ 622 5333
- ⑤ Free tours daily
- Tram: 9, 14, 20

Stadhuis– Muziektheater

- Map p. 100
- Waterlooplein 2
- Tram: 9, 14, 20

Waterlooplein

THE WATERLOOPLEIN DISTRICT IS DOMINATED BY THE vast Stadhuis-Muziektheater complex, known to Amsterdammers as the Stopera—an ironic reference to the 1980s "Stop the Opera" campaign, mounted by demonstrators who objected to the building of such a vast, expensive, and (in their view) elitist building in the heart of what was once the teeming and industrious Jewish quarter.

The Rembrandthuis (see pp. 102–103) is one of the few buildings to survive the postwar redevelopment of the Jewish quarter. It stands alongside **Sint Antoniessluis** (St. Anthony's Lock), from where there is a fine view northward down Oudeschans

The Waterlooplein market is the place to seek out exotic Asian textiles, crafts, and jewelry.

to the Montelbaanstoren (see p. 98). The lock mechanism survives, along with the lockkeeper's cottage, dated 1695, now a café called **De Slyswacht.**

The tall chimney you see to the right belongs to the massive **Gassan Diamond Works.** This is one of the few industrial buildings left in central Amsterdam, a reminder that diamond cutting and polishing was introduced to Amsterdam by Jewish refugees from Antwerp in the 17th century. Take one of its tours and see raw stones being turned into sparkling jewels and learn why Amsterdam

has been a center for this industry for the past 400 years.

On the opposite side of the road are the makeshift stalls of the Waterlooplein **flea market.** Itself a survivor from the pre-war city, when all the standholders were Jewish, the market extends around two sides of the Stadhuis, and sells everything from junk to new and recycled clothes, jewelry, and crafts.

South of the market you come to a simple **memorial slab** of polished black marble, set right by the water's edge, commemorating the victims of the Holocaust. Along the bank, with the barge-filled waters of the Amstel River to your right, you can enjoy extensive views that stretch from the **Blauwbrug** (Blue Bridge) in the east (see p. 188) to the distant spire of the **Munttoren** (see p. 63) in the west.

STADHUIS– MUZIEKTHEATER COMPLEX

A short way along the river bank toward the Blauwbrug, lies the **Stadhuis-Muziektheater** complex. As you enter the revolving doors between the two buildings, look for the sculpture of a trilby-hatted violinist bursting through the red marble paving to the left of the doors, a striking work that enlivens this otherwise dull corner.

Straight ahead is a scale model of the square Stadhuis (City Hall), from where Amsterdam is now administered, and the U-shaped Muziektheater, home to the

Netherlands Opera and National Ballet companies. Beyond are the **Vienna Theatercafé** and the **Boekmanzaal** (*free lunchtime concerts on Tues. at 12:30 p.m.*) and the Muziektheater ticket office. Just before the exit, a display explains all about the geographical datum known as **Normaal Amsterdams Peil** (N.A.P., or Normal Amsterdam Level). Because so much of the Netherlands lies below sea level, sea level itself cannot be used as the bench mark for establishing relative heights and depths, so N.A.P. is used instead. Beside the display, a mural shows a cross section of north Holland, revealing just how many well-known Dutch landmarks lie below the surface level of the North Sea, which is held back by artificial dikes and natural dunes.

The huge Catholic church near the Stadhuis-Muziektheater complex is the **Mozes en Aäaronkerk.** This grandiose classical building, now rarely used except for occasional organ recitals, was built between 1837 and 1841. Among the houses demolished to make way for it was the one in which the philosopher Baruch de Spinoza was born in 1632. ∎

Lovingly restored collectibles stand ready to decorate a buyer's home—yours?

Joods Historisch Museum
www.jhm.nl

🗺 Map p. 100

✉ Jonas Daniel Meijerplein 2–4

☎ 626 9945 (recorded information 625 4229)

🕐 Closed Yom Kippur

$ $$$

🚊 Tram: 9, 14, 20

Joods Historisch Museum & Jewish Amsterdam

JEWISH REFUGEES ARRIVING IN AMSTERDAM AROUND 1600 were not welcome. Denied civil rights and excluded from most established trades, they struggled to survive. Despite poverty and discrimination, many became wealthy and influential citizens. The Jewish Historical Museum charts their contribution to Dutch life, and the shattering of so many lives and hopes that occurred when Germany invaded the Netherlands in 1940.

The burly "Dokwerker" celebrates the anti-Nazi general strike of 1941.

Portugees-Israëlitische Synagoge

🗺 Map p. 100

✉ Mr. Visserplein 3

☎ 624 5351

🕐 Closed Sat., except for Sabbath Day service at 8:45 p.m.

$ $$

🚊 Tram: 9, 14, 20

This thought-provoking museum is one of the few reminders that Amsterdam's Jewish community ever existed. It is set in a complex of four Ashkenazik synagogues, built by Jewish refugees from Germany and Poland in the late 17th century. Those parts of the complex that survive in their original form are used to explain Jewish religious life and ritual. The remaining rooms and galleries document the flight of the Jews from repressive Catholic regimes in other parts of Europe, and their establishment of new lives in the Netherlands.

Protestant Amsterdam grudgingly tolerated the Jews who settled in their city, but placed many barriers in their path. Forbidden to own shops and barred from membership in the the city's trade guilds, the refugees slowly built their wealth as peddlers and market traders, later prospering as bankers and brokers, and introducing new crafts, including diamond processing, printing, and food production. Once they achieved full equality in 1796, when laws concerning Jewish emancipation were passed, which rescinded previous prohibitions, there was nothing to halt their entrepreneurship, and cottage industries became full-blown factory enterprises. The displays in the museum show what an important role the Jewish community played in leading Amsterdam into the industrial era.

One of the most successful of the community's entrepreneurs was Simon van der Bergh. As one of the Netherlands biggest butter producers, his company merged with the British Lever Brothers in 1929, to form Unilever, still one of the world's leading companies.

MONUMENTS TO JEWISH HISTORY

The Jewish Historical Museum encourages visitors to discover the main monuments commemorating the once-thriving community of some 80,000 Jews who lived in this area of tightly packed slums and alleys. Leaflets from the museum shop detail a self-guided discovery tour of Jewish Amsterdam.

One of these monuments, which stands opposite the entrance to the museum, is the **Arsenal** (*Nos. 6–8 Nieuwe Amstelstraat*), a 16th-century warehouse originally used to store bread, cheese, and peat, which were distributed to Amsterdam's poorest citizens as an early form of social security. The charity was administered from the handsome pedimented building of 1654 called the **Huiszittenaalmoezeniershuis,** around the corner to the left.

The huge early 17th-century **Portugees-Israëlitische Synagoge** (Portuguese-Israelite Synagogue) lies on the opposite side of the road from the museum.

Its instructive video is a good introduction to the synagogue. The entrance, to the left of the big brick building, faces onto the street called Mr. Visserplein, one of several local place-names that commemorate prominent members of the Jewish community. (Mr. Visser was the President of the Supreme Court of the Netherlands until the Nazi invasion, and he played a prominent role in the Dutch resistance.) Marie Andriessen's 1952 statue **"De Dokwerker,"** a burly long-shoreman, erected nearby, commemorates the 1941 general strike, led by Amsterdam's dockworkers and transport workers, in protest of Nazi treatment of the Jews. It stands on Jonas Daniël Meijerplein. Jonas Daniël Meyer (1780–1834) was the first Jew to be admitted to the Dutch legal profession, and a campaigner for Jewish civil rights.

East of the synagogue lies the Hortus Botanicus (Botanical Gardens; see p. 110), at the beginning of the wealthy Plantage suburb that became home to many of the city's most prosperous Jews in the late 19th and early 20th centuries. The **Hollandse Schouwburg** (*Plantage Middenlaan 24*) has a pediment carved with cavorting nudes, recalling its pre-war heyday when it was used as a theater. Now a roofless shell, it stands as a permanent memorial to the 1,000 or more Jews of Amsterdam who were rounded up and assembled here before being sent by train to the Westerbork internment camp, and from there to the death camps of Auschwitz and Bergen-Belsen. ∎

Jewish heritage and ritual are explained at the Joods Historisch Museum.

Modern glass houses protect precious plants in one of Europe's oldest gardens.

Hortus Botanicus

FOUNDED IN 1638 AS THE HORTUS MEDICUS—AN HERB garden for doctors and pharmacists—this is one of Europe's oldest botanical gardens. It is also one of the smallest. Shoehorned into a cramped site, it somehow manages to provide space for some 8,000 species of tropical and desert plants in state-of-the-art conservatories.

Hortus Botanicus
- Map p. 100
- Plantage Middenlaan 2A
- 625 8411
- $$$
- Tram: 7, 9, 14, 20

As Dutch explorers ventured farther and farther afield in the 17th century, they sent back a constant supply of rare and exotic plants. This wealth of new material provided the foundation for the pioneering research of Carolus Linnaeus (1707–1778), the creator of the classification system used to name all plants. It also proved handy to botanists looking for economically useful plants. In 1706 a coffee plant smuggled out of Ethiopia was brought here for propagation. Cuttings were then exported to Brazil, where the Dutch West India Company had plantations, to form the basis of what is now the world's largest coffee industry.

Amsterdam's gardens have always been used for entertainment as well as research. City notables were once granted privileged access to the botanical gardens to marvel at such curiosities as the monkey puzzle tree or the giant Amazonian water lily. A major attraction of the Palm House is the rare Cycad palm, which flowers very infrequently (one was planted 300 years ago, in the reign of King Willem II, making it the world's oldest potted palm). Here elevated walkways rise above the forest canopy with views down over the luxuriant foliage—the perfect antidote to a cold Amsterdam day. Today's visitors can also enjoy the sight of beautifully patterned butterflies dancing among the nectar-bearing plants, or explore the new climate-controlled greenhouses. ■

Nationaal Vakbondsmuseum

Even the brickwork forms part of the design at the Trade Union Museum.

THE NATIONAL TRADES UNION MUSEUM, HOUSED IN A charming Arts and Crafts building designed by Amsterdam school pioneer H. P. Berlage, is worth a visit just for the interior.

In 1894, Henri Polak established the ANDB, the Dutch Diamond Workers Union. By 1900, the union needed a headquarters building, and they asked Berlage, the most radical architect of his day, to supply the design. Remarkably, the building has survived almost untouched.

Berlage expressed his commitment to socialism in a building that bristles with symbolism. The castle-like battlements and tower of the exterior suggest the strength of union solidarity, while inside, the graceful stairwell is lit by a glass lantern symbolizing the light of the future. Monumental stone-carved friezes portray male and female laborers working at heroic tasks, and yet simple but elegant wooden furniture and Tiffany-style glass lamps show that Berlage did not want the ideal of beauty to be sacrificed in the battle for working-class power.

This is a very informal museum. Visitors can wander at will, exploring rooms that are remarkable for their design and furnishings, but that still function as meeting rooms and research facilities for people interested in trade union history.

Downstairs are a snack bar and a library full of early socialist books with colorful bindings, the volumes still redolent of pipe tobacco. The walls of these rooms, as well as the staircases, are lined with historic labor movement posters, many of them produced on the printing presses displayed in the basement.

Upstairs you will find photographs, trade union banners, and newspaper extracts charting the rise of trade union influence in the Netherlands. Though most of this is in Dutch, an English summary is available from the ground-floor information desk. ∎

Nationaal Vakbondsmuseum
www.fnv.nl/vakbondsmuseum
Map p. 100
Henri Polaklaan 9
624 1166
Closed Mon., Sat., & Sun a.m.
Tram: 7, 9, 14, 20

Artis

Artis
www.artis.nl

- Map pp. 100–101
- Plantage Kerklaan 38–40
- 523 3400
- $$$
- Tram: 6, 9, 14, 20
- Artis Express boat service links the zoo to Centraal Station

Artis

THE 19TH-CENTURY FOUNDERS OF AMSTERDAM'S ZOO signaled the seriousness of their commitment to research by naming the zoo Natura Artis Magistra (Nature is the Teacher of Art). Now known simply as Artis, this zoological garden combines numerous attractions (many of them indoors), making it the perfect place to visit on a cold or wet day.

Amster hamsters? The zoo's dam-building beavers are popular with all visitors.

The museum entrance is flanked by two indoor attractions. To the left lies the **Planetarium,** along with an exhibition of spectacular pictures, taken by the Hubble Telescope, which examines the universe and the future of space exploration. Shows are put on at hourly intervals, and although the soundtrack is in Dutch only, program notes are available in English.

On the right is the **Geological Museum,** which brings a rather static subject to life by looking at the interplay between geological processes and the history of life on Earth. Fossil evidence plays a major part in the displays that cover the heyday of the dinosaurs, major events such as earthquakes and volcanic eruptions, and the rise of the mammals.

The numerous **enclosures** surrounding the perimeter of the zoo have both indoor and outdoor viewing areas. If the weather is bad and the animals want to avoid the cold, everyone heads indoors, and vice versa if it's warm and sunny. It's amazing how quickly you get used to the feral smell that greets you as you enter the various animal houses.

The **gardens** are dotted with sculptures and monuments as well as flowering trees and shrubs, and numerous open enclosures where water birds, beavers, deer, and goats make their homes.

The newest part of the zoo, to the far left of the site, consists of a large area landscaped to resemble

Opposite: The zoo's gateway incorporates symbols of art, scholarship, and the natural world.

the African savanna, opened in 1999. You can watch the resident zebra, antelope, and gnu from the adjacent restaurant, while enjoying a large portion of excellent French fries, very popular with hungry children.

Continuing around the site, you come to the **Insect House,** where you will see the cockroaches, locusts, and tarantulas feeding—a fascinating sight as long as it does not come too soon after lunch.

If it does, head for the **Aquarium,** where fascinating displays in the new wing re-create different ecosystems. One shows the countless varieties of fish that teem in the waters of the Amazon River. Another presents the richly colorful life of the coral reef. Equally riveting is the brick-lined tank with bits of rusting bicycle littering the floor; this mock-up of a typical Amsterdam canal has more living creatures than you might expect, including eels and carp.

Larger water-loving creatures feature in the enclosures of the **Manatee and Hippo House,** full of wallowing, blubbery bodies that spend much of their time submerged. They may look ferocious but are in fact gentle vegetarians, living off a diet of lettuce and endive (manatees) and carrots, hay, and turnips (hippos). Keep your distance when the hippos are feeding. They use their own manure to mark their territory, and have a habit of spreading it far and wide with their tails. ■

The Plancius building, which now houses the Verzetsmuseum, was built in 1876 as the home of a Jewish choir.

Verzetsmuseum

NAZI GERMANY INVADED THE NETHERLANDS ON MAY 10, 1940, and for the next five years the Dutch lived under the tyrannical rule of an oppressive and foreign regime. The Verzetsmuseum (Resistance Museum) reveals the many ways in which they responded and conveys a very real sense of what life was like for ordinary people living through the war.

Verzetsmuseum
www.verzetsmuseum.org

Map p. 100

Plantage Kerklaan 61

620 2535

Closed Mon.

$$$

Tram: 6, 9, 14, 20

The main route through the museum is chronological and charts the events of the war, from the aerial bombing of Rotterdam in 1940 to the final cold winter when Allied blockades brought transportation systems to a halt and the Netherlands was starved of food and fuel. Peripheral displays provide a commentary on the main events by telling the stories of those individuals who were brave enough

to stand up to tyranny in countless different ways by working for the underground press or by using their skills to forge German-issued documents so that Jews and other persecuted victims could escape.

INVASION

The first group of displays looks at the response of Amsterdammers to the invasion of their city. When Austrian-born Arthur Seyss-Inquart arrived in Amsterdam as the new governor of the Nazi-controlled Netherlands, he believed that the Dutch would, once their initial concerns were quelled, accept and even welcome the new order imposed upon them. Documentary photographs show that, instead of grasping the hand of German friendship, the people made their feelings known by wearing white carnations on June 29, 1940, in celebration of the birthday of Prince Bernhard, the son-in-law of the Dutch queen. This public act of defiance was a symbol of mass support for a man who regularly broadcast messages of resistance and encouragement from his base in England, where he was serving as head of the Dutch Free Forces.

PROTEST

The next section tells the story of the General Strike of February 1941, using photographs, documentary film, and the recorded voices of those who took part. The General Strike was a public display of revulsion to the news that 400 Jews had been rounded up and deported. For two days, workers went on strike, bringing the city to a halt.

All pretense of friendship was dropped once the Nazis began forcing Dutch officials to implement a series of anti-Jewish measures. Letters, newspaper articles, and private diaries explain the dilemma this presented many officials: Should they stay in their positions and attempt to mitigate repressive laws? Or should they resign, knowing full well that a pro-German official would be appointed in their place?

Those who supported the first course of action formed the Netherlands Union to work with the Nazis. Union leaders could not agree upon an appropriate level of cooperation, however. In 1942 the union lost power to the National Socialist Party

(Dutch Nazi Party), and a puppet regime was formed under the leadership of Anton Mussert. Photographs show how eerily Mussert's appearance and behavior mimicked those of Hitler himself.

The brothers Kuyt listen to a radio in their Amsterdam hiding place in the spring of 1945.

RESISTANCE

The collapse of the Netherlands Union marked the last attempt at finding some sort of compromise with the Nazis. From then on, many Dutch dedicated themselves to outright resistance. The museum presents sobering accounts of the risks that people took to help Jews escape: distracting or befriending guards and getting them drunk; forging documents; smuggling children and babies away from danger; hiding people in cellars and attics; and producing and distributing 1,300 illegal newspapers that enabled resistors to keep in touch with one another at a time when all official news was censored.

The final section addresses issues of resistance in more general terms. Children's pictures and photographs of such renowned opponents of tyranny as Nelson Mandela help germinate the notion that everyone has a duty to fight oppression wherever it occurs. ■

Exploring Plantage & Maritime Amsterdam

Two adjacent districts, each with its own distinctive character, fill the space between the end of the canal circle and the eastern harbor. Plantage, with its zoo and botanical gardens, its former theaters and wide leafy streets, was a center for entertainment and relaxation in the 18th and early 19th centuries; later on it developed into a wealthy residential quarter. Only a narrow canal separates Plantage from the eastern docks—where, on a hot day, the warehouses still exude the unmistakable smell of pepper and cloves.

Start at **Hortus Botanicus** (see p. 110) and turn right, crossing the road over to the entrance to **Wertheimpark,** where stone sphinxes flank the gate of the city's oldest public park (created in 1895). Turn left down Plantage Parklaan and take the first right onto Henri Polaklaan, named for the founder of the Dutch trade union movement. To see inside one of the large and elegant villas lining this street, visit the **Nationaal Vakbondsmuseum** ❶ a short way up on the left (see p. 111). On the opposite side of the road, at Nos. 6–12, a plaque with a pelican feeding her young is the only reminder that this was the site of the Portuguese Jewish Hospital (the pelican is a symbol of self-sacrifice).

When you reach the entrance to **Artis** ❷ (see p. 112), turn left to walk down Plantage Kerklaan. Number 61, on the left, was built in 1875 as a concert hall and is now home to the **Verzetsmuseum** ❸ (see pp. 114–15).

At the end of the street, cross the Nijlpaardenbrug (Hippopotamus Bridge). This takes you over to the vast **Entrepotdok** warehouse complex ❹, which was built between 1708 and 1840 for entrepôt goods, stored here in transit before shipment to another country, and hence not subject to Dutch customs tariffs or import duties.

Walk along the dockside, with the boat-filled dock to the right, to an arch beside the Entrepotdok café (after No. 63 and before No. 66). Go through the arch and turn right at the other end of the passage, then take the next left, down a footpath and cycleway, to reach Hoogte Kadijk. Turn right here and walk across the next lifting bridge (a type of drawbridge) to the **Museumwerf 't Kromhout** ❺ (Kromhout Working Museum, *Hoogte Kadijk 147, tel 627 6777*), housed in the magnificent 19th-century iron sheds of the

Sphinxes guard the entrance to Wertheimpark, the location for the Auschwitz monument, designed by Jan Wolkers.

former Kromhout shipyard. The yard itself has been in operation since the 18th century, and the Kromhout Working Museum now specializes in the restoration of historic vessels. Displays here show what the Amsterdam docks looked like in their heyday, packed with tall-masted ships and bustling with activity.

From the museum return across the lifting bridge and, just beyond Hoogte Kadijk No. 119, turn right down Overhaalsgang. Straight ahead are the three manmade **Oostelijke Eilanden** ❻ (Eastern Islands), created in 1658 by filling in shallow stretches of the IJ River. They were needed to provide more space for wharves when the Dutch East India

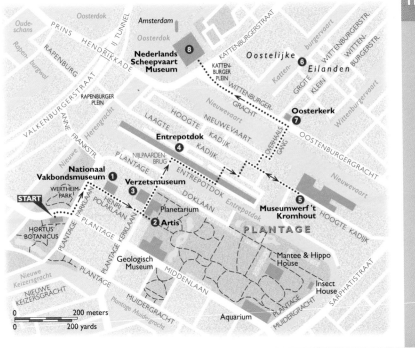

Oosterdok

Oude-schans

PRINS HENDRIKKADE

RAPENBURG

Ropenburgwal

IJ TUNNEL

Amsterdam

Oosterdok

Nederlands
Scheepvaart
Museum ⑧

KATTENBURGERSTRAAT

KATTEN-
BURGER
PLEIN

Oostelijke ⑥
Eilanden

burgervaart

WITTENBURGERSTR.

WITTEN-
BURGERSTR.

Wittenburgervaart

VALKENBURGERSTRAAT

ANNE FRANKSTR

RAPENBURGER
PLEIN

Nieuwe Herengracht

HOOGTE KADIJK

LAAGTE KADIJK

NIEUWEVAART

WITTENBURGER
GRACHT

Nieuwevaart

Katten-

GROTE

KLEIN

OOSTENBURGERGRACHT

Oosterkerk ⑦

OVERHAALS
GANG

Wittenburgergracht

Nationaal
Vakbondsmuseum ①

WERTHEIM
PARK

START

PLANTAGE

NIJLPAARDEN-
BRUG

HENRI
POLAKLAAN

Entrepotdok ④

Verzetsmuseum ③

PLANTAGE PARKLAAN

PLANTAGE KERKLAAN

ENTREPOTDOK

DOKLAAN

Planetarium

② Artis

Entrepotdok

Museumwerf 't ⑤
Kromhout

HOOGTE KADIJK

PLANTAGE

HORTUS
BOTANICUS

Geologisch
Museum

MIDDENLAAN

Mantee & Hippo
House

Insect
House

SARPHATISTRAAT

Nieuwe
Keizersgracht

NIEUWE
KEIZERSGRACHT

PLANTAGE

MUIDERGRACHT

Plantage Muidergracht

PLANTAGE

MUIDERGRACHT

Aquarium

0   200 meters
0   200 yards

🅜 Also see area map pp. 100–101
► Hortus Botanicus
↔ 1.3 miles (2 km)
⏱ 3 hours
► Nederlands Scheepvaart
   Museum

NOT TO BE MISSED
- Entrepotdok
- Nederlands Scheepvaart
  Museum

**The Entrepotdok warehouse complex
is a pioneering example of docklands
redevelopment.**

Company began its rapid expansion from the mid-17th century. It was here that Tsar Peter the Great toiled in the shipyards in 1697–98, working alongside ordinary Dutch carpenters, learning the shipbuilder's craft before returning to St. Petersburg to found the Russian navy.

This area has been comprehensively re-developed to provide modern apartment blocks. The 1671 **Oosterkerk** ⑦ (Eastern Church) survives, on the opposite side of the road to the lifting bridge; it has now been converted to offices and a concert hall. It was the main harbor of Amsterdam until the rail-road closed it off from the IJ River.

At the church, turn left down Wittenburg-ergracht, a busy road that leads to the huge sandstone building in classical style, built in 1656, that houses the **Nederlands Scheep-vaart Museum** ⑧ (Dutch Maritime Museum; see pp. 118–121). ■

Nederlands Scheepvaart Museum

THE NEDERLANDS SCHEEPVAART MUSEUM (DUTCH
Maritime Museum) is exhaustive in its coverage of the seafaring history of the Netherlands, with room after room of paintings, charts,
and model ships. Here you can learn about the subject from
Roman times onward, and marvel at the achievements of the
Dutch East India Company, while the children can play pirates on a
real tall-masted East Indiaman ship moored in the dock just outside
the museum.

**Nederlands
Scheepvaart-
Museum**

www.generali.nl/scheepvaart
museum

🅰 Map p. 100

✉ Kattenburgerplein 1

☎ 523 2222

🕐 Closed Mon. mid-
Sept.–mid-June

💲 $$$

🚌 Bus: 22

The building housing the museum
is almost as interesting as the dis-
plays it contains. Built in 1656 to
the severe classical designs of Dan-
iel Stalpaert, it is essentially a very
large and grandiose warehouse.
Here were stored all the goods
needed to equip the fleet of ships
entrusted with defending Dutch
naval interests and with protecting
Dutch harbors and merchant ship-
ping—a task that involved the
Netherlands in a series of long,
drawn-out wars with rival colonial
powers, notably England. Cannon
and other munitions were stock-
piled in the courtyard, while the

main building was used to store
sails, ropes, rigging, ships' victuals,
and fresh water. The building was
of such strategic importance that it
incorporated novel fireproofing
precautions—sand was stored in
the floor and ceiling cavities so that
it would drop through the burning
timbers and douse the flames in the
event of a fire. The perennial
problem of vermin was resolved by
employing an army of cats.

WAR & TRADE

The museum opens with a display
of early prints and topographical
drawings, showing Amsterdam

in 1544, 1597, and 1647, and revealing the rapid growth of the city and its dockyards, harbors, shipyards, and warehouses. Another map shows Amsterdam's trading relations—by 1640 the city was the entrepôt of Europe, trading products as diverse as Icelandic whale oil and Turkish carpets.

The next set of rooms is dominated by panoramic paintings of sea battles, a reminder that maintaining trade dominance was never a simple matter when others were eager to seize your ships or capture your trading colonies. Naval war was as much a part of 17th-century history as the rapid growth of trade with the Far East and the Americas, and ships became floating gun platforms as well as cargo containers.

INLAND VESSELS

Inland navigation was a vital aid to trade as cargo landed in Amsterdam had to be transported deep into landlocked Europe along the continent's waterways. The next section of the museum is devoted to all types of ingenious craft designed for use on rivers and canals, including ice yachts for navigating over frozen lakes, and even ornate barges for going to church on Sunday (pulled along by uniformed servants).

DUTCH EAST INDIA COMPANY

A large part of the Maritime Museum is devoted to the history of the Dutch East India Company, or VOC (see p. 26). Dutch maritime supremacy in the 17th century was built on the VOC's organizational capabilities. Within 60 years of its foundation, the VOC employed a private army, owned a huge fleet of warships to protect its interests, and virtually ruled vast swaths of the Indonesian archipelago. Its colorful history is illustrated here by

meticulous paintings and models of typical factories and Amsterdam's Oosterdok (Eastern Docks), built to service the needs of the VOC in the 1630s.

THE MODERN ERA

The final section deals with 19th- and 20th-century maritime history. As rivalry for trade heated up in the 19th century, new types of ships were developed for speed. Naval architects designed sleek clippers, finding the optimum balance between cargo weight and speed, as ships plied the oceans loaded with coffee, tobacco, sugar, and tea. Beginning in 1900, there was a new type of cargo—people emigrating from Europe to America, or cruising the Caribbean. This was the age of the steamship and the cruise liner— but also of the menacing iron-clad battleships of the two world wars.

Up in the attics (from where there are good views over the IJ to Centraal Station) are displays on modern tankers and container ships, and on watersports—everything from early yachts to sleek modern windsurfing boards, and even the Queen's golden sloop.

THE *AMSTERDAM*

For many visitors, the most entertaining part of the museum is outdoors. In the dock beside the museum several historic ships include a full-scale replica of a Dutch East Indiaman—the workhorse of the Dutch East India Company, which had a fleet of 1,500 such ships. Climbing aboard the *Amsterdam*, you are welcomed by English-speaking actors who play the part of the crew and answer questions about life on board.

The cramped quarters of the crew differ dramatically from the cathedral-like space of the hold: Here you can watch a video (with English subtitles) explaining the

Vereniging Museumhaven Amsterdam

🅰 Map p. 100
✉ Oosterdok
💲 $$$
🚌 Bus: 22

Listen to sailors' tales and discover what life was like on board the *Amsterdam*.

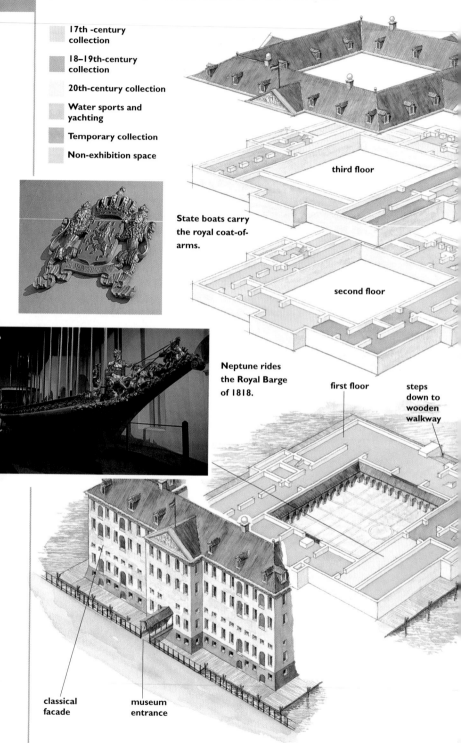

17th -century collection

18–19th-century collection

20th-century collection

Water sports and yachting

Temporary collection

Non-exhibition space

State boats carry the royal coat-of-arms.

third floor

second floor

Neptune rides the Royal Barge of 1818.

first floor

steps down to wooden walkway

classical facade

museum entrance

lucrative trade in spices and textiles. Orders for goods placed in Amsterdam typically took two years to fulfill, and the shipping companies could expect a profit of 250 percent on goods landed in the city. The downside was that up to a third of the poorly paid crew usually died on a voyage, either from disease or by drowning. It's a sobering thought that the original *Amsterdam*, launched in 1749, sank on its maiden voyage, when it was caught in a storm at Hastings, England.

full-size replica of Dutch East Indiaman

BACK TO THE CITY CENTER

Landscaping of the Amsterdam waterfront has created an attractive **pedestrian route** between the museum and the city center. As you exit the museum, turn right on busy Prins Hendrikkade, then look for a ramp leading down toward the big, green, ship-shaped NEMO museum. Before going down the ramp, look at the large 1641 **warehouses** on the opposite side of Prins Hendrikkade. These were built for the financially strapped West India Company (see p. 131), set up in 1621 to coordinate Dutch trade in the Americas and West Africa along the same lines as the more successful East India Company.

Going down the ramp, you will pass a modern bronze fountain featuring the sea goddess, Salacia, one of the sirens in Homer's *Odyssey*. To the right is the **Vereniging Museumhaven Amsterdam** (Amsterdam Harbor Outdoor Mu-

wooden walkway

Above right: Doors once used for unloading essential supplies now give views of the tall-masted *Amsterdam*, moored in the city's harbor.

seum), not so much a formal museum but a collection of restored and fully working historic ships moored in the Oosterdok.

Straight ahead is the NEMO museum (see pp. 122–23), designed by acclaimed architect Renzo Piano, built above the road tunnel that takes traffic under the IJ River. A flight of steps sweeps upward from the waterside to its rooftop;

short of climbing one of the city's church towers, this is as high as you can get in Amsterdam (topographically speaking), and there are terrific views across the rooftops and out to the skyscrapers of the suburbs.

The route back to the city center is via the two pedestrian bridges that cross from the NEMO museum to Oosterdokskade and from there to Centraal Station. As you go, you will pass the exotic **Sea Palace** (see p. 249), a floating Chinese restaurant on the northern bank of Oosterdok, and the big white Amstel Botel (see p. 249), a floating hotel, moored alongside. ∎

Plowing prow: Architect Renzo Piano has designed a museum perfectly suited to its harbor-side setting.

NEMO

NEMO
www.e-nemo.nl

- Map p. 100
- Oosterdok 2
- 0900 919 1100 (75c per min.)
- Closed Mon. during school vacations, April. 30, Dec. 25, & Jan. 1
- $$$
- Bus: 22

THE LATEST ADDITION TO THE AMSTERDAM WATERFRONT is a striking landmark—visible from many parts of the city—that resembles a green-hulled ship. Inside is a state-of-the-art science museum—the perfect place for inquisitive children on any day, but especially when it is cold or wet. NEMO, the new Metropolis Science and Technology Center, is one of the architectural highlights of Amsterdam, a thrilling 21st-century building that looks deceptively like a ship moored in the harbor.

Designed by Genoese architect Renzo Piano (co-designer of the Pompidou Centre, now the Centre Beauborg, in Paris), NEMO opened in 1997. The pinnacle of the hull, reached by a sweeping flight of terraced steps, offers an unrivaled panorama over the city. In summer, it has a popular café-restaurant with a beach motif. The expansive

view of Amsterdam from the pedestrian roof can be enjoyed year round.

Even children find the architecture thrilling, but not half so exciting as the exhibits, which are all interactive and cover real-life applications of modern science. Inevitably, the museum gets very busy, so it is best to be one of the first to

at a terminal and make decisions on buying and selling a range of shares. Every so often news items are broadcast on the screens above your head—your task is to guess what effect these announcements might have on your portfolio, and take action to maximize profits or minimize losses. Needless to say, the game is totally addictive.

Older children might look on this with contempt; if so, whisk them off to the **laboratory** on the third floor where they can don white coats and protective glasses, and conduct real experiments under the watchful eye of adult lab technicians. Alternatively, take them to the top floor, where the exhibits in "Journey Through the Mind" tackle the complex workings of the human brain, including how people react to various visual images. One experiment measures pulse rate and sweat excretion when you are confronted with a picture of a rose, a spider, or a nude. A new genetics exhibition is planned to open at the end of 2001.

Hunger alert: Catering at NEMO is fairly rudimentary—the one small café cannot really cope with the demand—but the situation is scheduled to be improved soon. For the time being, with no other cafés in the vicinity, you might want to bring a snack of your own. ■

NEMO is the number one Amsterdam attraction for those under 18.

arrive (it opens at 10 a.m.). To avoid the crowds, go straight to the top floor and work back to the second floor, the opposite route to that taken by most people. The only problem is that the opening exhibits are the most exciting and the ones that the children will probably enjoy most, so decide which is best for you.

The permanent exhibition, "Why the World Works," lets you experience what it feels like to escape the pull of gravity. It also invites visitors to witness the mysteries of chain reactions.

Then head upstairs to the second floor and see whether you can make it as the captain of an **oil tanker** or as a financial wheeler and dealer. The **Super Banker game** on the third floor lets you sit

Tropenmuseum

Tropenmuseum
www.kit.nl/tropenmuseum
- ⓐ Map p. 101
- ✉ Linnaeusstraat 2
- ☎ 568 8215
- 💲 $$$
- 🚋 Tram: 3, 7, 9, 10, 14. Bus: 22
- ⛴ Museumboot

THE TROPENMUSEUM (TROPICAL MUSEUM) IS ONE OF Amsterdam's best-kept secrets. This bright and lively museum, full of color and exotic sounds, provides an excellent introduction to the daily life, beliefs, and cultures of diverse peoples around the world. However, it lies off the beaten track, so fewer visitors go there.

Whatever the weather is doing outside, it's always warm and sunny in the Tropenmuseum, where the eight permanent exhibition areas give an account of life in Africa, Asia, India, and South America, while the central hall is used for temporary exhibitions highlighting some aspect of tropical culture. Whether it's textiles, music, religion, art, architecture, or cuisine, the displays will always be informative and fun. Children love the museum because it makes good use of video and sound to enhance the static displays and because it addresses issues that fascinate them. There is also a separate **Kindermuseum** (Children's Museum) attached to the Tropenmuseum, but the presentations there are exclusively in Dutch (*tel 568 8300*).

The Tropenmuseum also has a very good shop selling ethnic art—African masks, Indian jewelry, Japanese kimonos, Indonesian batik—and a relaxing restaurant where the buffet serves authentic dishes from around the world, as well as some delicious cakes and sweetmeats.

POLITICS & SOCIETY

The museum draws on vast collections built up over the years by anthropologists working in the former Dutch colonies. Rather than being shown as disassociated objects in display cases, exhibitions are put together within a reconstructed street, market, house, or temple to re-create as accurately as possible the real sights, sounds, and smells of the country in which they originate.

Nor is the museum backward looking. It shows life as it is lived now, be it in Bombay (Mumbai), Jakarta, or Mexico City. The implicit warning that emerges from many of the exhibits is that the way of life being depicted—often representing centuries of continuity and tradition—is on the verge of extinction.

Even so, the museum is not gloomy, and it presents many examples of cultures that have managed to embrace aspects of Western culture while remaining essentially themselves—and vice versa. On the third floor, for example, the displays on Islam include a reconstruction of a typical Arabic souk, or market, in the Syrian city of Halab (known as Aleppo in the West). Exploring the narrow alleys with their tiny shops, you turn a corner and encounter a teahouse, where men meet to drink sweet tea and watch television (which has taken the place of traditional storytellers). In the corner is a jukebox, and if you press the buttons you will hear not only examples of traditional Arabic music, but also popular Western music—from jazz to Hollywood movie themes—that have taken Arabic music as their inspiration. There are also displays on religion, including the extraordinary beliefs of different cultures.

MAN & ENVIRONMENT

One of the major themes explored by the museum is the relationship between town and country, for the

Opposite: Creativity is encouraged to soar in the cathedral-like central hall of the Tropenmuseum.

city is seen as the place where humans interact with each other, where cultures meet and blend. By contrast, people who inhabit the forest, savanna, or seashore live in relative isolation, and their culture results from interaction with their environment. The displays in the "Man and Environment" exhibit on the second floor are not judgmental—indeed, the experts whose words are captured on video and sound tracks tell us that the city is the environment of the future, a very good environment, enabling the efficient pooling of resources, and the creation of systems that protect the weak, such as health care.

If indigenous culture is under threat, it seems most likely to survive in the islands of the Asia Pa-

Even the gift shop at the Tropenmuseum abounds with exotica.

cific region and Oceania, simply because they are relatively remote. Here, religion and magic still play a central part in people's everyday lives, and the museum has some outstanding examples of the art that is produced as a by-product of those rituals and beliefs. Elaborately carved poles reach up, like rainforest trees, from the floor of the museum's central hall to its ceiling,

and there are symbolic animals carved in wood, and reconstructions of wooden houses, with areas reserved for the skulls of the ancestors where offerings are made. These are the tangible relics of ritual—and video footage fills in what the objects themselves cannot tell us about the music, the gorgeous clothing, flowers, masks, and food offerings. Even more vivid than the video are the occasional live performances of music, dance, and theater from around the world. Look out for posters advertising these events, or alternatively ask at the information desk.

AROUND THE MUSEUM
On leaving the museum, take a look at the building itself. Built in the eclectic style between 1916 and 1923, it features numerous statues and reliefs depicting scenes from life in the tropics, such as rice planting, bamboo harvesting, and temple worship. Around to the left, you pass the imposing facade of the **Instituut voor de Tropen,** the University of Amsterdam's Institute of Tropical Studies. Over to the right you will see the huge arch called the **Muiderpoort,** built in 1771. It may not look like much now (its mundane modern use is to house the library and information center of the Dutch Inland Revenue), but try to imagine it with an army marching through. In 1811, this was the spot where Emperor Napoleon chose to make his triumphal entry into the city, to be welcomed by many citizens, who saw him as a force for long-overdue legal and constitutional reform. From Muiderpoort, you will be able to see the sails of the splendid **De Gooyer** windmill, built in 1664, which stands six blocks northeast, beside the Nieuwe Vaart canal and next to the excellent microbrewery, Bierbruwerj't IJ. ■

Strolling along the banks of the quiet and leafy waterways of the northern part of the city's canal circle, with its profusion of beautiful buildings, is one of the great pleasures of visiting the city.

Northern canals

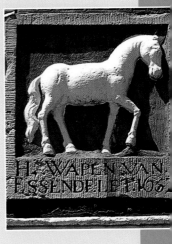

House plaque on Zandhoek

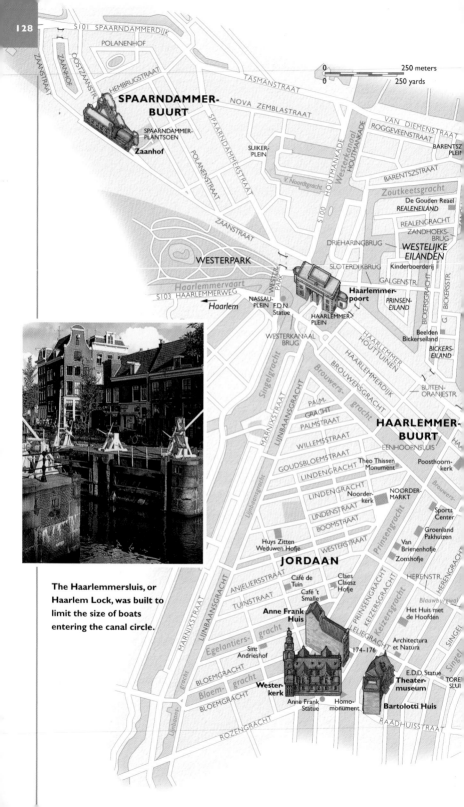

The Haarlemmersluis, or Haarlem Lock, was built to limit the size of boats entering the canal circle.

Northern canals

AMSTERDAM'S RAPID GROWTH CAN BE TRACED IN THE VARIOUS SCHEMES devised to expand it. The 14th-century city was just about contained by its medieval walls, but by 1420 the Singel canal had been dug to create more room for the city's burgeoning population. The main road out of Amsterdam to Haarlem became another focus for development, with its parallel Brouwersgracht, or Brewers' Canal, and it was immediately south of here that the northern section of the canal circle was dug at the start of the 17th century.

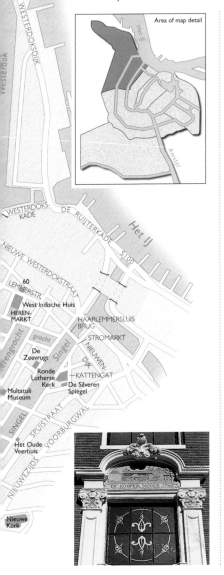

In 1609, Hendrik Staets, the municipal carpenter (see p. 34), came up with a novel idea for providing more land for housing, as well as more warehousing space and berths for merchants' barges. He proposed tripling the size of the city by wrapping three parallel canals around the ancient heart of medieval Amsterdam. This Grachtengordel, or Canal Circle, would eventually encircle the old city completely. The first phase, constructed between 1609 and 1660, is the part that forms the shape of a reversed letter J, or a fish hook, on the map. The adjacent Jordaan district, which wraps itself round the Grachtengordel like a sock, was conceived as an integral part of the plan—a place for factories and artisans, well removed from the more genteel residential areas of the city.

For about 50 years, beginning in 1609, this area was one big building site, as construction started from the northern end and proceeded southward. After this first phase was finished, the city had become transformed. The three canals of the Grachtengordel—Herengracht, Keizersgracht, and Prinsengracht—were now lined with elegant houses, nearly all of which have survived to this day, presenting an unbroken vista of uniform facades, individualized by ornate gables and fine doorways.

Even the most voracious student of historic architecture will find the effect overwhelming. Every building has a history, or some detail worth lingering over. The best approach is simply to take a leisurely stroll around a short stretch of the canal ring, enjoying the endless variety of detail that underlies the apparent uniformity. ■

Doorcases and fanlights create infinite variety among apparently similar canalside facades. Decorations and inscriptions gave clues to the owner's occupation.

Free of tourist haunts, the Haarlemmerbuurt district is real, lived-in Amsterdam.

Haarlemmerbuurt

HAARLEMMERBUURT IS THE NAME OF THE FORMER working-class district that lies on either side of the old road leading out of Amsterdam to the neighboring town of Haarlem. Today it is lined by small shops and inexpensive restaurants, and is a favorite place for young Amsterdammers to live because of its village atmosphere and low rents.

Haarlemmerbuurt
Map pp. 128–29

To get to Haarlemmerbuurt from the railroad station, head west up Nieuwendijk, a pedestrian-only tourist trap where McDonald's and a variety of respectable cafés lie sandwiched between the sex shops and the dope-peddling "coffee shops." **Haarlemmersluis Brug** (bridge) marks the unofficial frontier between the Amsterdam that most visitors know and the part of the city that is not so inviting.

THE OLD ROAD TO HAARLEM

Haarlemmerstraat begins on the other side of Haarlemmersluis bridge. If you followed the road for 10 miles (16 km), you would reach Haarlem itself (see pp. 222–23), the capital of North Holland province. Livestock were once brought into the city along this road, but the cattle markets and slaughterhouses were swept away in the late 19th century. Several shops retain decorative facades from that period. **Number 60,** a short way up on the right, has art nouveau tiles advertising the sale of *Koffie, Thee,* and *Cacao.*

Opposite No. 60 is the much earlier **West Indische Huis,** built in 1617 and used as the headquarters of the Dutch West India Company from 1623. The company was granted a monopoly on Dutch trade with the Americas and West Africa, but was never as successful as its sister company, the Dutch East India Company. For a brief period, the WIC controlled Manhattan Island in the United States, which it called Nieuw Amsterdam. The trading colony prospered under the governorship of Pieter Stuyvesant until English soldiers captured the island in 1664 and renamed it New York.

A variety of unique shops, interspersed with hardware stores and bakers, line the next stretch of Haarlemmerstraat. Set back a little from the street is the gaunt **Poosthoornskerk** (Post Horn Church) of 1860–63, built by P.J.H. Cuypers. The name of this striking building, a major landmark in the city, comes from an earlier clandestine church where Catholics met for secret worship above the stables belonging to the Amsterdam–Haarlem mail coach. The next bridge, **Eenhoornsluis,** crosses Prinsengracht. This is the only canal in the Grachtengordel that drains directly into the IJ River. Every barge entering the canal circle had to come through here, and the lock was deliberately built narrow as a defensive measure to limit the size of the boats allowed into the heart of the city.

On the other side of the bridge, the former canal becomes the **Haarlemmerdijk.** On the left, No. 39 is decorated with art nou-

veau tiles depicting an octopus and a seal, advertising the sale of fish. No. 43, a tea and coffee shop, has a ship's figurehead carved in the shape of a Tahitian maiden and a gable stone showing a ship at anchor—both represent the faraway and exotic origins of the products once sold here. This may also explain the symbolism of the porpoise on the gable stone of No. 45.

THE HAARLEM GATE

At the end of the street is busy **Haarlemmerplein,** with its bulky triumphal arch, known as the Haarlemmerpoort (Haarlem Gate) to locals. It is more correctly known as the Willemspoort (William's Gate) as it was built for the coronation of King William II of the Netherlands in 1840.

Another three-quarters of a mile (1.25 km) away you will come to Spaarndammerbuurt (see pp. 136–37), or you can explore the Westelijke Eilanden (Western Islands, see pp. 132–33) or the Jordaan (see pp. 138–43), or head back to the city center along pretty Brouwersgracht, the canal that runs parallel to the Haarlemmerdijk, two blocks south. Once lined by breweries (as the name suggests) this canal has many attractive bridges and fine warehouse conversions. ∎

FRESH HERRING

Amsterdammers like to stop for a portion of raw herring and chopped onions from the stand in the middle of the Haarlemmersluis bridge. Some hold the herring up in the air by its tail, tip their head back, and take great bites. Others cut the herring into bite-sized portions and eat them with a fork, or between a soft roll (*broodje haring*). ∎

The elegant head office of the Dutch West India Company

Westelijke Eilanden

CONSTRUCTION OF THE THREE WESTERN ISLANDS—
Prinseneiland, Realeneiland, and Bickerseiland began in 1621 well
away from the city center as a place where inflammable tar, used for
sealing the hulls of wooden boats, could be made and stored. Noisy
forges and shipyards, noxious fish-smoking houses, timber stores,
and shipbuilders' wharves once characterized the islands. Today, this
is a fascinating area of boatyards, converted warehouses, and artists'
studios, best explored on foot.

**Westelijke
Eilanden**
Map pp. 128–29

The railroad, built up on a high
embankment, was constructed
along the harbor in 1870, cutting
off the three Western Islands from
the rest of the city. Hidden behind
the high viaduct, the islands seem
to belong to a different world, with
their own tranquil, village-like
atmosphere. To reach them follow
the old Haarlem road through
Haarlemmerbuurt (see pp.
130–31) to **Haarlemmerplein,**
turning right to pass beneath the
railroad tracks.

Turning right just after the railroad bridge takes you down
Sloterdijkstraat and across narrow
Sloterdijkbrug, with views of
houseboats and rusting ships' hulls
awaiting restoration, and then over
to **Prinseneiland,** where working
timber yards sit side by side with
chic warehouse apartments displaying sail-shaped shutters. Ahead lies
Galgenstraat (Gallows Street), a
grim reminder that the gallows on
the opposite side of the IJ River
were once visible from this spot.

Turn left, past a warehouse block, then take a right, passing one of the island's boat-builders' yards, then turn left to cross pretty Drieharingbrug (Three Herrings Bridge), which takes you over to **Realeneiland.**

Turn right on Realeneiland, and down Realengracht, whose intrusive modern houses show how close the islands came to wholesale redevelopment in the 1960s. The Dutch author Jan Mens (1897–1967) led a campaign to conserve the islands' special character. One of his novels, *De Gouden Reael (The Golden Real;* 1940), was set here, in what was then a gritty dockworkers' district.

At the end of Realengracht, turn left into **Zandhoek** (Sand Hook), which looks like a scene reminiscent of the Golden Age. Sailing boats are usually moored in Westerdok, where the sand barges that gave their name to Zandhoek once unloaded. Sand was then in great demand for building and brickmaking.

**Right:
Warehouses built to store tar and timber now provide spacious homes.**

The houses on the left-hand side of Zandhoek have been beautifully restored. The two rows date from 1660, their lower facades built of timber, the fashion at the time. The houses have different gable designs, from the simple spout gables of Nos. 8–14 and the step gable of No. 6, to various versions of the bell gable and the slightly later cornice at No. 2 (probably an 18th-century replacement for the original gable).

Several of the houses retain their gable stones (although called *gevelstenen,* they often appear, as here, lower down). They provide a pictorial reference of the name of the house—hence the Golden Lion, the White Horse, Noah's Ark, St. Peter, and St. John. Number 14 is called De Gouden Reael and the gable stone depicts the Spanish real coin, a pun on the name of Laurens Jacob Reaal, the wealthy landowner after whom Realeneiland is named.

This house is today an excellent café specializing in French provincial food (see p. 251).

Crossing Zandhoeksbrug, ahead lies **Bickerseiland** (named after a 17th-century shipyard owner, Jan Bicker). The dull office blocks here show what the city fathers had in mind for the islands in the 1960s. Take the first right, and follow cobbled Bickersgracht as it turns left past a popular **Kinderboerderij** (Children's Farm), where the kids can feed the geese, ducks, rabbits, and goats. Take the second street on the left, Minnemoerstraat, then turn right onto Grote Bickersstraat. Here you can pause for a drink, snack, or dinner at 't Blauwe Hoofd Café, a popular spot with locals. Emerging from the underpass, walk up Buitenoranjestraat to return to Haarlemerdijk, from where you can explore Spaarndammerbuurt (see pp. 136–37) or the Jordaan district (see pp. 138–43). ■

Kinderboerderij

Map p. 128
Corner of Bickersgracht & Bickersstraat
Free (donations welcome)
Bus: 18, 22

Brown cafés & Dutch gin

In Amsterdam you are never far from a brown café *(bruin kroeg)*, so called because of the abundance of wood and the caramel color of the smoke-stained walls and ceilings. The traditional drink is jenever—Dutch gin— which has a much more pronounced juniper and citrus flavor than the better-known London gin. But tap beer is the main drink.

Brown cafés are a unique Amsterdam in- stitution. Their mellow patina and cozy atmos- phere are especially in- viting when fog or drizzle envelops the city or there is a chill in the damp sea air. Some at- tract a particular clien- tele. There are arty cafés; sports cafés; stu- dent haunts; feminist, gay, or lesbian joints; cafés known for their blues nights; or cafés

Gift idea: Dutch gin is still sold in antique-style salt-glazed ceramic bottles and jars.

justifiably renowned for their bagels or home-baked apple cake. On the whole, Amsterdam-mers tend not to barhop, preferring instead to make one café their regular haunt. The cafés function like the old village pump—the place where people from the immediate neighbor-hood gather after work or on weekends to gos-sip, read the newspaper, or discuss the latest news. Brown cafés are thus an extension of the home—a second living room where you can relax and enjoy the camaraderie of watching a soccer game on TV.

Most brown cafés are small. This facilitates socializing by forcing strangers and regulars alike to share tables. In the more traditional cafés, exotic woven rugs cover the tables to soak up spillage. This tradition dates back to the Golden Age, as you will discover when you view the paintings of tavern scenes in the Rijksmuseum (see pp. 192–97).

Incorrect coffee & gin

Equally traditional are the two archetypal café drinks: "wrong coffee" and jenever. "Wrong" or "incorrect" coffee is a literal translation of the Dutch *koffie ver-keerd;* if you ask for it, you will get coffee made with milk. The idea that white coffee is somehow "wrong"— that is, inferior to black coffee—is shared by the Italians, who look with mild suspicion on anyone found drinking cappuccino after breakfast.

Jenever is equally fraught with symbol-ism. It is considered manly to like *jonge jen-ever* (young gin) rather than the sweeter, creamier *oude jenever* (old gin, mellowed for several years in oak barrels). Both are deli-cious. If you buy into the "real man" ethic, you will avoid sipping the gin—served ice cold in short, stumpy glasses—in favor of knocking it back in a single motion, often followed by a glass of lager. This combination is known as a *kopstoot* (head butt); you have been warned.

Don't stint on food if you follow this course. Most cafés serve a range of appetizing and alcohol-absorbing snacks, from *broodjes* (sandwiches) and *tostis* (toasted ham-and-cheese sandwiches) to hearty soups, stews, omelettes, and salads. Best of all is the fra-grant combination of cinnamon and apple in the classic Dutch café dessert called *appelge-bak*—apple cake served with a large portion of *slagroom,* or whipped cream.

All these dishes are Dutch café standards. Some establishments—known as *eetcafés* and signaled by a chalkboard outside or a menu in the window—serve a greater range of dish-es, including specials of the day. ∎

Antique stoves (above) and oriental carpets on the tables (below) create a feeling of coziness in brown cafés.

Spaarndammerbuurt

SPAARNDAMMERBUURT (THE SPAARNDAM DISTRICT) IS the location for an Arts and Crafts housing estate built by the pioneering architects of the Amsterdam School. Postcards depicting buildings on the estate are sold throughout the city, though few visitors take the trouble to see the real thing, because it is so far from the center—but the effort of getting there is rewarded by a glimpse of a different side of Amsterdam.

GETTING AROUND

Bus No. 22 provides a fast link from here back to Centraal Station. Alternatively, you can return to Haarlemmerplein to explore the Western Islands (see pp. 132–33) or the Jordaan (see pp. 138–43). ∎

From Haarlemmerplein, the route to Spaarndammerbuurt lies across the Westerkanaal bridge. You will pass the **statue** of Ferdinand Domela Nieuwenhuis (1846–1919), the priest-turned-social reformer who summed up his own life in these words: "from Christian to anarchist." The statue, unveiled in 1931, shows the firebrand reformer in preaching pose above a carving of the chained Prometheus, the ancient god who liberated humans by giving them the gift of fire; in so doing he incurred the wrath of Zeus, who condemned him to eternal punishment.

ARCHITECTURE OF THE AMSTERDAM SCHOOL

The socialism that fired Domela also motivated the architects of the Amsterdam School, whose inspiring architecture lies at the other side of the railroad tracks to the right. From the statue, cross the road into Westerpark and follow the main path through the park to a subway beneath the tracks; go through and turn left, heading up Zaanstraat.

Walking up Zaanstraat, you will pass several uninspiring examples of 20th-century housing. These help you appreciate the inventiveness and ingenuity of the architects who designed Spaarndammerbuurt.

The most ornate buildings here, and the ones you will see on postcards, form a triangular block bounded by Oostzaanstraat,

Hembrugstraat, and Zaanstraat. The block is known as the **Zaanhof,** but locals call it Het Schip (The Ship), because of its streamlined shape, with a broad "stern," tapering to a narrow "prow."

DECORATIVE DETAIL

The prow is seen first as you approach the post office that forms the corner of the block. (The very plain post office interior comes as a disappointment after the expectations raised by the detailing of the exterior windows and brickwork.) The whole block, built between 1913 and 1915, is an experimental work on which architect Michel de Klerk lavished a huge amount of decorative detail. The bulging barrel-shaped **oriel window** on the corner of Hembrugstraat and Zaanstraat, and the curiously shaped **tower** that marks the prow of the ship on Hembrugstraat, are examples of his whimsical and inventive style, in which the building is treated as if it were a sculpture. Straight lines are rare, instead the brick walls billow and bulge, fold and curl in a way that lends the structure fluidity and plasticity.

The architects of the Amsterdam School, which flourished as an informal grouping of like-minded architects from 1912 to 1940, were often criticized for their obsessive attention to decorative detail, which added greatly to the cost of buildings that were intended as dignified

but low-cost dwellings for the city's poor. In this respect, the Amsterdam School had much in common with other Arts and Crafts movements, especially in the strong appreciation for the skills of the humble bricklayer, carpenter, and metal worker. Evidence for this is demonstrated in the playfully elegant shapes of the porches, staircases, doors, number plates,

and window frames of this block, all of which display consummate craftsmanship.

Michel de Klerk was also the architect of the housing block northeast of the Zaanhof, facing on to the garden square called Spaarndammerplantsoen. Several other housing blocks nearby are built in the same style, though they are not quite so decorative. ■

Bold and bulbous bay windows transform dull brick into an eye-catching feature.

A stroll through the Jordaan

The Jordaan district lies on the western fringe of the canal circle. It stretches for 1.5 miles (2.4 km) from north to south and is divided into a maze of tiny streets named after trees and flowers. Because of this, the French-speaking refugees who settled here in the 17th century called it Le Jardin—The Garden—a name which was later corrupted to Jordaan. It retains a remarkable village-like ambience.

Peaceful cloisters hide behind the Jordaan's maze of streets.

Start at **Palmgracht,** the northernmost street of the Jordaan district. The black facade of Nos. 28–38 has a gable stone depicting a turnip. The Dutch word for turnip is *raep,* and it's a pictorial pun on the name of Pieter Adriaenszoon Raep, who founded this **almshouse** in 1648, and whose coat of arms is proudly displayed above. This is one of the city's earliest *hofjes* (courtyards), so called because the almshouses were built, in the style of a religious cloister, around a communal courtyard.

Most hofjes were founded by wealthy citizens to house sick or elderly employees and their widows and orphans. There are dozens packed into the Jordaan, many with attractive gardens. Their existence is deliberately not publicized, because of the nuisance that intrusive visitors can cause residents. If you go for a closer look, respect the privacy of the occu-

pants (most hofjes close from 6 p.m. to 9 a.m.).

Walk to the end of Palmgracht, noting the many gable stones on the houses on both sides of the street. Turn left in Lijnbaansgracht. This street runs alongside boat-filled **Lijnbaansgracht ❶,** the canal that marked the outer edge of the city from 1660 until the mid-19th century. As you walk, note how many of the streets are named after plants: Palmgracht itself (Palm Canal—now filled in), followed by Palmstraat (Palm Street), Goudsbloemstraat (Marigold Street), and Lindengracht (Lime Tree Canal).

On leafy **Lindengracht,** cross the road to No. 167, where a gable stone depicting De Drie Linden (The Three Limes) records the restoration of this fine neck-gabled house in 1982. Next to it, the inscription above the entrance of Nos. 163–149 reveals that this is the **Pieter Jansz Suyckerhoff** (*hoff* is an archaic form

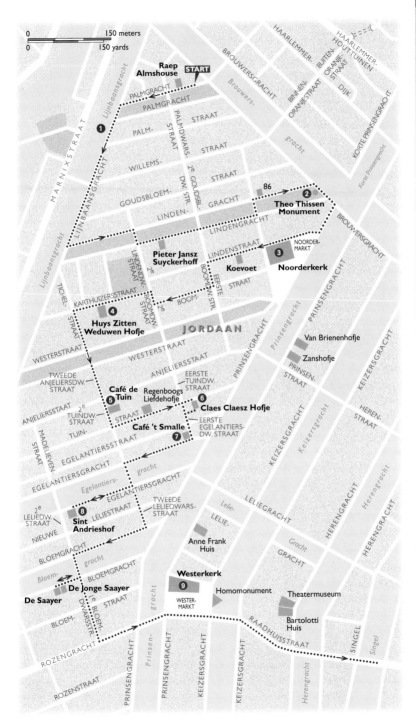

0 ——— 150 meters
0 ——— 150 yards

Raep Almshouse
START

HAARLEMMER.
HAARLEMMER.HOUTTUINEN
BROUWERSGRACHT
Brouwers
BUITEN.
BINNEN-ORANJESTRAAT
ORANJE-STRAAT
KORTE PRINSENGRACHT
DIJK

PALMGRACHT
PALMGRACHT

Lijnbaansgracht
MARNIXSTRAAT

❶

PALM-STRAAT
PALMDWARS-STRAAT
WILLEMS-STRAAT
2e GOUDSBL-DW. STR.

Brouwersgracht
BINNEN-ORANJESTRAAT

GOUDSBLOEM-GRACHT
LINDEN-GRACHT

86
❷
Theo Thissen Monument
BROUWERSGRACHT

LINDENGRACHT

Lijnbaansgracht

Pieter Jansz Suyckerhoff
LINDENSTRAAT
2e LINDENDW.STRAAT

NOORDER-MARKT
❸
Noorderkerk

Koevoet
BOOMDW.STR.
EERSTE BOOMDW. STRAAT
BOOM-

TICHEL-STRAAT
KARTHUIZERSTRAAT

❹
Huys Zitten Weduwen Hofje

JORDAAN

PRINSENGRACHT
PRINSENGRACHT

WESTERSTRAAT
WESTERSTRAAT

Van Brienenhofje

Zanshofje

PRINSEN-STRAAT

KEIZERSGRACHT

TWEEDE ANJELIERSDW. STRAAT
ANJELIERSSTRAAT

EERSTE TUINDW. STRAAT

HEREN-STRAAT

ANJELIERSSTRAAT
2e TUINDW.STRAAT

Café de Tuin ❺

Regenboogs Liefdehofje

❻
Claes Claesz Hofje

Keizersgracht

TUIN-STRAAT

EERSTE EGELANTIERS-DW. STRAAT

MADELIEVEN-STRAAT

EGELANTIERSSTRAAT

Café 't Smalle ❼

EGELANTIERSGRACHT

Egelantiers-gracht

EGELANTIERSGRACHT

Herengracht

2e LELIEDW.STRAAT
NIEUWE

❽
Sint Andrieshof
LELIESTRAAT

TWEEDE LELIEDWARS-STRAAT
LELIE-

LELIEGRACHT

HERENGRACHT

BLOEMGRACHT

Anne Frank Huis

Gracht

Bloem-gracht
BLOEMGRACHT

De Jonge Saayer

2e BLOEM-DWARSSTR.

Westerkerk
❾
WESTER-MARKT

Homomonument

Theatermuseum

De Saayer
BLOEM-STRAAT

Bartolotti Huis

ROZENGRACHT
PRINSENGRACHT
Prinsen-gracht
KEIZERSGRACHT
KEIZERSGRACHT
RAADHUISSTRAAT
Herengracht
SINGEL
Singel

ROZENSTRAAT

of hof), founded in 1670. Push open the door and go in to look at the courtyard. The pleasant gardens were originally used for drying laundry or for laying out cloth to bleach in the sun. Able-bodied hofje inmates were expected to work for the owners as cloth finishers, seamstresses or laundresses.

Leaving the hofje, turn right and check out the second-hand clothes shops, cafés, and Spanish tapas bars as you walk down the street, watching for unusual gable stones. **Number 86,** on the opposite side of the road, has a Dutch barge in full sail. At Nos. 55–57 you can see an amusing plaque showing a fish sailing through the branches of a tree, the date 1672 upside down, and an unpronounceable name: THCARGNEDNIL. Look carefully: This is Lindengracht spelled backward—the gable stone represents the trees of Lindengracht reflected in the waters of the (now filled-in) canal.

At the end of Lindengracht stands a monument ❷ to Theo Thijssen (1879–1943), the priest and educational reformer who did much to try and improve living conditions for the poor of the Jordaan. Thijssen wrote a semi-fictional novel, *Kees de Jongen* (*The Young Kees;* 1923), based on his own Jordaan childhood, and the bronze memorial, sculpted by Hans Bayens (1979), depicts Thijssen as a schoolmaster seated on a desk looking down at himself as a schoolboy.

Turn right, then immediately right again into **Noordermarkt,** the market square that was laid out in 1620 in front of the magnificent **Noorderkerk** ❸ (Northern Church), the last work of the great Dutch Renaissance architect Hendrick de Keyser (1565–1621). Following an extensive renovation in 2000, the church is open again for weekly concerts, and markets are still held in the square. On Monday you can pick up anything from old comics to decorative wall tiles at the flea market. On Saturday the

The square in front of the **Noorderkerk** has hosted a weekly market ever since the church was built in 1620.

Boerenmarkt (Farmers' Market) is held. Here standholders sell organic eggs, cheese, vegetables, bread, and much more.

The gables of the fine row of houses to the right of the church (on the northern side of Noordermarkt) reveal the kind of goods that were once sold here. Number 15 (with a pair of cloth shears) and No. 16 (with bales of cloth), indicating a tailor and a cloth merchant, stand alongside the butchers' houses (sporting a cow, a cock, and a lamb) and a freight carrier's (with a barge).

Continue up Lindenstraat, past No. 4, a house with a gable stone depicting King David and his harp, and No. 17, once a typical cozy Jordaan brown café (see pp. 134–35), but now an intimate and popular French restaurant called the Koevoet. Turn left onto Eerste

⬥	Also see area map p.128
▶	Palmgracht
⟳	2.2 miles (3.6 km)
⏱	2 hours
▶	Westerkerk

NOT TO BE MISSED
- Noorderkerk
- Claes Claesz Hofje

Boomdwarsstraat, and right onto Boomstraat (Tree Street), noting the different styles adopted by modern architects working in the district: No. 61 is a recent house built in the traditional style with a step gable and incorporating the gable stone of its predecessor, the Crowned Star; No. 68, opposite, is totally different, faced in aluminum whose colors (the three primaries, plus black and white) owe much to the paintings of the Dutch artist

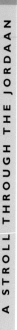

A STROLL THROUGH THE JORDAAN

Everyone who shops in the Jordaan flea market hopes to find a bargain.

"From the rose, sweet honey." A new gable stone upholds an ancient tradition.

Pieter Cornelis Mondrian (1872–1944).

Take the next right, Tweede Boom-dwarsstraat. All the streets running at right angles to the main streets are called *dwars straaten* (cross streets). They are numbered from east to west—*eerste* (first) and *tweede* (second)—followed by the name of the street they intersect. Hence Tweede Boomdwars-straat literally translates as "Second Tree Cross Street."

Take the next left, onto **Karthuizers-straat.** It is named not after a plant but after the medieval Carthusian monastery that once stood where the school playground is now located, on the right. Opposite, at Nos. 11–19, a row of five houses, dated 1737, bears the names of the Four Seasons (here Lent, Summer, Harvest, and Winter) under pictorial gable stones.

Next comes a long facade with wooden drying racks outside every window; this is the **Huys Zitten Weduwen Hofje ❹** (Alms-house of the Elderly Widows) of 1650, and the drying racks show that the inmates were expected to work for their accommodations. Go in through the main entrance to look at the courtyard with its garden and graceful water pumps. The Amsterdam coat of arms features

on one of the courtyard's classical pediments, with a trading ship on the other.

Coming out of the hofje, turn left, then left again onto **Tichelstraat,** looking for the gable stones at No. 33 (Batavia—the old Dutch name for Jakarta, capital of Indonesia) and No. 53 (a basket of coiled rope). Note, too, the excellent view of **Westerkerk** tower, leaning to the right, at the end of the street. Continue in the direction of the church, cross-ing wide Westerstraat onto Tweede Anjeliers-dwarsstraat. This marks the start of the Jordaan's main shopping street, where second-hand shops sit side by side with craft shops and small boutiques run by design coopera-tives. **Café de Tuin ❺** (*Tuindwarsstraat 13, tel 624 4559*), on the left in the next section of the street, is a good place to soak up the local atmosphere along with your coffee and apple cake.

Take the next left, onto Tuinstraat, passing another almshouse, **Regenboogs Liefde-hofje,** on the left. At the next junction—the one with Eerste Egelantiersdwarsstraat—look to your left for a gable stone showing the hand of God appearing from a cloud and wielding a hammer (the sign of a goldsmith); next to it a stone depicts a baker utilizing a long-

The Sower scatters his seeds; might this house have been constructed by a Mr. Saayer?

handled shovel to put loaves into his oven.

Cross over to the other side of Tuinstraat and continue down the street to the first house on the right, whose gable stone shows an organist and the words **Claes Claesz Hofje** ❻. Go back and turn left onto Eerste Egelantiersdwarsstraat to see the narrow entrance to this delightful hofje, restored in 1971. The atmosphere of this hidden hofje is enhanced by the strains of violin music echoing around the court, or the sounds of an operatic soprano in full flow, for it now provides accommodations for music students studying at Amsterdam's prestigious Conservatoire.

Turn left out of the hofje, and walk up to the atmospheric **Café 't Smalle** ❼ *(Egelantiersgracht 12, tel 623 9617)* on the next corner on the right. Founded in 1780 as the outlet for a gin distillery, this is one of the city's oldest traditional cafés, and it retains its 18th-century interior. It overlooks the Egelantiersgracht, which is lined with attractive 17th- and 18th-century houses. Among the finest are No. 50, on the right, with its gable stone of a bee flying towards a wild rose; No. 63, on the opposite bank, with a hooded falcon; No. 69, with a dove; and No. 87, with its two leather workers. Across the next

junction lies the **Sint Andrieshof** ❽, which is entered through a passageway lined with old Delft tiles. The courtyard is a tranquil haven, with a statue of Christ on the wall to the left.

Turning right out of the hofje, take the next right, Tweede Leliedwarsstraat, cross Nieuwe Leliestraat, and turn right on Bloemgracht, appropriately nicknamed the Herengracht (Gentlemen's Canal) of the Jordaan, because of its large and dignified houses. Cross the next bridge, then turn right, to see the step-gabled building at Nos. 87–91, designed by Hendrick de Keyser and known as The Three Hendriks. Next on the left is No. 81, called **De Jonge Saayer** (The Young Sower), depicting a child scattering grain across the newly plowed soil, perhaps built by the son of the owner of No. 77, **De Saayer** (The Sower).

Retrace your steps and take the next right, onto Eerste Bloemdwarsstraat, and head straight up to busy Rozengracht, then turn left up towards **Westerkerk** ❾ (see p. 145). This sudden return to traffic-filled streets highlights just how peaceful the Jordaan is. To get back to central Amsterdam, walk past Westerkerk and all the way up Raadhuisstraat, which will finally bring you to Nieuwezijds Voorburgwal. ∎

Theater Instituut Nederland

Commentaries in every language guide you around the riches of the Amsterdam Theater Museum.

THE THEATER INSTITUUT NEDERLAND IS A RESOURCE center covering the theatrical arts from the 17th century to the present day. The first floor has a small Theatermuseum whose exhibits change every few months; on the second floor is a library and archive of photographs and posters.

marks of Amsterdam's leading Renaissance architect, Hendrick de Keyser.

Bartolotti's neighbor *(Herengracht 168)* was built for the equally affluent Michiel Pauw, one of the founders of the Dutch West India Company. Pauw's much more restrained sandstone house was designed by Philip Vingboons in 1638. Vingboons invented the neck gable for this house, so called because its shape resembles the shoulders and neck of a wine bottle.

Inside the museum, costumes, set designs, puppets, and miniature theaters are displayed in rooms that are splendidly decorated with wall and ceiling paintings. Isaac de Moucheron painted the backgrounds, while Jacob de Wit was responsible for the languorous goddess Flora and her retinue of figures representing the Four Seasons, the Fates, and the Virtues.

The paintings are framed by exuberant plasterwork, as are the doors. Some of the best examples are in the hall and around the staircase: Look for the Maid of Amsterdam, symbol of the city, loaded down with gifts from the four corners of the Earth; for Neptune, the god of the sea; and for the beehive, symbol of diligence.

The latter can be found above the entrance to the small café, which looks onto the attractive rear garden, pleasant in fine weather. As befits a 17th-century house, it is a simple knot garden with box hedging clipped to form an intricate pattern. ∎

Theatermuseum, library & archive

⬛ Map p.128

✉ Herengracht 166–174

☎ 551 3300

🕐 Closed Mon., Sat. & Sun. a.m.

💲 $$$

🚊 Tram: 13, 14, 17, 20

⛴ Museumboot

The Theater Institute is housed in two adjoining houses that together illustrate the work of two eminent Amsterdam architects. The Bartolotti House *(Herengracht 170–172)* was built in 1617 for Guillielmo Bartolotti, one of the wealthiest merchants in Amsterdam. It is also known as the Gaudy House because of its flamboyant facade, which is decorated with urns, niches, scrolls, and masks—all of them the trade-

Westerkerk

IN HER FAMOUS DIARY, ANNE FRANK WROTE ABOUT THE companionship of the bells that rang out the quarter hours from the Westerkerk (Western Church), which lies a short way up Prinsengracht from her home. The bells still ring out—often with recognizable melodies—every 15 minutes.

Designed by Hendrick de Keyser, the church was begun in 1620 but not completed until 1638. The 278-foot (85m) **tower** is the tallest in Amsterdam. The golden crown that tops it is modeled on that of the Holy Roman Emperor, Maximilian I, who granted the city the right to use the crown in its coat of arms in 1489 in gratitude for loans from Amsterdam bankers.

Westerkerk has two splendid baroque **organs;** attending an organ recital is the best way to see the interior of the church, which is closed most of the time. The church was the last resting place of Rembrandt (see pp. 104–105), who was buried in an unmarked pauper's grave (restorers working in the church in 1997 discovered what they thought was his grave, but the contents disintegrated on exposure to the air). Living an extravagant life, often on borrowed money, the artist was forced into bankruptcy in 1658. He had to leave his fine house on Jodenbreestraat (see p. 102) for cheaper lodgings on Rozengracht, the Jordaan canal that lies just to the southwest of Westerkerk. Here he painted some of his greatest works, but never regained his popularity and died in poverty in 1669.

To the south of the church stands the small statue of Anne Frank (1977), the work of Marie Andriessen. Two pink granite triangles at the eastern end of the square on which the church stands, facing on to Keizersgracht, form part of the **Homomonument** (1987), a memorial to persecuted homo-

sexuals (the pink triangle was worn by homosexual victims of the Nazi holocaust). A third triangle sits on a terrace right by the edge of the canal and is usually strewn with flowers left by friends and relatives of AIDs victims. On the northern side of the church, the house at Westermarkt 6 has a plaque recording that the French philosopher René Descartes (1596–1650) lived here for several weeks in 1634. ∎

Westerkerk

- Map p. 128
- Prinsengracht 281
- 624 7766
- Church closed, except services and concerts. Tower closed Sun. April–Sept.
- Tower $
- Tram: 13, 14, 17, 20

Anne Frank Huis

www.annefrank.nl
- Map p. 128
- Prinsengracht 263
- 556 7100
- Closed Yom Kippur
- Tram: 13, 14, 17, 20
- Museumboot

Anne Frank Huis

WHAT IS IT THAT MAKES AN ALMOST EMPTY HOUSE ON Prinsengracht the most visited attraction in Amsterdam? It is, of course, the compelling story of the family that hid here during the Nazi occupation of the Netherlands, and the tragic story of young Anne Frank, whose dreams of becoming a writer ended with her premature death, at the age of 15, in the Bergen-Belsen concentration camp.

Anne Frank poured her soul into a secret diary during the Occupation.

The Anne Frank House is easily spotted by the long lines that build up outside during the peak holiday season (July and August, Easter and Christmas) so come early or late in the day if you want to avoid a long wait. It's hard to believe today that in the 1950s there were plans to demolish the house. At that time, the name of Anne Frank was almost unknown. Her father, Otto, was the only survivor of the eight people who hid in the *achterhuis*, the secret annex at the back of the house, from July 1942 to August 1944. During this time Anne kept a diary, filling three separate volumes and more than 100 loose-leaf pages with her thoughts and feelings.

Otto offered the diary to various publishers after the war. Initially, nobody was interested; then the first edited version was brought out by a small Dutch publishing house in 1947. When the diary was finally published in English, in 1952, right-wingers questioned its authenticity. Readers, attracted by the directness and immediacy of Anne's writing, felt differently. In 1955 the book was turned into a Broadway play and this served as the basis for the 1959 movie, starring Millie Perkins as Anne, that helped make the book the worldwide bestseller it is today.

Shortly after the arrest of the Franks, Miep Gies, one of the family's helpers, found Anne's diary lying forlornly on the floor. Recent restoration has not attempted to re-create the wartime appearance of the house. Instead, video screens set the scene with extracts from Anne's diaries and interviews with those trusted friends and employees who looked after the family and supplied them with food and fuel, at great risk to themselves, during the

two long years and 30 days they spent in hiding.

Like so many houses in Amsterdam, this one is divided into a front part and a back annex, the achterhuis, which had a variety of uses—some were used as warehouses or even clandestine churches. Otto Frank used the front as the base for his company, which specialized in spices, food additives, and flavorings. He had fled to Amsterdam from Frankfurt with his family in 1933, when Hitler's National Socialist Party came to power. Trapped in Nazi-occupied Amsterdam, Otto, his wife Edith and their daughters Margot and Anne, and the Pels family, Hermann and Auguste, with their son Peter, went into hiding in the achterhuis on July 6, 1942. They were joined in November by another refugee, Fritz Pfeffer.

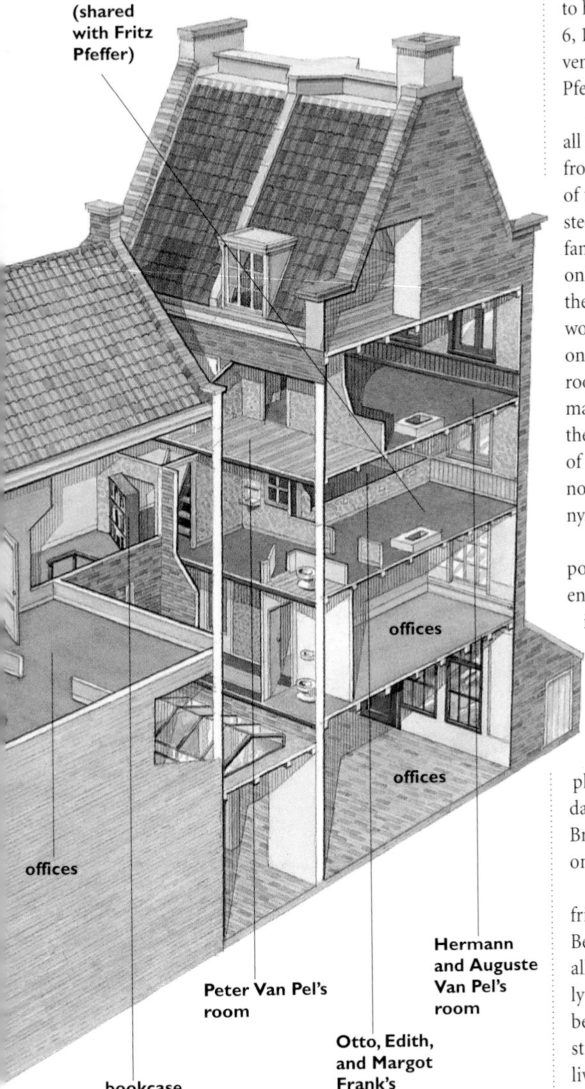

A simple wooden bookcase was all that separated the hiding place from discovery. Passing a replica of the bookcase, visitors climb the steep staircase that leads to the families' cramped quarters. The only remains from Anne's time are the pictures she cut from Hollywood movie magazines and pasted on the walls to brighten the dark rooms. There is also a newspaper map her father used for following the progress of the D-Day landings of 1944, and the slow liberation of northern Europe from Nazi tyranny.

Anne's story is all the more poignant because it came close to ending happily. Someone—never identified—reported the Franks' hiding place to the Nazis; the fateful knock on the door came on August 4, 1944. Anne was taken away to Bergen-Belsen, where she died of typhus in March 1945 (the exact date is not known), days before the British arrived to liberate the camp on April 15.

According to an old school friend who was with her in Bergen-Belsen, Anne believed that all the other members of her family were dead. That friend firmly believes that Anne might have struggled on and found the will to live if she had only known that her father was still alive. ■

Anne Frank's bedroom (shared with Fritz Pfeffer)

offices

offices

offices

bookcase doorway

Peter Van Pel's room

Otto, Edith, and Margot Frank's bedroom

Hermann and Auguste Van Pel's room

The House with the Heads vies for the title of Amsterdam's finest Renaissance residence.

Grachtengordel North

THE NORTHERN PART OF AMSTERDAM'S CANAL CIRCLE, from Brouwersgracht to Raadhuisstraat, is a fascinating blend of patrician houses, almshouses, houseboats, cafés, and shops. The area's three canals show subtle differences in architectural style and social pretension. Traditionally, the Herengracht (Gentlemen's Canal), nearest the center of Amsterdam, has been the abode of the wealthiest citizens. The Keizersgracht (Emperor's Canal) was more for the merchant class, while the Prinsengracht (Prince's Canal) has a mix of warehouses and more modest dwellings.

One of the finest examples of an aristocratic Golden Age house is the **Bartolotti Huis,** home to the Theatermuseum (see p. 144), at Herengracht 170. The house was built for wealthy Guillelmo Bartolotti, whose brother-in-law built an equally flamboyant house—**Het**

Huis met de Hoofden (The House with the Heads)—nearby on Keizersgracht (named after the Holy Roman Emperor). To find it, continue down Herengracht, and turn right onto Leliegracht. Along this short canal are several good antique shops and one of Amster-

dam's best specialist bookshops—**Architectura et Natura**—at No. 22. Those with an interest in architecture, gardening, or natural history should step in and browse the stock, which has a large selection of English-language books.

Towering over its neighbors at the end of the street is an unusually tall building, **Keizersgracht 174–176,** built in art nouveau style, with a mosaic high up in the corner tower. It depicts a child watched over by a guardian angel, the symbol of the insurance company for whom the building was constructed in 1905. Today Amsterdammers refer to it as the Greenpeace building, because it houses the headquarters of the environmental activist group.

RENAISSANCE HOUSES

The House with the Heads lies a short way down on the right, at **Keizersgracht 123.** Canal-boat tours all stop here to look, for this is one of Amsterdam's most celebrated Dutch Renaissance houses. Built in 1622, it has a very fine elevated neck gable (shaped like the neck of a wine bottle) rising from a facade enlivened by blank niches and columns of painted sandstone, contrasting with the delicate brickwork. The name of the house refers to the six heads set in the facade, which depict the classical deities Apollo, Ceres, Mars, Pallas Athene, Bacchus, and Diana.

That, at least, is the official explanation. A more colorful theory holds that the heads were placed here to commemorate the bravery of a servant girl who beheaded six burglars with an ax when they tried to rob the house in the owner's absence. The architect is unknown, but the house bears a strong resemblance to the style of Hendrick de Keyser (see p. 151); it may have been the work of his son, Pieter.

SIDE STREETS & RADIAL CANALS

Off Keizersgracht lies Herenstraat, a fascinating shop-lined side street with tempting cafés (such as Expresso Corner, on the corner of Herenstraat and Herengracht) and artful window displays. Here you can browse for antiques, books, crafts, cut flowers, jewelry, clothes, and toys. Several shops specialize in art deco and art nouveau, while others offer various oriental crafts and antiquities.

Back on Keizersgracht, look across the canal to see the way that some of the houses lean at precarious angles. That is usually a sign that the pile foundations were inadequate or that they have rotted or broken. Amsterdam's subsoil is soft and unstable, so deep piles were driven through the upper layers of peat, clay, and thin sand to the more solid sand bed that lies between 16 and 23 feet (5 and 7 m) below ground level. The piles, made of pine or birch, were used to support a platform of oak plates, atop which the brick walls were built.

Skimping on the foundations—by using too few piles, by driving the piles in at an angle rather than vertically, or by making the piles too short—usually resulted in subsidence. Rotting, too, can cause houses to sink. For these reasons, piles are now made of reinforced concrete.

You may notice that all the houses on the left-hand side of the canal—from No. 90 all the way down to No. 46—have facades of equal width. This is because housing plots along the canal circle were initially sold with precisely 98 feet (30 m) of frontage. Developers frequently subdivided these into three narrower plots. Occasionally the plots were divided into two; less often, the whole plot would be used

Architectura et Natura

Ⓜ Map p. 128
✉ Leliegracht 22
☎ 623 6186
🕐 Closed Sun.
🚋 Tram: 13, 14, 17, 20

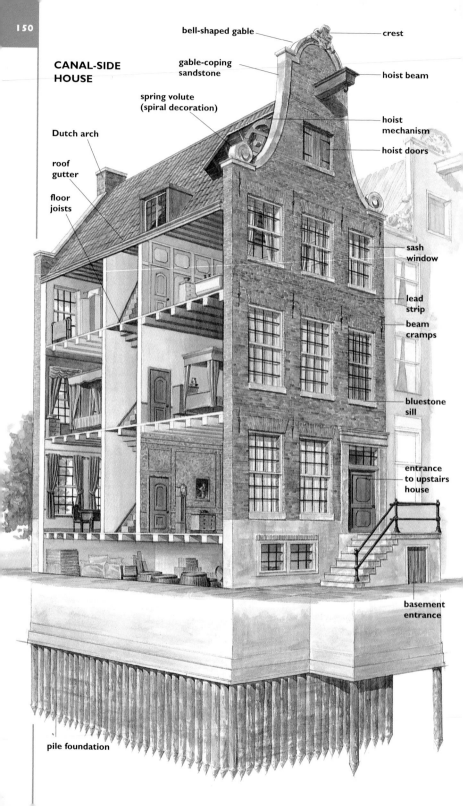

CANAL-SIDE HOUSE

bell-shaped gable

crest

gable-coping sandstone

hoist beam

spring volute (spiral decoration)

hoist mechanism

Dutch arch

hoist doors

roof gutter

floor joists

sash window

lead strip

beam cramps

bluestone sill

entrance to upstairs house

basement entrance

pile foundation

Hendrick de Keyser

Hendrick de Keyser (1565–1621), a sculptor from Utrecht, was put in charge of municipal building projects in Amsterdam in 1595. He designed the city's three great 17th-century churches, pioneering a new Protestant style for the Zuiderkerk (1614), the Noorderkerk (1620), and the Westerkerk (1621).

De Keyser's style—the pinnacle of Dutch Renaissance architecture—is unmistakable. His facades have been likened to the tiers of a wedding cake, with one story piled on top of another, and each one slightly smaller than the layer below it. ∎

Crowning glory: De Keyser's tower for Westerkerk

to accommodate a single palatial town house. Local taxes were levied on houses according to the width of their facade, so only the very wealthy could afford to build and live in the largest houses.

BOATS & WAREHOUSES

Nearly all of these houses were built for merchants, hence the hoisting beams that project from the gables, from which a pulley and tackle could be hung for lifting goods up to the roof space. The gable windows, through which the goods were hoisted, differ in size and shape from those in the lower facade (furniture is still winched through the windows because the staircases in most canalside houses are narrow and steep).

The canals themselves were not the underutilized waterways of today. Each of the three Grachtengordel canals is 82 feet (25 m) wide, broad enough to accommodate four lanes of shallow-drafted barges or lighters (the boats used to unload larger ships docked in Amsterdam harbor and

convey goods to the houses of individual merchants). Up to 4,000 ships could, and often were, berthed in the canal circle, and the wide quays, now sadly used as parking lots, once bustled with porters delivering goods by sledge, cart, or wheelbarrow.

Trees have always been a feature of the canals—though many of the big elms of old have succumbed to disease and have been replaced by tougher, younger trees.

Some of the buildings nearest to the port were built exclusively as warehouses. As you continue down Keizersgracht, note the three **Groenland Pakhuizen** (Greenland Warehouses) at Nos. 40–44 (on the opposite bank), which once contained huge tanks used for the storage of whale oil. Built in 1621 by the Greenland Whaling Company, the step-gabled buildings fell out of use when whale hunting ended in 1819 and have since been converted to housing. A short way farther down the street is an unusually large building, formerly a Jesuit church, now a sports center. This church was built in 1835 on the site of an earlier clandestine church, and its sober classical exterior respects the style of surrounding buildings, though it once had the kind of highly ornate, statue-filled interior more normally associated with Jesuit churches.

PRINSENGRACHT

At the bottom of Keizersgracht, turn left onto Pastoorsbrug to walk along Brouwersgracht (see pp. 155–56), and then turn left up the western bank of Prinsengracht (named after Prince William of Orange). There is a good view across the canal to the Jordaan district and its fine church, the **Noorderkerk,** designed by Hendrick de Keyser in 1620 (see p. 140). On this side there are some well-restored houses at Nos. 1A, 3, and 5, bearing gable stones carved with reliefs of St. Peter, St. Paul, and the Apostles who met the resurrected Jesus on the road to Emmaus. Number 1A has a neck gable with carved sandstone side cheeks, a style that was current from 1640 to the 1770s. Slightly later in date are the bell gables of Nos. 3, 5, and 7, a style introduced about 1660 and lasting until the 1790s. Most houses along this bank have simple flat cornices, however, a style that came from France in the late 17th century and became increasingly popular up until the 19th.

Gables were one way to give your house individuality and to distinguish it from houses of similar size and materials on either side. The number and the disposition of the windows was another way. Many of these houses have very large windows because, although glass was expensive, it helped to cut down the weight of the facade, making the house less liable to subsidence. Doors, fanlights, and railings all add to the variety, and most

of the houses along this stretch have basements, so that the ground floors begin about 5 feet (1.5 m) above street level. The entrance is reached via a flight of steps, or *stoop*, with cast-iron balusters and hand rails. The basements were often used for storage or as servants' accommodation and they have a separate hatch or low door to provide access. Keep an eye out for these delightful details as you walk up by the canal.

ALMSHOUSES & HOUSEBOATS

The rhythm of equal-size houses is broken by Nos. 89–133, a block with high windowless walls. You

can push open the small door to enter the peaceful courtyard of the **Van Brienenhofje,** an alms-house built in 1804 by Arnout Jan van Brienen on the site of a former brewery. Legend has it that van Brienen founded the alms house after he accidentally locked himself inside the strongroom of his house *(Herengracht 182)*. In danger of suf-focating, he knelt and prayed, promising to devote his life to the needy if he were rescued—which, in due course, he was.

A short way up the canal is another almshouse, built on a more modest scale. Nos. 159–171 are known as **Zonshofje** (Sun Court) and consist of houses originally built for elderly members of the Mennonite religious community in 1765. You can go into the *hofje (Closed Sat. & Sun.),* and enter the quiet courtyard with its clock and a depiction of Noah's Ark and a large sun with a smiling face. Both "The Sun" and "Noah's Ark" were names given to clandestine Catholic churches that stood on this site before the almshouses were built.

If you continue up Prinsengracht from here, the next building of note you will reach is the Anne Frank Huis (see pp. 146–47); beyond that lies the Westerkerk (see p. 145). To return to the city center, turn left at the church and go back to Dam Square via Raadhuisstraat. ■

Amsterdam is a paragon of early town planning that has stood the test of time.

Singel & Brouwersgracht

THE NAME SINGEL PROBABLY DERIVES FROM *CINGEL*, meaning a "belt." This canal marks the line of the 15th-century city wall, and it loops around to join the Amstel River, in the south, to form a moat encircling the medieval city. At the northern end of Singel is Brouwersgracht (Brewers' Canal), dug between 1585 and 1612 and one of the prettiest of the city's many canals.

Singel & Brouwersgracht

Map pp.128–29

SINGEL

Singel was once lined with merchants' warehouses, but it gained its residential character in the 17th century, when the canal circle (see p. 129) was dug. A good place to take in the views up and down this canal is the **Torensluis**, a wide bridge to the west of Nieuwe Kerk (see pp. 58–59), where locals and visitors come to sit and enjoy the sunshine. The great width of the bridge (138 feet/42 m) is due to the presence of a tower that served as a military prison until it was demolished in 1829; prisoners were also kept in cells underneath the bridge.

A large **statue** of Eduard Douwes Dekker (1820–1887), a government official who wrote plays, novels, and poetry under the pen name of Multatuli (Latin for "I have suffered greatly"), now occupies the site of the tower. Dek-

ker's radical (and often humorous) novels about life in Amsterdam and in the Dutch colonies made him a great influence on Dutch social reformers. A small **museum** devoted to his life and work is tucked inside the nearby house where he was born (*Korsjespoortsteeg 20, closed Mon. & Wed.–Fri.*).

Singel has the appearance of being frozen in time, but the view is a constantly changing one. The most recent addition can be seen at **Blauwburgwal,** Amsterdam's shortest canal, to the north: Looking across the canal to the right you will see No. 109, with its prominent postmodernist facade, built in 1994. The bridge itself was constructed in 1652 to replace an earlier ferry; which explains why the house at Nos. 83–85, decorated

with Ionic pilasters and swags, is known as **Het Oude Veerhuis** (The Old Ferryhouse).

Across the bridge is No. 64, with its gable dated 1637, in contrast to the 19th-century neo-Renaissance house with step gables at No. 62 and the early 20th-century house in art deco style at Nos. 46–48. More elegant than all of these is No. 36, the building known as **De Zeevrugt** (Produce of the Sea). Built in 1736 for a shipbroker, the cornice above the tall door depicts a ship, and the Louis XV-style roof cornice Mercury, god of trade.

BROUWERSGRACHT
Many bridges cross Brouwersgracht as the city's four main canals—Singel, Herengracht, Keizersgracht, and Prinsengracht—all flow into

Unlike most city bridges, Torensluis is wide enough to accommodate both traffic and a café.

this canal, which acts as a busy terminus for craft that still use the canals, principally the glass-topped tourist boats.

Originally this was an industrial canal, lined with factories and warehouses, which benefited from their proximity to the port. Local brewers didn't draw their water from the canal—it was too foul with discharges from the breweries themselves, and from other nearby businesses involved in drying fish, curing leather, rendering whale blubber into oil, and manufacturing soap. Instead, water barges brought in fresh water from outside the city.

Today Brouwersgracht is a desirable, quiet, and tree-shaded residential street that is close to the city center. Some of its houses still

Traveling the canals by boat affords a novel perspective of the city.

bear evidence of their earlier use: No. 48 has two huge fish carved on either side of the gable, and No. 52 has the gable stone of a chairmaker. To the right is **Herenmarkt** (Gentlemen's Market Square), with its children's playground backing on to the **West Indische Huis,** the former headquarters of the Dutch West India Company (see p. 131).

SINGEL

Back on Singel, the **Haarlemmersluis bridge** (see p. 130) leads across to the eastern bank of the canal. The *sluis* (lock) beside this bridge once controlled the water level in the whole canal system by holding the water back when the tide went out. Now that the IJ River is dammed, and no longer tidal, the lock remains permanently open.

To the right of the bridge is **Stromarkt,** once the site of the city's Straw Market, where thatching materials and animal bedding were sold.

If you walk up Singel a short way you will pass No. 7, which is often said to be the smallest house in Amsterdam because the facade is only as wide as the door (in fact, this is the back entrance to a much bigger building on Jeroensteeg). Just beyond is the huge bulk of the **Ronde Lutherse Kerk** (Round Lutheran Church), a splendid building of 1668 designed by Adriaan Dortsman. Known locally as the Knitting Basket, because of its green copper dome, it's an unusual feature in a city of towers and spires. The church burned down several times and was rebuilt in the mid-1990s exactly as before. Now it's used as a conference center and concert hall, operated by a hotel.

Next door to the church on Kattengat are two of the city's most interesting buildings, **De Gouden Spiegel** (The Golden Mirror) and **De Silveren Spiegel** (The Silver Mirror). Built in 1614 by Hendrick de Keyser, they both have step gables, a style introduced around 1600, which continued to be popular until the 1670s. The buildings now house a restaurant, De Silveren Spiegel. From here it's a short walk up Kattengat and then left down Hekelveld to return to Centraal Station. ∎

You can find it all in the southern canal district: casinos and nightclubs, earnest debating societies, a street devoted to antiques, and a shopping center built around a chess set.

Southern canals

The Magere Brug

Southern canals

THE SOUTHERN PART OF THE GRACHTENGORDEL STRETCHES FROM
Raadhuisstraat all the way around to the Amstel River. Originally the canal circle ended at
Leidsegracht. Following a 48-year hiatus, work began on the next stretch, southeastward
to the Amstel, in 1660. Many of the people who bought plots on the new stretch were the
extremely wealthy heirs of merchants, manufacturers, and bankers. The houses they
built were far grander than those of earlier generations, earning this part of the canal
circle the nickname Gouden Bocht (Golden Bend).

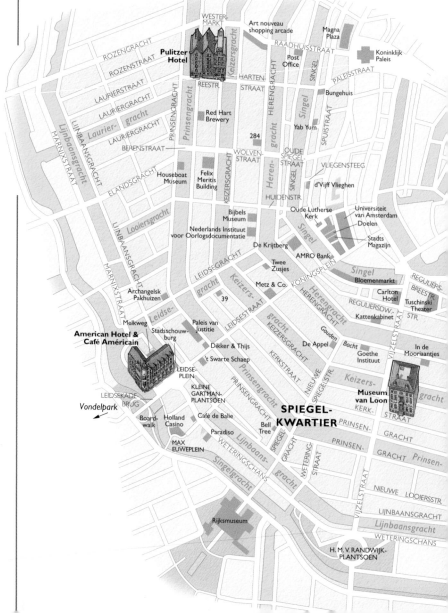

The residential tranquility of the area was shattered in the mid-19th century, however, when new thoroughfares were driven through the Golden Bend linking the city center with the newly developing suburbs around the Museum Quarter and Vondelpark (see pp. 206–208). As a result, the area has seen more recent redevelopment than the northern stretch, and has a greater mixture of buildings—not just elegant houses and attractive antique shops and art galleries, but also churches and theaters, brothels and hotels, university faculties and the homes of former squatters, as well as the lively nightlife of Leidseplein and Rembrandtplein.

Toward the Amstel end, the character of the canal circle changes yet again. The river, alive with the bustle of barges and spanned by elegant bridges, provides a wide-open vista to contrast with the enclosed world of the Golden Bend. ■

The artistic tradition is vibrantly alive in the city that gave the world Rembrandt.

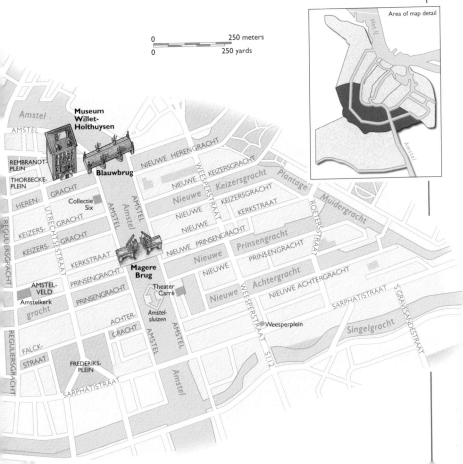

The monumental former post office headquarters is now a popular upscale shopping mall, the Magna Plaza, open seven days a week.

Singel & Spuistraat

SLUMS AND ROTTING WAREHOUSES ALONG THE SOUTHERN stretch of the Singel canal were swept away during 19th-century redevelopment, and more would have been demolished during the 1980s were it not for the activities of squatters, who defied the authorities and won the day. As a result, this corner of Amsterdam is a kaleidoscope of architectural styles from several centuries.

Singel & Spuistraat

Map p. 158

Raadhuisstraat was cut through the canal circle in the 1890s to create a tram route linking the city center and the western outskirts. Where the street crosses the Singel canal, you can look back for a fine view of the rear of the Koninklijk Paleis (Royal Palace; see pp. 54–57). High on his pediment above the palace, Atlas carries the world on his shoulders while, below, figures symbolizing the peoples of the earth offer gifts to the Maid of Amsterdam. As you look back at the palace, to the left lies the huge and flamboyant **Magna Plaza,** built by Cornelis Hendrik Peters in 1889 and a splendid example of the eclectic style, borrowing architectural elements from the Romanesque, Gothic, and

Renaissance periods. Originally built as the city's main post office, it is now a shopping center with a splendidly arcaded atrium.

In the other direction, you will see the present post office on the opposite bank of Singel. Beyond, running round the southern curve of Raadhuisstraat, is an art nouveau **shopping arcade,** built in 1898 by the Van Gendt firm of architects, its canopy decorated with crocodiles and dragons.

SQUATTERS & BROTHELS

Turning down Singel, the first building on the left after Paleisstraat is the eight-story **Bungehuis** (*Singel 239*), constructed of gray limestone in the 1930s for the Bunge Trading

Company, whose founder, Julius Carl Bunge, disliked superfluous decoration. Despite this, the main entrance around the corner on Spuistraat is a good example of art deco design (the building now houses various Amsterdam University faculties). A short way farther down Spuistraat, Nos. 214–216 has a garishly painted facade, a monument to the squatters' movement of the 1970s and '80s, when young people moved into empty properties to protest against the lack of affordable housing in the city.

Back on Singel, No. 295 looks innocuous, but has one of the city's most exotic interiors, with an unusually large number of bedrooms, each equipped with baths and cocktail bars. This is **Yab Yum,** Amsterdam's most expensive and luxurious brothel.

FRUIT & FLIES

Farther down Singel is an area of small shops specializing in postage stamps, coins, and antiquarian books. The alleys running off to the left all lead over to the sidewalk cafés of **Spuistraat,** a popular spot for Amsterdammers to meet for a drink after work.

This stretch of Singel used to house the city's fruit market. Look for No. 367 where Adam and Eve and the serpent in the Garden of Eden, the symbol of the Fruitsellers' Guild, are carved on the gable stone. The existence of the market might explain the names of the adjacent **Vliegensteeg** (literally "Fly Alley") and its venerable restaurant, **d'Vijff Vlieghen** (The Five Flies; see p. 253).

On the opposite bank, No. 390 has a splendid gable depicting Apollo and Minerva, gods of the sciences and the arts. Farther down, at No. 446, looms the huge Jesuit church of St. Francis Xavier, built in 1883. Known as **De Krijtberg** (The Chalk Hill) after a chalk warehouse that once stood on the site— and that doubled as a clandestine Catholic church in the 18th century—this house of worship is well worth a look. Inside, check out the ornate Gothic-revival rood screen and stained-glass east window.

CHURCHES & SHOOTING GALLERIES

From the church, there is a good view across Singel to the simple **Oude Lutherse Kerk** (Lutheran Old Church; see p. 62) now used by the University of Amsterdam for academic ceremonies. Farther down, the grand double-fronted building you see is the former

Doelen building, radically altered in 1773 but originally constructed to allow members of the city militias to practice shooting with their longbows and crossbows. Next to it, the **Stadts Magazijn** (City Arsenal) retains its original 1605 facade, with its wide, flat-topped gable decorated with scrollwork, built for the storage of weapons used by the militias. All of these buildings, from the Arsenal up to the church, have now been converted into a library for the University of Amsterdam. ■

Dragons and heraldic beasts decorate the leadwork of the art nouveau arcade in Raadhuisstraat.

An eclectic mix of styles typifies the later period of canal building.

Grachtengordel South

WALKING AROUND THE PART OF THE CANAL CIRCLE THAT stretches from Raadhuisstraaat to Leidsegracht, you'll run across scores of interesting architectural details to see and savor. The grand houses here are far from cheap to buy or rent—many have been turned into offices for advertising, design, or fashion companies—but the overall character remains residential.

When the canal circle was built, shops and workshops were deliberately restricted to the short cross-streets linking the radial canals. Wolvenstraat, two blocks south of Raadhuisstraat and one block over from the Singel canal (see pp. 160–61), is a typical example. It can be reached down Oude Spiegelstraat (named after Pieter Spiegel de Oude, who owned land in this area in the 17th century). Continue across the next bridge toward Wolvenstraat, looking over to the right as you go, across to **Herengracht No. 284.** This has a splendid sandstone facade dating from 1728. If you walk down for a closer look, you will see that the central bay has window frames heavily ornamented with acanthus leaf carvings, and an ornate crest rises from the roof cornice. The architect is not known, but the obsession

the buildings on the left, Nos. 314–316, as you reach the western bank of Keizersgracht. You might date this elegant building to the middle of the 17th century because of its step gable, small-paned sash windows, and fine brickwork. Actually, it was only constructed in 1935 by A.A. Kok, an architect who believed in using the traditional idiom for new buildings constructed in the historic city center. It's a perfect example of architectural good manners, not observed by every architect whose work is found along the Grachtengordel.

As you turn right down Keizersgracht, you come to Nos. 298–300, a glass-and-concrete building of 1955 that was regarded as revolutionary in its time but now just looks jaded and out of place. Is this preferable, though, to the kind of bland historicism represented by the buildings on the opposite bank, Nos. 271–303, all of which have been constructed since 1955, some as recently as 1984? The debate continues among architects, critics, and city council planners and is renewed every time a site comes up for development within the canal circle.

Several surplus churches have been saved by converting them to new uses.

SQUATTERS TURNED TENANTS

Among the older buildings on Keizersgracht are Nos. 294–292, a pair of 1730 houses with elongated neck gables and side pieces decorated with seashells and marine motifs. Farther down Keizersgracht, Nos. 252 to 242 form a group of buildings that were squatted in during the late 1970s and which were the scene of violent battles when riot police attempted to evict the occupants. In the end, the city council agreed to restore the buildings and rent them to the former squatters at a subsidized price. Needless to say, such a policy enrages some Amsterdammers,

with symmetry is apparent in the way the off-center front door has been made very plain so as not to distract from the central axis.

WOLVES, STAGS, & BEARS

Beyond No. 284 lies Wolvenstraat, whose name means "Wolf's Street." All the cross-streets to the north and south of here have names associated with the fur trade: Reestraat and Hartenstraat (Stags and Deer), Berenstraat (Bears), Huidenstraat (Hides), and Runstraat (Bark, used in tanning). Clearly this was once an area that thrived on dealing in furs and hides, though the furriers' shops have now been replaced by a medley of small but excellent cafés and restaurants, specialty shops, and art galleries.

Crossing the next bridge, note

This annual canalside concert is staged by the upscale Pulitzer Hotel, a major patron of the arts.

who resent the fact that lawbreaking squatters have ended up living cheaply in palatial and prestigious canal houses that are beyond the means of many ordinary and law-abiding citizens.

PULITZER HOTEL & RED HART BREWERY

Shop-lined **Reestraat** is a good place to stop for a coffee—perhaps in the upscale Pulitzer café on the corner with Keizersgracht. The café is part of the **Pulitzer Hotel** (see p. 252), which occupies a whole block of 17th- and 18th-century canalside houses and warehouses running from Keizersgracht to Prinsengracht. Peter Pulitzer, grandson of the newspaper publisher who founded the annual Pulitzer prizes for journalism, literature, music, and drama, founded the hotel in 1968. All of the rooms and public areas have works of art on the walls, and sculptures dot the fine gardens (much of the art is for sale). In summer the hotel hosts a music festival with musicians performing on barges moored in the Prinsengracht, and the audience spread along both banks of the canal.

Turn left down Prinsengracht and note the medallions set high in the facade of Nos. 357–359, showing the deer trademark of the former **Red Hart Brewery,** which occupied these premises from around 1612 to 1841. Brewers in Amsterdam dealt in fresh water as well as beer. In the days before drinking water was supplied by tap, they imported fresh water by barge both for their own use and for sale to the public. Farther down the street, the plain building at No. 415 was the home of Johannes Commenius (1592–1670), the Moravian priest who wrote a pioneering treatise on educational theory, the *Didactica Magna,* and who was the first to advocate the use of pictures (today's "visual aids") as a learning tool.

PETER THE GREAT

The next left is Berenstraat, another shop-lined cross street, with the **Houseboat Museum** (see pp. 168–69) on the opposite bank. At the end of Berenstraat, you have a view across Keizersgracht to No. 317, another relatively plain house with a distinguished former resident: Peter the Great, the tsar of Russia, quite literally turned up on the doorstep in December 1716.

The owner of the house was Christoffel Brants, a merchant who had spent much of his early life in Russia, where he became a friend of the young tsar (they were both fascinated by shipbuilding). When

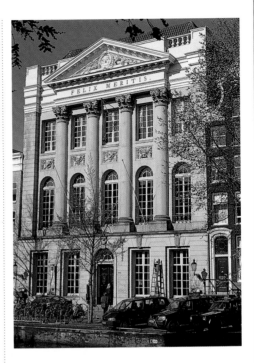

The Felix Meritis Building, once home to Amsterdam's leading academic society, is now an innovative theater.

Peter set off on his tour of Europe, traveling incognito, he called on his old friend without any prior warning. Reminiscing about the past, Peter is said to have drunk a great deal of beer before falling asleep on the hard floor of Brants' bedroom. Once the city council heard that the tsar was in town, it hastily prepared a reception for the ruler and persuaded him to move into the Herengracht house of the Russian ambassador (see p. 180).

FELIX MERITIS

On this side of the canal, at No. 324, is another building with Russian connections: The **Felix Meritis Building** was used as the headquarters of the Dutch Communist Party from 1945 until 1968. This was just one episode in the building's varied history. It was built in 1787 for the Felix Meritis society (whose name, meaning "Happiness through Merit," is

Bijbels Museum

Map p. 158

Herengracht 366

624 2436

Closed Sun. a.m.

Tram: 1, 2, 5

Museumboot

carved beneath the pediment). This institution was set up to further interest in the arts and sciences. Behind the well-proportioned classical facade was an auditorium where the society's lectures took place. Upper rooms in the building were designed for use as artists' studios, and there was an astronomical observatory on the roof.

Intellectual Amsterdammers were proud of their Temple of Enlightenment, but others were less impressed. Napoleon was brought here for a reception after his grand entry into the city in 1811, but he had hardly set foot through the door before he beat a hasty exit, complaining that the auditorium stank of tobacco smoke. On another occasion, Brahms conducted a performance of his *Third Symphony* in the building and departed with the stinging criticism that his hosts were "good people but bad musicians." It was this rebuke that spurred the city to build the Concertgebouw (see p. 206) and set up a permanent professional orchestra.

Fire destroyed the interior of the Felix Meritis Building in 1932 and, in its rebuilt form, it housed the Communist Party, which briefly enjoyed mass support because of the role that it played in the resistance to the Nazi occupation. In 1968 the building was renamed the Shaffy Theater after the actor Ramses Shaffy, but its diet of avant garde and experimental drama failed to attract large audiences, and the Shaffy finally closed in 1989. The building was then rescued by the Felix Meritis Foundation, which now runs it as a theater for the promotion of European arts—dance, music, and drama—with a lively summer school. There is a café to the left of the entrance, a popular meeting point for young arts enthusiasts and a relaxing place to gather your thoughts.

Opposite:
Mirrors take the neck pain out of viewing Jacob de Wit's ceiling paintings in the Bijbels Museum.

BIJBELS MUSEUM

At the next junction, turn left across the bridge and walk down Huidenstraat, then turn right onto Herengracht. A short way down is the **Bijbels Museum** (Bible Museum). The sandstone buildings are identifiable as the work of Philip Vingboons because of the ornate neck gables (invented by him in 1638 and first used for the building that now houses the Theatermuseum; see p. 144). This group of buildings dates from 1660 and his client was Jacob Cromhout, a merchant whose trademark, a crooked stick, appears on a plaque on the facade. The building combines classical elements (the pedimented windows, for example) with baroque (the garlanded ox-eye windows in the attic story). The interior retains its stately period details and ceiling paintings by the celebrated Jacob de Wit, not to mention the best preserved 17th-century kitchens in Holland and a lovely back garden with terraces and pools. The museum itself exhibits archaeological finds, models, and religious objects relating to the history, content, and influence of the Bible. One of its most celebrated exhibits is a large-scale model of the Biblical city of Jerusalem and of the Temple, the focus of Jewish worship, which the Romans destroyed in A.D. 70.

Just beyond the museum is another very decorative building, Nos. 380–382, built between 1888 and 1891 for a tobacco millionaire. The facade borrows its style from the French Renaissance châteaus of the Loire Valley. The building now houses the **Nederlands Instituut voor Oorlogsdocumentatie** (Dutch Institute for War Documentation; *closed Sat. and Sun.*). It is worth a visit just for a look at the opulent neo-Renaissance interiors. ■

Houseboats

Some 2,400 licensed houseboats ride at anchor inside Amsterdam's boundaries (many more are docked illegally). Of those 2,400, about 750 are tethered within the city center. This aquatic life style came about through the happy confluence of two factors: the postwar housing shortage and the modernization of the Dutch cargo fleet, the latter of which made available a number of surplus ships. The 1960s and '70s saw a boom in houseboat living as hippies and political activists embraced this inexpensive alternative way of life.

Best of both worlds: A boat and a bike equal an unusual home and the freedom to roam.

Walking up Prinsengracht, you'll quickly discern that the section of the canal circle from Raadhuisstraat to Leidsegracht boasts an unusually high number of houseboats. These watercraft range in style from beautifully restored seagoing sailbarges to ramshackle sheds. In theory if rarely in practice, no houseboat is supposed to exceed 50 feet (15m) in length nor rise higher than 8 feet (2.5m) above the waterline.

Houseboat Museum

To learn more about this unique way of life, the best place to start is the Houseboat Museum, moored opposite Prinsengracht 296 (Tel 427 0750, www.houseboatmuseum.nl, closed Mon. & Tue., tram: 13, 14, 17, 20). If you will be visiting Amsterdam for a week or longer, you could also sample life aboard a houseboat rather than in a hotel room. Several Amsterdam companies acting as agents for owners who rent their boats out on a weekly basis or longer; see p. 244 for details. ■

Rising costs

Living on a houseboat is no longer a cheap option. The cost of mooring licenses has soared because of a city council decree that no new permits will be issued. A sound boat will therefore cost you dearly. An ark—a square platform, often of steel or concrete, with a brick or timber superstructure—can be had for less.

Concrete hulls are relatively maintenance-free, but owners of steel or iron-hulled boats must check for signs of corrosion every three to four years; the typical result is an expensive trip to the shipyard. Here the boat is taken out of the water and the hull cleaned with a high-pressure hose to remove water plants and shellfish. Loose rivets are replaced and new steel plates are welded on where the hull has corroded to less than 0.2 inches (4 mm) thick.

As well as regular maintenance and annual premiums, there is also the cost of paying for a connection to the city sewage system. Until recently, houseboat toilets flushed straight into the canal; foul water from the canal system was then pumped into the North Sea and replaced with fresh water from the IJsselmeer—the manmade lake, once an ocean inlet, that lies east of Amsterdam. New laws stipulate that every boat owner has until 2005 to link to the nearest sewer.

Given all these expenses—not to mention property tax and diesel fuel, plus such standard costs as running water, electricity, telephone, and cable TV—living on a boat is no cheaper than buying a conventional apartment. Why, then, would anyone bother? The answer has more to do with the heart than the head. Some people just won't have it any other way: They love their boats and everything related with life afloat. ■

Life inside a canal barge is more spacious and comfortable than you might imagine. When you're on the move, the view topside is forever changing.

Leidsegracht, seen here at the corner of Keizersgracht, has a mix of fine 17th- and 18th-century canal houses.

Leidsegracht

LEIDSEGRACHT IS AN UNUSUAL CANAL IN THAT IT CUTS across the canal circle. In fact, it marks the end of the first section of the Grachtengordel, constructed from 1609 to 1660, and the beginning of the second phase of 1660 onward. The name "Leiden canal" indicates that this was where boats traveling the inland waterways between Amsterdam and Leiden once moored.

Leidsegracht

Map p. 158

The buildings that line the canal include several large warehouses where goods that were essential to the functioning of the city were unloaded. Number 88, the **Archangelsk Pakhuizen** (Archangel Warehouse), is named after the Russian port with which the warehouse owner, Egbert Thesingh, carried out his trade. He imported timber for shipbuilding, including ships' masts, and in turn Thesingh exported luxurious fabrics to the Russian Imperial Court. At No. 108 is the city stonemasons' yard. It was here, on the edge of the 17th-century city, that the stone and bricks used for constructing municipal buildings were unloaded, stored, and worked.

The adjacent bridge takes you across to the south bank of the canal with a view to the right of the massive former dairy, now the famous **Melkweg** arts center (see p. 174). In the bad old days, according to Amsterdam folklore, unscrupulous milkmen delivering milk by barge would adulterate it by adding canal water to the churns. So widespread was this practice that a new market in guaranteed fresh milk was created. The farmers would lead their cows to your door and milk the beasts before your eyes!

CORNELIS LELY

On the other side of the canal is **No. 39,** a simple spout-gabled building where Cornelis Lely was born in 1854. Lely was the engineer

Dutch province of Flevoland, whose provincial capital—Lelystad—was named to honor the engineer.

Farther along the street, there are good views, especially at night, when the arches of the bridges are outlined by strings of white lights. Look at the side cheeks of the neck gable at No. 11, decorated with a carving of intertwined snakes and lizards. The motif is unique in Amsterdam. Some say the snakes symbolize the financial entanglements of the first owner, a silversmith, who got himself deeply into debt.

THE GOLDEN BEND

Where Leidsegracht joins the Herengracht you will see a pretty pair of identical late 17th-century houses, Nos. 396 and 398, known as the **Twee Zusjes** (Two Sisters). No. 402 is a fine sandstone house, in the style of Philip Vingboons, with an unusually ornate curving *stoop* (the name is the same in English) dating from 1750. No. 408, also in similar style, has a fine ornamental fanlight above the door, while No. 412 is the work of Vingboons himself, who built it in 1667. These and the houses opposite are in the much grander style of the so-called Golden Bend (see pp. 178–81). ■

who transformed the Netherlands by planning and supervising the construction of the Afsluitdijk (Enclosing Dam), which was completed in 1932, three years after his death. The dam cut the shallow tidal Zuider Zee off from the North Sea. With the dam in place, the Zuider Zee was transformed into a freshwater lake (now called the IJsselmeer), parts of which have been reclaimed to create some 70 square miles (1,800 sq. km) of new land. Much of this forms the new

This Leidsegracht café preserves the expanse of expensive glass that confirmed the owner's affluence.

Bulbs, cut flowers, or potted plants: You'll find them all at the floating Flower Market.

Koningsplein & Leidseplein

NARROW KONINGSPLEIN IS ONE OF AMSTERDAM'S MAIN shopping streets, where upscale department stores stand cheek by jowl with discount stores and fast-food joints. In places the street is so narrow that trams have to line up to pass, while pedestrians and bicycles dodge each other along the crowded sidewalks.

Koningsplein

Map p. 158

Koningsplein starts at the Bloemenmarkt (Flower Market; see p. 63), with its floating flower stands. The market has been here since the 17th century, and the tradition of selling flowers from boats moored in Singel canal began in 1862.

Standing at the market and looking back toward the city center, you can see the **AMROBank,** an attractive Arts and Crafts building in the style of the Amsterdam School, with owls and stylized human faces carved on the facade. Also on the opposite bank stands the huge brick complex of 1896–97, which comprises the city's defunct indoor swimming baths and the former public records office; it is now a huge shopping mall.

Heading away from the center are the big, late 19th-century stores, many of them with corner towers or domes, a feature of Koningsplein and of its northern continuation, Leidsestraat. A good example of early shop design at the point where the street crosses Herengracht is the art nouveau clothing store that has an almost unbroken wall of plate glass running around the first three stories, thanks to the innovative use of iron framing, a relatively new technique when the store was built in 1901.

METZ & CO.

Just before the next bridge, on the right, is another pioneering commercial building, the textiles, furnishings, and clothing store, **Metz & Co.** (see p. 261). It was built for the New York Life Insurance Company, which wanted an exact copy of its existing office in Vienna, hence its Viennese appearance. Metz & Co., founded back in 1740, moved into the building in 1908. It was, and remains, a progressive company, selling the designs of artists and small artisan businesses, rather than mass-produced products. In keeping with that adventurous tradition, the company commissioned the radical Dutch designer and architect Gerrit Rietveld (1888–1964) to design a rooftop extension for the store in 1933. Rietveld was a leading member of the group of artists known as De Stijl (The Style), who espoused simple geometric designs in bold primary colors, a style that greatly influenced the Bauhaus and modernist movements. Rietveld's glass and metal gallery survives, though altered, as a rooftop restaurant; it's well worth a visit if you feel like splurging to enjoy its unusual views, which stretch across the rooftops of Amsterdam's canal circle and Museum Quarter.

Along Leidsestraat is **Dikker & Thijs**, a renowned hotel and restaurant on the right at the corner of Prinsengracht, housed in a former insurance company office of

1915. To the right, running all the way down Prinsengracht to Leidsegracht, stands the massive somber-looking **Paleis van Justitie** (Palace of Justice). It was built between 1825 and 1829 on the site of the city orphanage that was torn down to make way for it. Farther down Leidsestraat, No. 88, on the right, has a tile portrait of Christian Huygens (1629–1693), the Dutch scientist who developed Galileo's observations on pendulum motion and invented the first pendulum clock.

LEIDSEPLEIN

Leidsestraat leads into the open expanse of **Leidseplein,** one of Amsterdam's main nightlife centers and a popular meeting place for young backpackers. In winter a

Metz & Co.'s Viennese-inspired department store has a fine rooftop restaurant.

Metz & Co.
🅰 Map p. 158
✉ Leidsestraat 34–36
☎ 520 7020

Leidseplein
🅰 Map p. 158

Stadsschouwburg

Map p. 158

Leidseplein 26

624 2311

Box office:
Mon.–Sat. 10–6

Tram: 1, 2, 5, 7, 10, 20

skating rink is set up in the square, and in summer tables spill out on to the sidewalks from the scores of restaurants lining the square and nearby side streets. These range from inexpensive but well-regarded places, such as the **Tandoor,** at No. 19, to gourmet temples, such as **'t Swarte Schaep** (The Black Sheep, see p. 254). There are plenty of fast-food outlets, but not enough to justify the square's nickname, La Place de la Mayonnaise.

Neon lights advertising discos, cinemas, and nightclubs add to the square's variety. Culture vultures come for the plays and ballets put on at the **Stadsschouwburg** (City Theater) on the right, built in 1894. Others come for the two renowned rock and world-music venues, Melkweg and Paradiso. **Melkweg** (Milky Way; see p. 265) lies down the lane to the right of the Stadsschouwburg, on Lijnbaansgracht. Housed in a converted dairy, it has evolved from being a center of hippie happenings in the 1970s into a multimedia arts center offering a varied program of everything that is cool and hip, from avant garde cinema to world-music festivals.

THE AMERICAN HOTEL

Beyond the Stadsschouwburg is the **American Hotel** (see p. 252). If you are in the mood for a coffee, there are few more atmospheric places in Amsterdam than the hotel's splendid Tiffany-style **Café Américain.** Built in 1904, the hotel has been progressively stripped of its art nouveau style by successive modernizations, but the café survives in all its glory, complete with stained-glass windows and delicate chandeliers. Staying open until late, it is a favorite haunt of stylish night owls, who often meet early risers coming to the café to enjoy its excellent breakfasts.

Across the road stands the **Leidsekade Brug** (bridge), with its art deco granite columns carved as sea monsters, and its wrought ironwork, suggestive of waves. This bridge marks the edge of the pre-19th-century city, and the water to the right formed a defensive moat around Amsterdam until parts began to be filled in the 1860s.

A boardwalk on the left runs along the waterside skirting the glass walls of the Holland Casino. It leads to the **Max Euweplein,** a public space named after Max Euwe, the Dutch chess player who was world champion from 1935 to 1937. A giant chess set in the square attracts a crowd as players pit their wits against each other. Beside the chess set, a water rill gives off the soothing sound of cascading water.

Various other sculptural works lie dotted around the plaza, and if you walk through the adjacent shopping center, you will come to the columned entrance, where the classical pediment bears the beautifully lettered Latin inscription: *"Homo Sapiens non Urinat in Ventum."* This fun bit of epigrammatic Latin affirms optimistically that humankind does not piss in the wind. This reminder that we do not strive entirely in vain could apply to the eminent artists, authors, and activists who come to give talks at the **Café de Balie,** a highbrow café and cultural center, to the left on Kleine Gartmanplantsoen.

To the right, housed in a converted church is **Paradiso** (see p. 265), the popular nightspot offering live rock music from around the world. The small triangular patch of green opposite it deserves a closer look for the sculptures of lizards scuttling across the grass and along the top of the low retaining wall, a lovely piece of humor that sets these municipal gardens apart from others in the city. ∎

Opposite:
The Tiffany-style Café Américain

Old Amsterdam is reflected in an antiques store-front in the Spiegelkwartier.

Spiegelkwartier

THE SPIEGELKWARTIER (SPIEGEL QUARTER) IS NAMED after the little Spiegelgracht. Literally translated, it means "Mirror Canal," but the name has nothing to do with reflections: Hendrik Spiegel was mayor of Amsterdam at the time the canal was dug in 1660, and it was named for him. Today, the Spiegelkwartier is renowned for its antique shops and art galleries, selling everything from rare 17th-century maps and tribal art to ultramodern paintings.

Spiegelkwartier
Ⓜ Map p. 158

The shop windows along Spiegelgracht (and its continuation, Nieuwe Spiegelstraat) are filled with artistically arranged displays of nautical instruments, Louis XVI furniture, art nouveau lamps, and Roman statuettes. The area developed as the antiques sector of Amsterdam as far back as the 1880s, shortly after the nearby Rijksmuseum (see pp. 192–97) opened to the public. The street's proximity to the museum meant that it was used by art lovers walking from the city center to the Museum Quarter (see pp. 190–210). Little by little, all of the antique dealers in Amsterdam

attractive and reasonably priced botanical prints or old navigational maps.

On Spiegelgracht, **Heinen** *(No. 13)* specializes in hand-painted Delftware, while the **Galerie Wuyt** *(No. 32)* and **Spiegeling Art** *(No. 26)* sell paintings and old master prints.

In Nieuwe Spiegelstraat, the shockingly bright colors of the Amazonian artifacts on offer at **Tribal Design** *(No. 52)* interrupt the cozy patina of wood and canvas. The **Amsterdam Antiques Gallery** *(No. 34)* has numerous dealers under one roof selling everything from Russian icons and Japanese woodcuts to pewter plates and art deco statuettes.

Farther down, the **De Appel Center for Contemporary Art** offers changing exhibitions of contemporary artists' work, with a full program of lectures and a well patronized café.

On the right, the **Spiegelhof** is the latest arrival on the scene, a modern arcade sheltering several more upscale antique shops. The **Galerie Lieve Hemel** *(No. 3)*, has intriguing displays of paintings, sculpture, silverware, and jewelry by modern artists and artisans.

If the prices in the Spiegelkwartier exceed your means, take a stroll along Kerkstraat, which cuts across Nieuwe Spiegelstraat. Here you will find shops selling crafts and pictures at more affordable prices.

Today, the stretch that runs east from Nieuwe Spiegelstraat up to Leidsestraat forms an important part of Amsterdam's nightlife, and is home to several gay bars, hotels, and shops. Westward, Kerkstraat runs all the way round to Plantage, dotted with a mix of squats, low-cost housing, small neighborhood stores, budget hotels, and inexpensive cafés. ∎

began to gravitate to this street to take advantage of the passing trade.

If you have a particular interest in antiques or Oriental and African arts and crafts, you'll make slow progress down Spiegelgracht, where every shop window is like a museum display, and where even the cafés seem to possess an extra special dose of antique charm. Across Prinsengracht, on Nieuwe Spiegelstraat, the temptations include antique jewelry and Delftware, clocks and candelabra, Golden Age furnishings, paintings, and silverware. The prices can be every bit as high as you would expect to pay for a genuine Old Master painting, but not everything bears a telephone-number price tag; you will also find

Amsterdam Antiques Gallery

✉ Nieuwe Spiegelstraat 34

🚋 Tram: 6, 7, 10

⛴ Museumboot & Canal Bus

Works of art both new and old can be found in the Spiegelkwartier's fascinating shops.

De Appel Center for Contemporary Art

🗺 Map p. 158

✉ Nieuwe Spiegelstraat 10

☎ 625 5651

🚋 Tram: 6, 7, 10

⛴ Museumboot & Canal Bus

The still waters of the Herengracht mirror the splendor of the Golden Bend.

Gouden Bocht

THE GOUDEN BOCHT (GOLDEN BEND) EARNED ITS NAME from the magnificence of its houses. Here they are much larger than elsewhere on the canal circle. Adding to their grandeur is the use of sandstone instead of humble brick for the frontages. In style, they are classical rather than homey Dutch. In place of neck and bell gables, you will see elegant pillars, cornices, and pediments.

Kattenkabinet

www.kattenkabinet.nl

- Map p. 158
- Herengracht 497
- 626 5378
- Closed Sat. & Sun. a.m.
- Tram: 1, 2, 5, 16, 24, 25

Herengracht 466, on the corner of Nieuwe Spiegelstraat and Herengracht, is a good example of this style, built between 1669 and 1671 by Philip Vingboons and known as the Eagle because of the bird carved on its pediment. Next door, No. 468 and its neighbor, No. 470, built for two brothers-in-law in 1665–69, once shared a common facade of exceptional width. Subsequent owners included the Nazi tyrant Hermann Goering. The buildings were thoroughly overhauled in 1949, when No. 470 was converted into the **Goethe Instituut.**

No. 474 (1666) is unusual in that it is the only single-width house on this stretch of the canal, thus providing a scale against which the grandiose proportions of the surrounding properties can be measured. Its neighbor, No. 476 (1667), has an opulent brick facade broken up by stone Corinthian pilasters, said to result from the owner's passion for the architecture of Andrea Palladio. The baroque stone cornice, featuring an eagle, coats of arms, and symbols of trade and navigation, was a 1730 replacement for the original pediment. No. 482, at the end of this stretch, dwarfs all its neighbors. The block was built in 1918–1926 as offices for the Nederlandsche Handel-Maatschaapij (Dutch Trading Company).

On the opposite bank of Herengracht, No. 507 is a pleasing building (1666) with Corinthian pilasters, making its neighbor, No. 505, look rather antiquated, with its old-fashioned bell gable. No. 497 houses the unusual and idiosyncratic **Kattenkabinet,** a gallery entirely devoted to art with a feline theme (and, this being Amsterdam, it comes as no surprise to discover that one or two of the drawings have an erotic theme). Be grateful for this opportunity to see inside a grand house, and, if you happen not to be one of the world's greatest admirers of the feline species, keep your views under your hat!

CRYPTIC INSCRIPTION

Number 495 was built for Jan Six, son of the more famous but identically named Jan Six, who was a patron of Rembrandt. The house is unusual in having a balcony above the front door, whose brasswork contains an inscribed quotation from the Roman writer and historian Sallust (86–34 B.C.): *"Omnia Orta Occidunt"* ("All Creation Passes Away"). The letters of the inscription also contain the date of the building (MDCCVII—1707) in cryptic form. Jan Six the younger got himself embroiled in a long and costly legal battle with his neighbor at No. 493, Anthony van Hemert, who built a coach house in his garden (accessed from the rear of the property), which Jan Six disliked because it overlooked his garden. After fighting all the way up to the highest court in the land, Six failed to have the coach house demolished; van Hemert was instructed merely to reduce the size of its windows.

Number 475, a good bit farther down Herengracht, is regarded as one of the finest of the canal circle's 18th-century houses. Built in 1733, it has a richly decorated central bay carved with volutes and foliage rising to a crest. On one side of this is seated a female figure represent-

Opulent plasterwork signals 18th-century Amsterdam's taste for the classical.

ing Plenty; on the other side, two children can be seen shaking apples from a tree.

In the past, the building was attributed to the French designer Daniel Marot (1661–1752), one of the Protestant refugees who arrived in Amsterdam from France after their rights to freedom of worship were annulled by the Revocation of the Edict of Nantes in 1685. Marot introduced the baroque Louis XV style to Amsterdam, but historians now believe that this building was constructed by another architect, who based it on the published engravings of Marot.

SERVANTS' QUARTERS

Running parallel to Herengracht, one block north, is the colorful Reguliersdwaarsstraat, a street lined with good restaurants and gay bars and shops. Several of those farther east on the right-hand side of the street are housed in low two-story buildings. These are the former garages and coach houses of the grand houses on Herengracht.

Reguliersdwaarsstraat emerges onto busy Vijzelstraat. This is not a particularly attractive thoroughfare, being dominated by traffic and lined with bulky modern buildings. The huge **Carlton Hotel,** on the left, dates from 1929; in its day, this was the most luxurious hotel in the Netherlands. Its construction marked the start of a scheme to widen and develop Vijzelstraat to form a wide avenue linking central Amsterdam to the southern suburbs. This controversial scheme, which would have involved the demolition of several fine buildings, was abandoned during the 1930s Depression. But fate took a hand in 1943 when a British Halifax bomber crashed at the back of the hotel, its bombs and fuel causing fires that destroyed many nearby buildings. That explains the presence of the bulky and unfriendly office block on concrete stilts, built in 1964, to the rear of the Carlton Hotel.

PETER THE GREAT & NAPOLEON

Aesthetically, the townscape improves once you turn left at the first canal to return to Herengracht. The first building, No. 527, has a fine facade in Louis XVI style, with fluted Ionic pilasters rising to a pediment carved with an imperial eagle. This was once the Russian embassy, and it was here that Peter the Great, tsar of Russia, stayed during his visits to Amsterdam to study shipbuilding. Famous for his alcoholic excesses, the tsar had to pay a large sum of money for repairs to the house following his visit, during which the wall paintings were vandalized. A later visitor, Napoleon Bonaparte, displayed greater decorum when he came by in 1811.

On the opposite bank of the canal is No. 52, the official residence of Amsterdam's mayor, flying a flag with the Amsterdam coat of arms on it. To the left, you will see

Johan Thorbecke, the father of Dutch democratic government

Opposite: Neptune rides a sea monster at Herengracht 510.

that Nos. 504–510 form a group of four neck-gabled houses with boldly carved sidepieces. They depict, in turn, rampant heraldic dogs holding the owners' coats of arms, scrolls ending in a lion's foot motif, tritons cavorting in the waves and blowing their trumpets, and Neptune riding a dolphin while brandishing his trident.

Similar nautical motifs appear on this side of the canal, at No. 535, which has art nouveau seahorses forming a frieze around the door, and at No. 539, with its sea gods reclining on the roof cornice and its caryatids supporting the first-floor balcony.

L'ERREUR

On the opposite bank, No. 514 is known as **In de Mooriaantjes** (At the Moor's) because of the black marble busts that flank the balcony above the entrance. The busts have often caused misunderstanding. The house was built for the Salm brothers as the headquarters of their insurance company and the busts are 18th-century Italian, but their presence has led many to believe that the house was that of a slave trader.

The hero of *La Chute (The Fall),* Albert Camus's 1950 novel, makes this assumption when he passes the house. Political radicals opposed to what they perceive as symbols of repression have repeatedly threatened to smash the sculptures.

Farther down, at No. 526, is another building with a neck gable flanked by monstrous fish. At this point, the canal is interrupted by leafy **Thorbeckeplein** (see pp. 182–83), named after Johan Thorbecke (1798–1872), the first prime minister of the Netherlands, whose statue looks away from the topless bars and tawdry clubs that surround the square, one of the busiest nightlife spots in the city. ∎

Tuschinski Theater

🄰 Map p. 158
✉ Reguliersbreestraat
26–28
☎ 0900 1458
🚋 Tram: 4, 9, 14, 20

Rembrandtplein & Thorbeckeplein

REMBRANDTPLEIN AND THORBECKEPLEIN ARE TWO adjoining squares ringed by sidewalk cafés. By day this is the haunt of drunks, dopeheads, and homeless tramps; by night it is lit by neon lights flashing to the pounding beat of Amsterdam nightlife.

The statue of poor old Rembrandt, in the middle of the square that bears his name, now wears a drab coat of graffiti-proof paint. He seems out of place in a square given over to the antithesis of high art. A lone beacon of culture, the **Tuschinski Theater** (see p. 264) lies to the west of the square on Reguliersbreestraat. This twin-towered building bristles with wrought-iron decorations, looking like a palace of entertainment in the futuristic city created by Fritz Lang for his 1926 film *Metropolis*. Founded by Abram Tuschinski (a Polish Jew who died at Auschwitz), the movie theater opened in 1921, and the glitzy art deco furnishings have just been restored to their original glory.

To the north of Rembrandtplein is another small square ringed by bars and nightclubs. Originally

Late-night lounging amid the lurid lights of Rembrandtplein

known as Kaasplein (Cheese Square), because it was once the site of the city's cheese and butter market, it was renamed Thorbeckeplein in 1876 in honor of Johan Thorbecke, the reforming politician elected first prime minister of the Netherlands in 1848.

SEVEN BRIDGES

Thorbecke's statue, at the southern end of the square, looks up **Reguliersgracht.** The name of this canal refers to the Reguliers (Regulars), a monastic order whose monastery here burned down in 1532. Plans to fill in the canal to create a tramway were successfully opposed at the beginning of the 20th century, thus preserving what is arguably the most picturesque stretch of canal in Amsterdam.

The canal is at its most photogenic at the junction with Keizersgracht, a spot known as the Seven Bridges because of the number of hump-backed bridges in the view —three on the junction itself. At night the outlines of the bridges are illuminated by strings of white lights, making the view even more attractive.

All the houses surrounding the junction lean in a pronounced manner, adding to the appeal. These tilting facades result not from subsidence but are a deliberate feature of buildings that had warehouse storage space in their lofts. The facades were built "in flight"—tilting forward, so that goods being winched up to the loft had sufficient clearance, and were not in danger of banging or dragging against the front.

The **Museum van Loon** (see pp. 184–85) lies on the opposite bank of Keizersgracht. Continuing up the canal brings you to the start of the Amstel walk (see pp. 186–88). If you do so, watch for Reguliersgracht Nos. 57 and 63, on the left. Both are built in the style known as "Carpenter's Gothic," so called because they were built by carpenters to show off their skills in decorative woodwork. ■

Rembrandtplein shows its calmer face by day.

Symmetry and order pervade the pretty garden at the Museum van Loon.

Museum van Loon & Museum Willet-Holthuysen

TWO HOUSES ON THE GOLDEN BEND THAT RE-CREATE THE atmosphere of bygone times are within a short walk of each other. The Museum van Loon and the Museum Willet-Holthuysen both offer a feast of Golden Age opulence.

Museum van Loon

- Map p. 158
- Keizersgracht 672
- 624 5255
- Closed Tues.–Thurs.
- $$$
- Tram: 16, 24, 25

MUSEUM VAN LOON

The imposing Museum van Loon occupies two adjacent houses. At No. 674, statues of the Roman deities Minerva, Ceres, Mars, and Vulcan decorate the parapet. The last two, symbolizing war and metal-work respectively, indicate the source of the original owner's wealth. Jeremias van Raey, a Walloon refugee (see panel) who dealt in iron and armaments, became rich enough to hire Adriaan Dortsman to build these houses for him in 1672. Van Raey lived at No. 674 and let No. 672 to the painter, Ferdinand Bol (1616–1680).

The van Loon connection dates from 1884, when Jonkheer van Loon, the wealthy descendant of one of the founders of the Dutch East India Company, bought the house as a wedding present for his son. The family portraits inside give a good

Willet was a passionate collector of art, and his marriage to the wealthy Holthuysen allowed him to refurbish the house as a showcase for his glass, silver, and porcelain.

The opulent furnishings of the upper rooms include wall paintings of romantic rural scenes. In the **Blue Room,** you can imagine visitors playing cards into the wee hours beneath ceiling paintings by the celebrated artist Jacob de Wit (1695–1754) showing "Dawn Chasing Away the Darkness of Night." Across the hallway, chandeliers light the splendid ballroom, while the more intimate dining room is set for a grand dinner.

On the floor above, Willet created a **Kunstkammer**—Cabinet of Curiosities—in the turret room; designed as a showcase for treasured items from his collection. ■

Walloons

Walloons were Protestants from southern Belgium and northern France. Like the French Huguenots, they were persecuted after the Revocation of the Edict of Nantes in 1685, which rescinded their right to freedom of religious worship. ■

Museum Willet-Holthuysen

- Map p. 159
- Herengracht 605
- 523 1822
- $$$
- Tram: 4, 9, 14, 20

Oriental silk fabrics at the Museum van Loon look as fresh as the day they were woven.

idea of the lifestyle of the van Loons at the end of the 19th century, though most of the decorations date back to an earlier age. The elegant staircase incorporates the initials of the 18th-century owners, Willem von Hagen and Catherina Trip, and plaster friezes of the same era celebrate the joys of gardening and music. The walls of the **Painted Room** are covered in a canvas depicting an imaginary Italian landscape with classical ruins and ships.

MUSEUM WILLET-HOLTHUYSEN

You enter the Museum Willet-Holthuysen through the basement kitchens, where elaborate meals were once prepared for the wealthy guests of the owners, Abraham Willet and Sandrina Holthuysen.

A walk around the Amstel River

This last section of the Grachtengordel, abutting the western bank of the wide Amstel River, leads to the edge of the canal circle. Construction here came to a halt in the 17th century. This explains why many of the buildings on the opposite bank of the Amstel are of relatively recent vintage; they date from the mid-19th century, when the semicircular belt of canals enclosing the medieval core Amsterdam was finally completed.

Suntrap café, a popular spot beside the timber-built Amstelkerk

Start at the big, windy square called **Amstelveld** (Amstel Field). The existence of such a large open space in the canal circle indicates that the pattern of building familiar from earlier stretches of the Golden Bend (see pp. 178–81) has now broken down. This final stretch of the canal circle feels very much on the fringe of things, and the houses in the area are mostly small and later in date.

Dominating Amstelveld is the 1669 **Amstelkerk**, looking like a New England church, with its white-painted clapboard construction. It was built as a "preaching barn" and

was intended to be temporary, pending the construction of a new brick and stone church. A century later, the church had still not been built and the "barn" was beginning to acquire the appearance of a permanent structure, with ancillary buildings up against its walls, providing homes for the verger and bailiff. By the 19th century, it became obvious that no new church would be built, and the congregation paid for the remodeling of the interior, which is now largely used for musical recitals. A café stands up against the sunny south-facing wall of the church and is a popular spot with

0   150 meters
0   150 yards

Also see area map p. 159
► Amstelveld
↔ 0.9 mile (1.4 km)
⊕ 2 hours
► Blauwbrug

NOT TO BE MISSED
- Magere Brug
- Museum Willet-Holthuysen
- Blauwbrug

parents who bring their children to play in the adjacent playground.

Walk east, down Kerkstraat, with its boutiques and art galleries, to the **Magere Brug ❶**, one of Amsterdam's most famous landmarks (outlined by white lights at night and floodlit during the summer). The name is often translated as "Skinny Bridge," but a more faithful translation would be "Meager Bridge," a reference to the disproportionate fragility of its timber construction in relation to the might of the Amstel River, which it crosses. Originally built in the 17th century, it was almost entirely reconstructed just after World War II—desperate Amsterdammers had used the timbers as

firewood during the last winter of the war. The bridge is still operated by hand, and you will see large barges passing through, since this branch of the Amstel provides a link from the IJ River to the inland waterways system of the southern Netherlands.

The view across the Amstel River takes in the Stadhuis–Muziektheater building.

Looking across the river, you will see the **Theater Carré** *(Amstel 115–125, tel 622 5225)* to the right, with its ballooning green roof. Built in 1887 as a permanent tent for the Oscar Carré Circus, the theater is best known today for staging concerts and Broadway musicals.

At the Magere Brug, turn left down the Amstel. Turn left again down **Keizersgracht.** Nos. 818–822 form a striking group of houses in a style that was already antiquated when they were built in 1672. (Their style of gable went out of fashion in the early 16th century.) No. 802 is a late 19th-century former dairy (built for the Plancius company, which prided itself on supplying milk untainted by drowned cats, rats, or mice!) while the highly ornate No. 766, with its art deco windows and balcony, was once the premises of a baker. In the early days of the canal circle, such a commercial site would have been relegated to the side streets, but here it occupies a prime canalside position.

Turn right at Utrechtsestraat and right again to return down the opposite bank of the Keizersgracht. Halfway down, at No. 745, is a unique sight: a house with a garage. The garage door once led to a coach house and

stable block in the garden to the rear of the house. For 300 years the passage of horses, coaches, and carriages, and latterly of motor cars and vans, was the cause of constant disputes between the owners and their neighbors. The owners voluntarily gave up the use of the garage in the 1970s, but for three centuries it enjoyed the unique status of being the only canalside property in Amsterdam with vehicular access.

Here is the beautiful ornate doorcase of No. 605, the **Museum Willet-Holthuysen ②** (see pp. 184–85). On the opposite bank to the museum, Nos. 568 and 570 have gables featuring giant polar bears and lizards, a splendidly exotic piece of decoration.

Return to the Amstel and turn left for a view of the **Blauwbrug ③** (Blue Bridge). The name derives from the fact that its timber predecessor was painted blue, with bridge lamps topped by imperial crowns and set on granite columns clasped by ships' prows. Built in 1884, the Blue Bridge draws its inspiration from the Pont Alexandre III in Paris. Straight ahead lies the bulky **Stadhuis–Muziektheater ④** (see pp. 106–107), clad in the white marble that has given rise to its local nickname: "the set of dentures." ∎

The Museum District marks the hinterland between the Old Amsterdam of canals and cobbled streets and the New South—that is, the Amsterdam of the early 20th century.

Museum District & the New South

Detail from Rembrandt's "The Night Watch"

Museum District & the New South

AFTER THE FLURRY OF BUILDING THAT MARKED THE 17TH CENTURY, Amsterdam endured 200 years of relative stagnation. Only in the second half of the 19th century did the city begin to grow again. When it did, major overcrowding resulted. Various harebrained schemes—including a proposal to fill in Amsterdam's canals and build on them—were proposed to relieve the congestion. Thankfully, none of these were implemented. The urgent need to find outlets for the growing city was finally addressed in 1900, when architect H. P. Berlage was commissioned to design an expansion scheme.

Berlage's proposal resulted in the creation of the new Amsterdam Zuid (Amsterdam South) district. Developed from 1917, Amsterdam Zuid includes three major art museums, the world-renowned Concertgebouw concert hall, and the Amsterdam Conservatoire, where the city's brightest young musicians polish their skills. Together these form the Museum District, which also has

numerous grand Arts and Crafts houses and villas, as well as some of Amsterdam's most upscale stores. A number of the district's largest houses have been converted to hotels, with the result that many visitors find themselves based here for the duration of their stay. Although lacking the character and intimacy of the city center, the district offers convenient access to the major museums and to the nightlife of Leidseplein, just a short walk away.

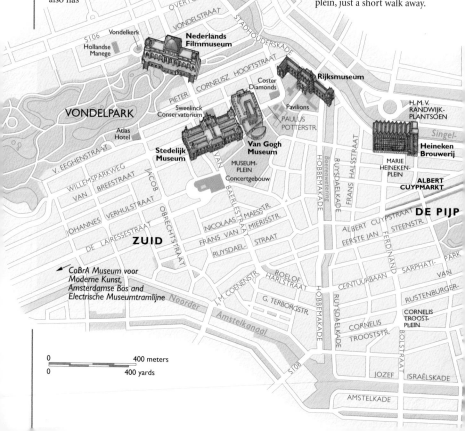

Anyone staying in this area should also explore the green spaces of Vondelpark, with its tea gardens, ornamental shrubs, and duck-filled lakes, used by many Amsterdammers for tai chi, jogging, or in-line skating. The park is also the venue for festivals and national celebrations such as the Queen's Birthday (April 30).

Tucking into freshly made vanilla waffles at Albert Cuypstraat, home to Europe's largest street market

Farther south and east, grand houses give way to more utilitarian dwellings in the district known as De Pijp, where you will find Amsterdam's lively, mile-long street market, on Albert Cuypstraat. Few visitors penetrate the suburbs that lie beyond—though they contain some outstanding examples of pioneering urban architecture in the area known as De Dageraad (The Dawn). Perhaps more popular with most visitors, the area also includes the former Heineken Brouwerij (Heineken Experience; see p. 210), now functioning as a museum with a difference—visitors get the chance to sample the city's world-renowned brew. ■

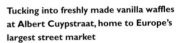

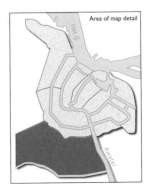

Area of map detail

Rijksmuseum

FROM A CORE OF PAINTINGS PUT TOGETHER BY THE DUTCH Royal Family in the 18th century, and originally displayed in the Royal Palace, the Rijksmuseum has grown to today's leviathan. Think of any famous Dutch artist of the Golden Age, and his works—often his finest—will be found here.

Rijksmuseum
- Map p. 190
- Stadhouderskade 42
- 020 674 7000
- $$$
- Tram: 2, 3, 5, 6, 7, 10, 12, 16, 20
- Museumboot

Because the museum is so big, it's a good idea to plan to spend all day here. Even if you're not an art buff, there's at least a half-day's worth of essential viewing. Upon arrival, you are confronted by two entrances—east or west. It doesn't really matter which one you take, so just head for the entry with the shortest line (these build up in summer, but they move quickly). Whichever entrance you choose, stairs lead up to a mezzanine floor, where the museum shop is also located. Turning your back on the shop, you face the so-called **Gallery of Honor,** where the museum has thoughtfully placed all the most celebrated works in the collection so you need not look far to find them.

GALLERY OF HONOR

Every painting here seems specially chosen to reveal Dutch art in all its vibrancy and variety—from religious pictures, portraits, and still lifes, to morality tales, tavern and winter scenes, and sea battles.

One of the artists represented here is Vermeer (1632–1675), whose pictures show scenes from everyday life, painted with such an assured feeling for the effects of light that they seem to glow with luminescence as in his "Woman Reading a Letter" (ca 1665).

Some paintings are easier to read, despite the mists of time. The artist Abraham van den Tempel (1622–1672) depicts "David Leeuw with His Family" (1671) as the epitome of marital unity and happy

Vermeer's enigmatic "Woman Reading a Letter" is pregnant with hidden meaning.

family life by showing them making harmonious music. Alongside, the "Merry Family" (1668) by Jan Steen (1626–1679) depicts the same subject, but there is an underlying sinister parody of harmony, with everyone, including the children, engaged in a drunken tavern song. If the moral isn't obvious, the artist has inscribed the title in Dutch—"*Soo De Oude Songen, Soo Pijpen De Jonge*" ("As the Old Sing, So the Young Chirp")—so beware of setting a bad example.

REMBRANDT

The Rembrandt paintings are the highlight of the gallery. "The Syndics of the Drapers' Guild" (1662; see p. 195) is a brilliant and compelling work that shows Rembrandt transforming a commonplace subject into a work of genius. This one stands out because the penetrating, inquisitive, judgmental eyes of the guild officials are focused on us. The Syndics wear the haughty half smiles of people who are confident of their own superiority. As they look down on us, they make us feel like candidates at an interview—or prisoners in the dock. "The Jewish Bride" (ca 1665; see p. 105) is another study in bourgeois complacency. The title is potentially misleading, because nobody knows what Rembrandt intended by the work. What we see is a portrait of a married couple dressed in their most gorgeous finery, the man placing his hand on his wife's breast in a gesture that could be interpreted as loving and

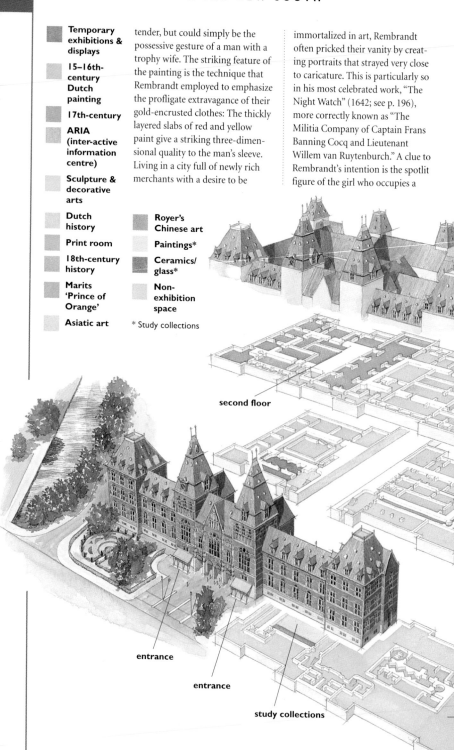

Temporary exhibitions & displays

15–16th-century Dutch painting

17th-century

ARIA (inter-active information centre)

Sculpture & decorative arts

Dutch history

Print room

18th-century history

Marits 'Prince of Orange'

Asiatic art

Royer's Chinese art

Paintings*

Ceramics/glass*

Non-exhibition space

* Study collections

tender, but could simply be the possessive gesture of a man with a trophy wife. The striking feature of the painting is the technique that Rembrandt employed to emphasize the profligate extravagance of their gold-encrusted clothes: The thickly layered slabs of red and yellow paint give a striking three-dimensional quality to the man's sleeve. Living in a city full of newly rich merchants with a desire to be

immortalized in art, Rembrandt often pricked their vanity by creating portraits that strayed very close to caricature. This is particularly so in his most celebrated work, "The Night Watch" (1642; see p. 196), more correctly known as "The Militia Company of Captain Frans Banning Cocq and Lieutenant Willem van Ruytenburch." A clue to Rembrandt's intention is the spotlit figure of the girl who occupies a

second floor

entrance

entrance

study collections

Right: Riotous behavior is rampant in Jan Steen's "Merry Family."

Below: Stern and sober citizens fill Rembrandt's "Syndics of the Drapers' Guild."

central position in the painting. What is she doing here, with her golden dress, her moneybag, and a dead cockerel hanging from her waist? She seems to be laughing at the posing pretensions of the militiamen, and the cockerel could be a punning reference to the name of Captain Cocq.

DUTCH ART

The remainder of the museum is divided into three main areas. The first floor of the east wing is devoted to **Dutch art**, and there are plenty of masterpieces to study

and admire in this packed network of rooms. Room 201, immediately east of the shop, is hung with works by the so-called Flemish Primitives. The "Seven Works of Mercy" (1504), by the anonymous Master of Alkmaar (early 16th century) is typical of the period and style. This series of panels depicts the core Christian act of charity, from feeding the hungry to giving hospitality to strangers, and is full of contemporary detail and color. In the same room is the glowing "Adoration of the Magi" (1510) by Jan Mostaert (1475–1556), in which

"The Night Watch" by Rembrandt is the master's most celebrated work.

MOVIES & REFRESHMENT

Having toured the highlights of the collection, check out what movies are showing in the auditorium, just off the shop area in the west wing. Movies on art-historical themes are shown here continuously in various languages. A self-service café on the floor below offers refreshments. ■

all the main figures—Mary, Joseph, and the Three Kings—are set in a recognizable Dutch landscape and dressed in the most lavish and fashionable clothing of the day.

In the 17th century, artists no longer confined themselves to religious subjects. Hendrick Avercamp (1585–1634) was one of the first Dutch artists to paint landscapes for their own sake, instead of as a background to a biblical story, and his "Winter Landscape with Skaters" (1608; see pp. 28–29), in Room 208, is a perfect example of the new genre.

Equally meticulous, painted with a draftsmanlike concern for perspective, are the church interiors by Pieter Saenredam (1597–1665). The two paintings in Room 214— "St Bavo's Church in Haarlem" (1637) and the "Mariakerk in Utrecht" (1641)—look like photographic records of the buildings, but are much more. Saenredam's contemporaries would have viewed

these pure white churches, stripped of statues, wall paintings, and stained glass, as a celebration of the enlightenment and rationality of Protestant beliefs.

The prosperity of the Netherlands in the 17th century fueled the demand for paintings, as wealthy patrons commissioned pictures of themselves, their homes, their ships. One outstanding example is the "Portrait of Isaac Massa and his Wife" (1622) by Frans Hals (1581–1666), a picture full of emblems of marital fidelity, such as the ivy that clings to the tree behind the smiling couple, the prominently displayed wedding rings, the peacocks in the garden (symbol of Juno, goddess of marriage).

SCULPTURE & DECORATIVE ARTS

The whole of the west wing is given over to **Sculpture and the Decorative Arts.** Some of the finest exhibits are also the earliest. In Room 238, for example, don't miss the 11th-century oliphant (a hunting horn fashioned from elephant ivory), or the 13th-century Limoges reliquaries, made from jewel-like enamel to contain the relics of saints. Room 239 has 10 bronze statuettes from the tomb of Isabelle de Bourbon (1476), which depict members of her family in various tender postures expressing grief, mourning, and loss. Among outstanding religious sculptures are three carved oak panels (Room 241) by Adriaen van Wessel (1417–1490) depicting the Nativity, with the three kings riding through a rocky landscape.

Other exhibits include three reconstructed rooms decorated with period furnishings to illustrate the history of changing taste. Equally revealing as a barometer of style are the two very popular dolls' houses displayed in this section (Room 164). Both were made in the early 18th century and depict in miniature detail the furnishings and domestic arrangements of a patrician house of the age. One step down again in the basement is the art nouveau collection (Room 34), well worth seeking out for the complete 1909 room moved here from a house in Frederiksplein.

An annex to the rear of the main museum is used to display costumes and textiles, as well as Asiatic art. The costume displays change regularly so the fragile textiles are not exposed to the light, but you can usually count on seeing court costumes, children's clothes, and domestic attire. The highlight of the Asiatic Art collection is the 12th-century bronze figure of the Dancing Shiva (Chola dynasty, southern India), the Hindu deity whose nature combines the opposites of creation and destruction, visible and invisible, masculine and feminine.

DUTCH HISTORY

The third part of the Rijksmuseum, in the east wing, makes imaginative use of paintings and objets d'art to illustrate key events in Dutch history. Room 102 contains paintings that are not great masterpieces, but come into their own when presented in this context, illustrating the use of windmills to drain the landscape and create new agricultural land, the building of ships in Amsterdam docks and the hunting of whales in Spitsbergen. The history of the Dutch East India Company is also illustrated by objects rescued from the ships that sank en route between Europe and Asia over the 300 years of colonial trade. Don't miss the realistic canvas showing a meeting between the victorious commanders after the Battle of Waterloo (1815), in Room 110. Painted by Jan Willem Pieneman nine years after the event, it still manages to capture the atmosphere of the battlefield. ■

Early contortionist goes through the motions in the Rijksmuseum's sculpture collection.

The walls are alive with the sound of color: paintings from van Gogh's Arles period

Van Gogh Museum

STANDING OUT FROM THE GRAND NEO-GOTHIC VILLAS that line Paulus Potterstraat is a building of stark—some would say almost brutal—simplicity. This white concrete cube, designed in 1963 by the renowned Dutch modernist Gerrit Rietveld, serves as the perfect foil for the vibrantly colorful works of van Gogh and his contemporaries.

Van Gogh Museum

www.vangoghmuseum.nl

- Map p. 190
- Paulus Potterstraat 7
- 020 570 5200
- $$$
- Tram: 2, 3, 5, 12, 16, 20
- Museumboot

Be prepared for lines at the entrance of this most popular of Amsterdam museums (these are shorter at the start, and towards the end of the day). If possible visit on a Monday morning. Once inside, you will discover that the museum is not just about van Gogh: It's about the artist in the context of the art and culture of his time.

THE CONTEXT

The **first floor** exhibits paintings from the mid-19th century to illustrate the wealth of artistic ideas and styles current at the time, and to which van Gogh was exposed as he developed his own artistic interests. These paintings range from an erotic portrait by Gustave Boulanger (1824–88) depicting "Phryne" (1850), the archetypal femme fatale and mistress of the ancient Greek sculptor Praxiteles, to the photographic realism of the English Royal Academician Alma-Tadema (1836–1912), here represented by a historic scene in which "The Emperor Hadrian visits a Romano-British Potter" (1884). These paintings rooted in past artistic traditions contrast with the early works of the Impressionists and Pointillists, and the inspired landscapes of artists such as Gustave Courbet (1819–1877) and Anton Chantreuil (1816–1873). A few of van Gogh's own still lifes and landscapes are tucked into this section as if to prove that his own works were very much a product of the time.

Bottles" (1885), and "Women Winding Yarn" (1885). Van Gogh was immensely proud of these works, in which he strove to paint the wintry landscape and the honest features of the peasants he saw every day while living with his parents at their rectory in Nuenen. "The Potato Eaters" (1885), his first large-scale painting, marks the culmination of this period. Painted in dark colors and depicting a group of peasants eating a supper of plain potatoes, van Gogh regarded it as his finest work to date. As he explained to his brother in a letter: "I have tried to make it clear that those people eating potatoes in the lamplight have dug the earth with those very hands they put in the dish, and so it speaks of manual labor, and how they honestly earned their food." Instead of the success and acclaim he expected for this picture, however, its uncompromising ugliness failed to impress any of his family and friends.

VAN GOGH

The **middle floor** of the museum is devoted solely to van Gogh, and the paintings are displayed chronologically, in five groups—the Netherlands, Paris, Arles, St. Rémy, and Auvers-sur-Oise. These mirror the major stages of his short and turbulent life. During this time, van Gogh was astonishingly productive: The 100 or so major works that you see in this museum were produced in the space of just ten years, during which time he made over 800 paintings, 1,000 drawings, and an untold number of sketches and watercolors.

The Netherlands 1880–1885

Van Gogh was 27 years old in 1880, when he decided to become an artist (see pp. 202–203). The early works displayed show the novice van Gogh copying pictures from books, and producing sketches—at first clumsy, but growing in competence. Typical of his work at the time is "View of the Sea at Scheveningen" (1882), "Cottages" (1883), "Congregation Leaving the Reformed Church at Nuenen" (1884), "Still Life with Earthenware

Paris 1886–1888

For once, van Gogh was not deterred. Instead, he moved to Paris where he mixed with other young artists and began to experiment with new techniques, from the light and airy style of the Impressionists, to the use of layers of dots to represent the vibrancy of natural light, a technique known as *pointillisme*. Paintings such as "The Courtesan" (1887) and "The Bridge after Rain" (1887) show that he was also very fond of Japanese paintings at this time. Their use of powerful colors and strong lines seems to have had a lasting effect on his developing style, which is represented here by several "Self Portraits" (he painted himself because he was too poor to afford a model). In these paintings, it is possible to see the emergence of that bold use of color that is the artist's trademark.

Amsterdam, Van Gogh Museum (Vincent Van Gogh Foundation)

Multimillion-dollar art: Van Gogh's sunflower paintings—only five exist—have fetched world-record prices.

Arles 1889–1890

Paris was still a period of experimentation, but the move to Arles in 1888 saw van Gogh find his true style. He went to this sunny town in Provence in search of warmth and tranquility, but he seems to have found much more—the light of the south and the intense colors of the landscape simply set him alight, and in 1888 he poured out works that display his delight in the colors of the changing seasons: "The White Orchard," "The Pink Peach Tree," "Wheatfield," and "The Harvest," for example.

These paintings could not be further removed in style and tone from his somber and labored early works, and from this time onward, van Gogh seems to have abandoned realism altogether in his preference for simple subjects given emotive force by the use of warm and vibrant colors. The predominant colors of his palette were yellow, orange, ocher, and green, as can be seen in the paintings of 1889, which include "The Yellow House" (where he lived), "The Bedroom," "Gauguin's Chair," and one of five paintings of "Sunflowers" that he made at this time.

St. Rémy 1889–1890

Van Gogh painted pictures to decorate the walls of the Yellow House, which he rented as the base for an artists' colony. He persuaded Paul Gauguin to join him in Arles, but no sooner had Gauguin arrived than Vincent began to suffer a series of seizures. During one of these attacks, the two artists quarreled. Afterwards, van Gogh attempted to cut off his ear, and Gauguin fled back to Paris. Van Gogh decided to seek help from a doctor who admitted him to the mental health clinic at St-Rémy, near Arles.

Thus was van Gogh's brief period of astonishing achievement and productivity cut short by illness. He was initially forbidden to paint because of the effect that art had on his emotions. In 1890, as he appeared to recover, he was allowed to work again. Happy days produced such vividly realized art as the well-known and much-loved "Irises" and the festive "Almond Blossom," showing pink and white flowers etched against a turquoise sky. Days of gloom produced the several paintings of tangled stems and rotting leaves that are all entitled "Undergrowth," and some darkly brooding paintings on biblical themes, such as the "Pietà" (the dead Christ in his mother's arms) and the "Raising of Lazarus."

Auvers-sur-Oise 1890

In May 1890, van Gogh was considered well enough to leave the St. Rémy clinic, and he settled in Auvers-sur-Oise, an artist's village

near Paris. Here he was befriended by Paul Gachet, a doctor and amateur artist, who watched over van Gogh's health as he produced a great number of works, including portraits of the doctor and his daughter, and paintings of the old thatched houses of Auvers. Art historians have studied these paintings from the last weeks of his life for clues as to his mental state. They include tortured abstract depictions of "Tree Roots," and a series of panoramic landscapes, with titles such as "Wheatfields under Thunderclouds" and "Wheatfields with Crows," which have been interpreted as reflections of van Gogh's deepening depression. His letters home offer few clues to the reason for his suicide, though they do contain hints that he was worried about his lack of commercial success as an artist; not for his own sake, but rather because he felt that he was a financial burden on his brother. Whatever the reason, Vincent van Gogh tragically shot himself in the chest on July 27, 1890, and two days later died from his wounds.

TOP FLOOR & ANNEX

The **third floor** displays pictures that inspired van Gogh: Japanese prints, and works by Monet, Pissarro, Gauguin, and Cézanne. There is also a study collection consisting of smaller works by van Gogh, as well as a comprehensive library of books, and computers linked to the museum's website.

The museum displays only a fraction of its collection, but in June 1999 a new annex opened linking the main museum by a subterranean tunnel. Used for temporary themed exhibitions, this striking building of serene gray stone and metallic surfaces was designed by the Japanese architect Kisho Kurokawa. ∎

Van Gogh's rendering of his rustic bedroom at Arles draws its impact from its simplicity.

Vincent van Gogh

One of the great ironies of Vincent van Gogh's life is that the artist whose work now commands world-record prices at auction scarcely sold a painting in his own short lifetime (1853–1890). Today his popularity can be judged by the fact that poster shops worldwide sell millions of copies of his work each year.

Van Gogh's artistic career began in 1880, when he was rejected as a trainee minister, and ended with his suicide in 1890. Within those ten short years, he produced 2,000 works of art—an average of one every two days. Some of them were dashed off in a moment of inspiration; others were the result of meticulous studies and preliminary sketches. No matter how they were composed, each represented an astonishing achievement for a man who did not begin to paint until he was 27 years old.

Art & commerce

Van Gogh's interest in art did not come entirely out of the blue. Three of his uncles were art dealers, and he himself joined the firm of Goupil and Cie, the international art dealers, in July 1869. His apprenticeship with Goupil took him to The Hague, Brussels, London, and Paris at a time of artistic ferment.

Van Gogh was eventually fired from Goupil's, but his brother, Theo, was promoted to manager of the Montmartre branch. Vincent later moved in with Theo, sharing rooms in a part of Paris that was the heart of the artistic universe. He relied on his brother for financial support for the rest of his life, .

The life of an aesthete

Van Gogh was far from extravagant in his use of money. What little he had he spent on paint, brushes, and canvas—and on candles, which he wore around the brim of his hat so he could continue to work at night. Food was rarely a consideration—his diet consisted of little more than stale bread. He himself acknowledged in letters that chronic under-nourishment and lack of sleep—aggravated by a fondness for copious quantities of coffee and alcohol—may have precipitated his suicidal emotions. The physician who admitted him to the St. Rémy asylum noted his symptoms as "acute mania with hallucinations of sight and hearing." Van Gogh's predisposition to depression was reinforced by a failed attempt to set up an artistic colony in Arles, as well as by a quarrel with the one artist who joined him there—Paul Gauguin. All things considered, van Gogh's suicide at the age of 37 came as little surprise.

Recognition

Van Gogh firmly believed himself to be a misfit and a failure. Yet in the year he died, the art world began to notice him. His paintings were exhibited in Paris and Brussels, and reviewers began to single out his work, praising the intense emotional quality of his palette and his sympathy for the sun-flooded landscapes of southern France.

In September 1890, shortly after Vincent's death, Theo—who had inherited all of his brother's artwork—mounted a memorial exhibit in his Paris apartment. His own health was not good, however, and he died in January 1891. Vincent's legacy remained largely intact, forming the core of the collection that is now displayed at the Van Gogh Museum and in the Kröller–Müller Museum, near Arnhem. The few paintings that were sold from the collection rarely come to auction—but when they do, they consistently notch record prices. Such is the demand for the works of a man who now probably ranks as the world's favorite artist. ■

Amsterdam, Van Gogh Museum (Vincent Van Gogh Foundation)

Left: Van Gogh with bandaged ear, an honest self-portrait
Above: The swirls of this wheat field (the same one where he shot himself) may reflect the tortured restlessness of van Gogh's mind.
Right and below: In the "State Lottery" and the "Potato Eaters," van Gogh celebrates the quiet dignity of ordinary people.

Amsterdam, Van Gogh Museum (Vincent Van Gogh Foundation)

Stedelijk Museum
- Map p. 190
- Paulus Potterstraat 13
- 020 573 2737
- $$$
- Tram: 2, 3, 5, 12, 16, 20
- Museumboot

The Stedelijk Museum is home to new works and modern classics, including Karel Appel's "Composition" (1951), above.

Stedelijk Museum

THE STEDELIJK MUSEUM IS MORE LIKE AN ART GALLERY than a museum—the displays are constantly changing to show the latest work of mainly Dutch contemporary artists. This gives it a cutting-edge feel, and because it's so new, the art provokes strong reactions: People either love it or hate it.

PERMANENT COLLECTION

The first floor of the museum displays a small number of key works from the permanent collection, including paintings by Cézanne (1839–1906), Piet Mondrian (1872–1944), Kasimir Malevich (1878–1935), Pablo Picasso (1881–1973), and Georges Braque (1882–1963)—all pioneers of new forms of art. None of them was content to work within the constraints of inherited tradi-

tions. Instead they wrestled with philosophical questions about the nature of art, and the distinctive qualities that set it apart from other forms of human endeavor, expressing their answers in terms of pure pattern, shape, and color—abstract representations encapsulating the so-called painterly values.

KASIMIR MALEVICH

The museum has a particularly rich collection of work by Kasimir Malevich, presented on the ground floor (along with quotations from his unpublished essays) as an example of one artist's personal pilgrimage from representational art to pure abstraction. From the early studies of peasant life that Malevich made around 1904, he began to develop a much simpler style, with the same colorful and direct expressive power as Russian folk art.

Then, under the influence of Picasso, he created collages from letters, fragments of text, simple shapes, and figures, deliberately designed to challenge our notions of common sense and logic. Even so, there is a logic to the pictures—you can still detect the eyes and brain of the artist creating aesthetically pleasing patterns and combinations.

As if to break free of even this last vestige of formal composition, Malevich eventually produced what he called his "Suprematist" works—defining Suprematism as "the supremacy of pure sensation—form, color, technique—disassociated from any recognizable form." His first such painting was a black square on white canvas. Clearly he failed in his objective: A square is still a recognizable form. Malevich realized this too, and the ultimate in pure painterliness was reached in 1915, when he produced the white canvas that is displayed here, without title.

DEVELOPING A UNIQUE PERSONAL STYLE

Having effectively taken abstract art as far as it could go, Malevich presented artists with a challenge—what next? Wrestling with that dilemma, successive artists have decided to reject the notion of a single monolithic entity called art; instead, they now argue that there are as many different forms of art as there are artists. This liberating realism has inspired artists to

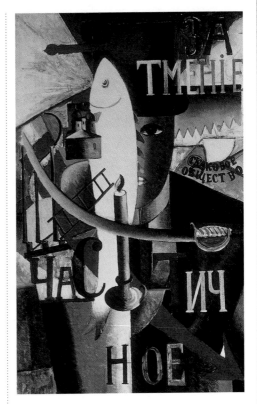

develop their own unique styles. One of the most successful among Dutch artists was Piet Mondrian, who began his career as a landscape painter in the 1890s. His unique compositional style, based on horizontal and vertical lines, is instantly recognizable—the museum's "Composition with two lines" (1931) is an example of his radical work.

A grand staircase leads from the first floor to the second-floor galleries, where new works are displayed, ranging from very large installations to small photographs. Visiting the museum is a matter of serendipity—a journey of unexpected discoveries. You might not like everything you find along the way, but you can be sure it will be thought provoking. ∎

"Symbols and Dreams," a work by Kasimir Malevich

Tempting shops supplement the world-class galleries of the Museum Quarter.

A walk around the Museum Quarter & Vondelpark

The Museum Quarter has undergone a transformation in recent years with the landscaping of Museumplein, the construction of bold new buildings, and the restoration of some old favorites. In addition, the area has a fine park and some of Amsterdam's best shopping.

Begin at the massive **Rijksmuseum** (see pp. 192–97). It's worth spending some time looking at the terra-cotta friezes and portraits that decorate the outside of this neo-Renaissance building depicting artists and various kinds of artistic endeavor.

As you walk through the echoing groin-vaulted underpass that leads to the back of the museum, street musicians taking advantage of the flattering acoustics here will entertain you. At the rear of the museum, small formal gardens decorated with classical statues give way to **Museumplein ❶,** once a vast parking lot for the tour buses bringing visitors to the Museum Quarter, and now an expanse of green grass dotted with pavilion-like buildings of glass and steel, housing shops and cafés (the lot is underground). Across the Museumplein you will see the **Concertgebouw** (see pp. 44 and 264), the classical building with the golden lyre on its pediment, home to the world-famous Concertgebouw Orchestra.

Turning right from the back of the Rijksmuseum onto Paulus Potterstraat, the eclectic-style building you will see on the right-hand side of the street, with its corner turrets topped with witches-cap roofs, is home to **Coster Diamonds ❷** (*Paulus Potterstraat 2–6, tel 305 5555*), where you can take a free tour and see demonstrations of

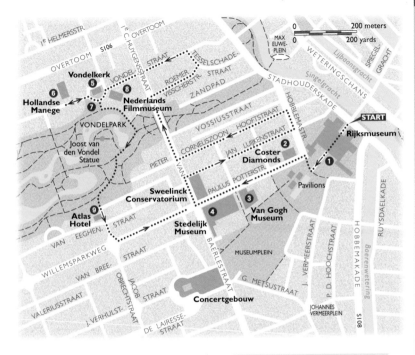

diamond cutting. Beyond this lies the cubist
Van Gogh Museum ❸ (see pp. 198–201)
and the red-brick, neo-Gothic **Stedelijk
Museum** ❹ (see pp. 204–205).

At the end of Paulus Potterstraat, turn right
along Van Baerlestraat, with the **Sweelinck
Conservatorium,** Amsterdam's highly regarded music school, on the right. The next
right, onto Jan Luijkenstraat, takes you past
numerous fine late 19th-century buildings with
art nouveau balconies (No. 102) and door surrounds (Nos. 92 and 94), stained glass (No. 64),
and tile pictures of Aesop's Fables (No. 60).
There are plenty of projecting oriel windows
at second-floor level, and the building at the
end of the street is decorated with a frieze of
dancing cherubs.

Turn left here and left again onto Pieter
Corneliszoon Hooftstraat, where you can indulge in a spot of window shopping on Amsterdam's most upscale shopping street. Back
on Van Baerlestraat, turn right and cross a
bridge that doesn't have a canal running underneath: Instead you look down on a footpath leading to leafy Vondelpark (see p. 208).
Take the first right, Roemer Visscherstraat, to
see a charming group of houses (Nos. 20 to

> 🅜 Also see area map p. 190
> ▶ Rijksmuseum
> 🕒 2.2 miles (3.5 km)
> 🕒 3 hours
> ▶ Rijksmuseum
>
> **NOT TO BE MISSED**
> - Shops on Pieter Corneliszoon
>   Hooftstraat
> - Houses on Roemer
>   Visscherstraat
> - Vondelpark

30) built in 1894 in the national styles of
England, the Netherlands, Russia, Italy, Spain,
France, and Germany.

Turn left onto Tesselschadestraat and left
again onto Vondelstraat, passing more grand
19th-century houses, now converted to hotels
or Amsterdam University faculties. Cross Eerste
Constantijn Huygensstraat and continue down
Vondelstraat toward the **Vondelkerk** ❺,
which lies straight ahead, bristling with spirelets
like Sleeping Beauty's castle. Inspired by
German Gothic church architecture and

A statue to the Shakespeare of the Netherlands, Joost van den Vondel, in the Vondelpark

completed in 1880, this romantic church (now converted to offices) is the work of Rijksmuseum and Centraal Station architect P. J. H. Cuypers (1827–1921); many regard it as his finest work. Continue past the church and you will see the Arts and Crafts-style house on the left (Nos. 77–79) that Cuypers built for his own use in 1899. This style is characterized by its use of details derived from rural and vernacular architecture.

A little farther along a surprising sight (and smell) greets your senses: At No. 40, on the right, an ordinary domestic-looking facade disguises the entrance to the **Hollandse Manege ⑥** (*Vondelstraat 10, tram: 1, 6*), an indoor riding school built in 1882 and modeled on the Spanish Riding School in Vienna. If you love horses, go in quietly to watch the riders practicing their dressage beneath an iron roof decorated with horses' heads.

Returning toward the church, take the gate beside Cuypers' house that leads into **Vondelpark ⑦**. This 112-acre (45 ha) green lung stretches for a mile (1.5 km)

westward and is Amsterdam's year-round playground; in winter it throngs with joggers, skaters, cyclists, and dog-walkers. Just beyond the entrance on the left is the pavilion that houses the **Nederlands Filmmuseum ⑧** (*Vondelpark 3, tel 589 1400, films $$, tram: 1, 6*), which shows new movies and material from its huge archive; there is also a pleasant café-restaurant with an outdoor terrace. On the right as you continue along the main path is a statue of the poet and playwright Joost van den Vondel (1582–1674), often dubbed the Shakespeare of the Netherlands, after whom Vondelpark is named. Keep the ponds and statue to your right as you bear right away from the city center, then take the next left path. This will take you out of the park onto Jacob Obrechtstraat, past the **Atlas Hotel ⑨** (see pp. 256–257), with its decorative art nouveau tiles. Similarly fanciful houses line Willemsparkweg (the third street on the left after you emerge from the park), which leads you back to Paulus Potterstraat and the Rijksmuseum. ■

Dishing out samples at the deservedly popular Heineken Experience

More places to visit in the Museum District & the New South

ALBERT CUYPMARKT

Albert Cuypmarkt is said to be Europe's biggest street market. True or not, there is enough here to exhaust even the most avid shopper, with everything on sale from bicycles to wedding dresses and thermal long johns to sexy underwear. The mile-long street has exotic fruit and vegetables, fish of all kinds, poultry, flowers, cheeses, and household goods for sale, all at bargain prices, not to mention street performers and much good-natured banter.

The market is in a densely packed neighborhood in the southwest of the city known as **De Pijp** for reasons that are lost in the mists of time, though some say it's because the streets are long and narrow, like the stem of an old-fashioned clay pipe *(pijp).*

De Pijp was, until recently, a poor area of cheap housing serving newly arrived migrants to the city. In the last two decades, as house prices and rents in central Amsterdam have soared beyond many people's means, it has become something of a bohemian quarter, favored by artists, intellectuals, writers, musicians, and composers, adding a new element to this colorful part of the the city.
 Map pp. 190–91   ✉ Albert Cuypstraat
🕐 Closed Sun.   🚊 Tram: 4, 16, 24, 25

AMSTERDAMSE BOS & THE ELECTRISCHE MUSEUMTRAMLIJNE

Amsterdam Wood is a giant park on the city's southwestern outskirts, carved out of an area of agricultural land as part of a job-creation scheme in the 1930s depression era. More than 5,000 unemployed people worked here to create the now-mature woodlands, the boating lakes, and the artificial hill used for winter sports. There is a small visitor center, the **Bezoekerscentrum het Bosmuseum** *(Koenenkade 56, tel 676 2152),* with displays on the park's history and wildlife.

A popular way to get to the park is by taking

a ride on the veteran tramcars of the Electrische Museumtramlijne (Electric Tramline Museum). Trams operate between Haarlemmermeer-station and Amstelveen (at the southern tip of the Amsterdamse Bos), a 20-minute trip. A variety of rolling stock from all over Europe, dating from 1908 to 1958, is used. Those antique trams and streetcars that are too fragile to run along the line are displayed at the Haarlemmermeerstation, itself a historic build-ing. The tramline skirts the Amsterdamse Bos, with good views of the Olympic Stadium, built for the 1928 Olympic Games.

🅰 Map p. 190 ✉ Haarlemmermeerstation, Amstelveenseweg 264 ☎ 020 673 7538 ⏱ Trams only run Sun., April 23–Oct. 29 💲 $ 🚊 Tram: 6, 16. Bus: 170, 171, 172

CoBrA MUSEUM VOOR MODERNE KUNST

The CoBrA Museum of Modern Art is located in the southern suburb of Amstelveen, and, as its name suggests, the collection focuses on the art produced by members of the CoBrA move-ment, formed in 1948 and named from the initial letters of the cities of Copenhagen, Brussels, and Amsterdam. Their aim was to explore and portray the unconscious, resulting in abstract and figurative work depicting dreamlike figures or demons from mythology, or bright abstract images drawn in bold pri-mary colors as if by children. There is much to enjoy here if you are interested in this influ-ential art movement, whose leading members were Asgar Jorn (1914–1973), Karel Appel (born 1921), and Corneille (born 1922).

🅰 Map p. 190 ✉ Sandbergplein 1–3, Amstelveen ☎ 020 547 5050; www.cobra-museum.nl ⏱ Closed Mon. 💲 $$$ 🚊 Tram: 5. Bus: 170, 171, 172

DE DAGERAAD & THE GEMEENTARCHIEF AMSTERDAM

De Dageraad (The Dawn) is an area of Amsterdam School architecture in the south of the city, centered around Pieter Lodewijk Taakstraat. Built in 1918–1923, the buildings make adventurous and playful use of brick and tile work, projecting windows, turrets, and clocktowers. Four blocks west, along Tolstraat, a fine neo-Renaissance building stands on the banks of the Amstel River. Completed in 1895,

it served as the town hall for this part of the city, then known as Nieuwer-Amstel. Today it houses the **Gemeentarchief Amsterdam,** the Amsterdam City Archive, which mounts temporary exhibitions of photographs and documents relating to the city's history. It is also a useful resource for anyone visiting Amsterdam to trace his or her ancestors, since it maintains a comprehensive computerized archive of information, gathered from tax and property registers going back to the early days of the city, on who lived in the city, where, and when.

🅰 Map p. 191 ✉ Amsteldijk 67 ☎ 020 572 0202 ⏱ Exhibitions daily, but reference library closed Sat. in July & Aug. 🚊 Tram: 3, 4, or metro to Wibautstraat station

HEINEKEN EXPERIENCE

Heineken is Amsterdam's native brew—or was until the brewery closed in 1988, a victim of its own popularity. This inner-city brewery simply couldn't produce enough beer to satisfy the city's thirst, not to mention the interna-tional demand. The brewery was moved to a new plant in Den Bosch in the southern Netherlands, to the relief of Amsterdammers, who frequently complained about the smell.

The old brewery has been given a new lease on life as a visitor attraction, one of the most popular in Amsterdam because of the free samples that are served at the end.

The exhibitions take in the history of brew-ing from ancient Assyrian origins to today. Interactive displays explain the brewing pro-cess and the unique Heineken recipe, which was developed by Gerard Adridan Heineken when he acquired the brewery in 1864. An important ingredient in the brew is the yeast, developed for the firm by one of Louis Pas-teur's students, whose formula remains a closely guarded secret. There is no doubting the popularity of the result: Heineken's facto-ries in various parts of the Netherlands can turn out well in excess of one million bottles a day, and that is just to satisfy the thirst of drinkers in the Netherlands—worldwide con-sumption is simply staggering.

🅰 Map p. 190 ✉ Stadhouderskade 78 ☎ 020 523 9239; recorded information 523 9666 ⏱ Closed Mon. 💲 $ 🚊 Tram: 6, 7, 10, 16, 20, 24 ■

A msterdam is an excellent base for exploring the Netherlands. From the bulb fields of Haarlem to the modern architecture of Rotterdam, there is much to see within a short distance from the city.

Excursions

Windmill on the Ijsselmeer

Excursions

RENT A BIKE FROM CENTRAAL STATION AND YOU COULD BE CYCLING through gentle Dutch countryside, admiring birds, flowers, and pretty villages, in less than 20 minutes. Take a train from Centraal Station and you could be at the heart of Haarlem in about the same time. The Netherlands is a very small country, and the integrated transportation system offers frequent and reliable train and bus services. This makes it very easy to get out of Amsterdam and explore the Dutch countryside, or visit cities that have played such an important part in European history.

Within an hour's travel from Amsterdam are the great cities of Utrecht, Rotterdam, Leiden, Haarlem, Delft, and Den Haag (The Hague)—all of them places with resonant names, all players on the great stage of world history. The Treaty of Utrecht, signed in 1579, ended 100 years of warfare and ushered in the Golden Age of European prosperity. Rotterdam is the port (now the biggest in the world) from which the Pilgrims set sail in 1620 on their historic voyage to the New World. Settlers from Haarlem gave their name to what is now the New York neighborhood, and Delft is renowned for distinctive blue-and-white pottery produced in the town since the 17th century. The name of The Hague is inextricably linked with the concepts of peace and humanity, thanks to the establishment here of the United Nations International Court of Justice (1946) and the European Court of Human Rights (1959).

But these cities are far more than just famous names. They are all very distinctive and attractive places, with a vibrant cosmopolitan mix of shopping centers and art-filled museums, clubs and bars, and quiet leafy canals—something for everyone. Only Rotterdam, bombed into surrender by the Nazis at the outbreak of World War II, has lost its historic city center, though it has compensated by encouraging modern architects to create some of the most daring and innovative buildings anywhere in the world. ■

The searing colors of spring attract flower-lovers to the gardens of Keukenhof.

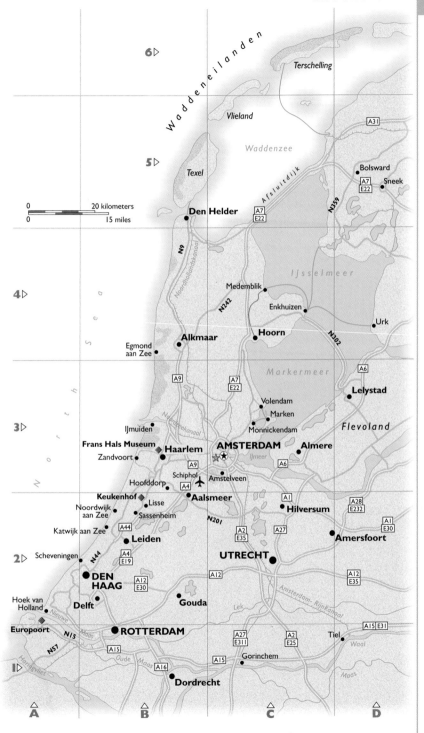

Waddeneilanden

6▷

Terschelling

Vlieland

Waddenzee

A31

5▷

Texel

Bolsward

A7
E22

Sneek

0   20 kilometers
0   15 miles

Den Helder

A7
E22

N9

Noordhollandskanaal

N359

IJsselmeer

4▷

Medemblik

Enkhuizen

Urk

N242

N302

Alkmaar

Hoorn

Egmond
aan Zee

Markermeer

A6

A9

A7
E22

Lelystad

3▷

Volendam

Marken

Flevoland

IJmuiden

Monnickendam

Noordzeekanaal

Frans Hals Museum

Zandvoort

Haarlem

AMSTERDAM

Almere

A9

IJmeer

A6

Hoofddorp

Schiphol

Amstelveen

A4

Keukenhof

Aalsmeer

A1

Noordwijk
aan Zee

Lisse

Hilversum

A28
E232

Sassenheim

N201

A1
E30

Katwijk aan Zee

A44

A2
E35

A27

Amersfoort

Leiden

2▷

Scheveningen

N44

A4
E19

UTRECHT

A12
E35

**DEN
HAAG**

A12
E30

A12

A12

Amsterdam-Rijnkanaal

Hoek van
Holland

Delft

Gouda

Lek

Nieuwe

Maas

Tiel

A15 E31

Waal

Europoort

N15

ROTTERDAM

A27
E311

A2
E25

N57

Oude

Maas

A15

Maas

1▷

Haringvliet

A16

A15

Gorinchem

Maas

Dordrecht

△   △   △   △
A   **B**   **C**   **D**

North Sea

Biking in Waterland

This bike ride shows how easy it is to get out of Amsterdam and experience the Dutch countryside. The route covers a distance of 22.5 miles (36.5 km), with an additional 5 miles (8 km) for the optional extension to Marken. There are cafés and shops providing refreshment stops, but it's always a good idea to carry your own extra water. (For details on renting bikes, see p. 239.)

From the rear of **Centraal Station** (see p. 49) take the free ferry that crosses the IJ River. On the northern bank, follow the canal towpath that lies straight ahead. When you reach the first lock, you will see the first of a

Below top: Level pathways free of car traffic make cycling a pleasure.
Below bottom: Waterside houses in pristine Broek in Waterland

series of fingerposts marked with a hexagonal ANWB cycleway symbol. These are helpfully placed at every junction you come to. Follow the signs for Broek in Waterland.

Continue along the canal, past boats, anglers, and colorfully painted houses. After five minutes, a sign directs you across a bridge to the opposite (right-hand bank) of the canal. For a short time, the canal and bike path run parallel to a busy main road, but another ten

Door decoration reflects maritime traditions.

minutes on, at **Het Schouw**, bear right, to pass under the road, and leave the main Noord-hollands Kanaal to follow the Broekvaart, a smaller side canal.

Passing numerous small dairy farms, you will reach **Broek in Waterland ❶** after 15 minutes. This village is famous as the place where Napoleon was forced to take his boots off when he came to see the mayor in 1811. The villagers were obsessed with cleanliness because they didn't want alien bacteria to infect the culture they used for making cheeses. Today it remains pristine, a village of beautiful timber houses, some in pastel hues, others painted gray in token of mourning for those who lost their lives and livelihoods following disastrous floods in 1825. The church, founded in 1573, has splendid woodwork and

stained glass. If biking has made you hungry, try De Witte Swaen (The White Swan), a café set in a lovely 1596 house at the point where you enter the village, offering 40 different varieties of pancakes.

> ⊠ Also see area map p. 213 C3
> ▶ Centraal Station
> ⟷ 27.5 miles (44.5km) with optional excursion to Marken
> ⏱ 8 hours
> ▶ Centraal Station
>
> **NOT TO BE MISSED**
> - Broek in Waterland
> - Zeedijk

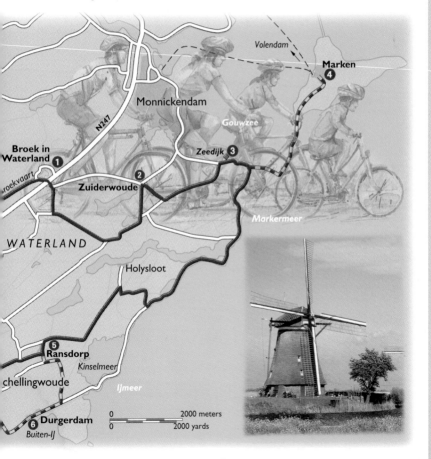

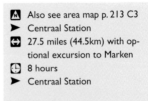

From the café, follow signs to Zuiderwoude, passing beneath the main road through a tunnel. Cross the next canal bridge, but 200 yards (220 m) on, having crossed the next bridge, turn right following signs to Zuiderdorp. At the junction follow the Zuiderdorp sign left, but at the next junction, go left, following the green hexagonal signs that say "Aeën en Dieën."

The track leads straight to the village of **Zuiderwoude** ❷, little more than a water-side church and a cluster of houses around the main square, reached in 25 minutes from Broek. You might like to stop for ice cream at the candy store just before the bridge leading into this tiny village. Another 25 minutes of cycling take you to the **Zeedijk** (Sea Dike) ❸, which is all that stops Waterland from being flooded by the IJsselmeer. Climb the dike to look out over the boat-filled expanse of water. Away to the right is the village of Marken, reached by a long causeway. If time is a consideration, you may wish to start the return journey; otherwise it really is worth the ride along the causeway to this historic village.

Marken ❹ was an island until 1959, and the inhabitants built their wooden houses on artificial mounds called *werfs*. Space on the mounds was limited, so the timber houses, painted black and green, are attractively crowded together. Because it is such a tourist attraction, you will find older ladies of the village posing for photographs in traditional costume in front of their houses, which double as souvenir shops. Plenty of cafés cluster around the small harbor, serving mussels and pancakes. An express boat service departs from the harbor every 30 to 45 minutes for the equally attractive fishing villages of **Volendam** and **Monnickendam**, which lie farther north on the shores of the IJsselmeer (the last boat back is at 5:30 p.m.; you can take your bike for a small extra payment).

Back on the mainland, the route back to Amsterdam simply involves following the dike-top path. After ten minutes or so the "Aeën en Dieën" path will take you off the dike and in-land toward Holysloot. You do not want to go to the village, though; instead, take the first left turn you come to, signposted **Ransdorp** ❺. Take the next turn right, also signposted Rans-dorp, and head for the church when you reach

the village. This stands opposite the attractive 1652 town hall. The Gothic brick church tower is well worth climbing for expansive views across the polder to Amsterdam *(Open mid-April–end Sept., 11–5 Sat. & Sun., and daily, except Mon., in July & Aug.)*.

The easiest way to get back to Amsterdam now is to continue past the church and go right across the lifting bridge when you reach the end of the village. Follow signs to **Schellingwoude** until the path reaches the banks of the IJ, then turn right along the river bank following signs for Centrum, until you return to the IJ ferry. As you leave Ransdorp, you will see the village of **Durgerdam** ❻

in the distance to the left. If you still have energy, you might like to visit this pretty village of waterside houses, then continue around the dike-top path to return to the main route at Schellingwoude.

Whichever route you take, you will bike through land rich in wildlife. The ditches that drain the agricultural land are full of snipe, shellduck, and mallard, not to mention the numerous heron. Depending on the season, there are yellow flags and purple loosestrife in flower among the stands of reed mace and water reed. The song of the lark will accompany you, as well as the haunting cries of oyster catchers and curlews.

Marken's old houses are built on low mounds threaded with waterways to protect them from flooding.

If you get bitten by the cycling bug, remember that there are some 12,000 miles (19,200 km) of *fietspaden* (cycle paths) to explore in the Netherlands, creating a network that will take you to all sorts of places that cars cannot go. Every VVV tourist information center in the Netherlands sells maps and guides detailing local routes, and ANWB, the Dutch motoring organization, produces numerous guide books detailing cycling routes. ■

Enkhuizen

🅰 Map p. 213 C4

Visitor information

✉ Tussen Twee Havens 1

☎ (0228) 313164

Enkhuizen

THE FASCINATING ZUIDERZEEMUSEUM IN ENKHUIZEN IS A living history museum that covers 3,000 years in the life of the village, from Bronze Age settlement to a prosperous herring port. Getting to the museum is an adventure in itself, traveling backward in time from modern railroad to steam train and then to paddle steamer.

All aboard for the *stoomtrein* (steam train) from Hoorn to Medemblik.

Although you can go straight to Enkhuizen by train (see panel), it's much more fun, especially if you have children, to take the normal train service from Centraal Station to Hoorn, then join the steam train service that goes from Hoorn to Medemblik, where you continue your journey by paddle steamer. Make sure you arrive in Hoorn in plenty of time to catch the 11:05 a.m. steam train. This departs from the **Museumstoomtram** (Steam Train Museum), and you can buy an all-inclusive ticket at the museum covering the rest of the journey, including entry into Enkhuizen's Zuiderzeemuseum.

As the sturdy little antique steam train pulls you through the Dutch

countryside, you get an intimate view of neat and productive suburban gardens, open countryside, apple and pear orchards, dairy farms, and fields full of colorful blooms such as daffodils, tulips, roses, carnations, and chrysanthemums, depending on the season, grown for the cut-flower trade. The journey to **Medemblik** takes 65 minutes. On arrival, the guard leads everyone on a Pied Piper march through the town's main street and down to the harbor, where one or more steamers wait for the next leg of the journey. The steamers depart at 12:45 p.m.; you can buy refreshments on board or bring your own picnic. The journey to Enkhuizen

takes 90 minutes, so there is plenty of time for contemplating the views, which take in numerous small coastal towns, and hundreds of leisure craft darting about the surface of the IJsselmeer.

THE IJSSELMEER

Until 1932, the IJsselmeer was known as the **Zuider Zee** (Southern Sea). For centuries it provided the people of Holland with an outlet to the North Sea for fishing and trade. Continual silting meant that it was too shallow for modern shipping, so the Noordzee Kanaal was dug to provide a more direct route from Amsterdam to the North Sea and opened in 1876. High tides always brought the risk of flooding to the regions bordering the Zuider Zee, and a particularly destructive flood in 1916 led to the revival of an idea, first proposed by Cornelis Lely in 1891, of closing off the Zuider Zee altogether. This led to the construction of the **Afsluitdijk,** the Enclosing Dike, built by sinking rafts of woven willow laden with stones and concrete. The final section of the dike was completed in 1932, beginning the slow transformation of the saltwater Zuider Zee into today's freshwater lake.

Villages around the Zuider Zee flew flags at half-mast on the day the dike was officially opened. For them, the loss of access to the sea meant an abrupt end to their long-established maritime and fishing industries. All have since adapted to the new conditions: Leisure boats now fill the harbors, and visitors flock in summer to enjoy the unspoiled character of these former fishing towns, with their numerous seafood restaurants.

ENKHUIZEN

Enkhuizen has prospered more than most by virtue of the

Museumstoomtram, Hoorn

✉ Antwoordnummer 137
☎ (0229) 214862 (information), (0229) 219231 (reservations)
🕐 Closed Nov.–March

Zuiderzeemuseum, Enkhuizen
www.zuiderzeemuseum.nl
✉ Wierdijk 12–22
☎ (0228) 318260 (information line); (0228) 351111 (inquiries)
$ $$$

ENKHUIZEN DIRECT

If time is limited, you can take a train directly to Enkhuizen. Trains leave daily from Centraal Station at 19 and 49 minutes past the hour, from 6:19 a.m. to 11:49 p.m. ∎

Once a defensive tower, the Hoofd-toren in Hoorn now presides over a boat-filled harbor.

Zuiderzeemuseum, which attracts thousands of visitors to the village every year. The museum is in two parts: the **Binnenmuseum** (Indoor Museum) and the **Buitenmuseum** (Outdoor Museum). The steamer docks alongside the entrance to the latter so that you step from the boat straight into a village frozen in time. Historic buildings—cottages,

churches, shops, farms, and barns—have been rescued from all over the Netherlands and reconstructed here to form a complete community, with costumed guides to explain life as it was prior to the enclosure of the Zuider Zee.

It takes a couple of hours to see the Outside Museum, but leave some time for the Indoor Museum, which is housed alongside in the

HOORN

The route back to Enkhuizen's railroad station is clearly signposted and is a ten-minute stroll from the indoor museum. On your way back to Amsterdam (or in the morning, if you have time) it is worth stopping in **Hoorn** for a taste of Dutch provincial life. The little fishing town has two distinct centers—the main square and the harbor.

The main square is dominated by the splendid **Westfries Museum,** with its flamboyant facade flanked by larger-than-life stone lions and Hoorn's coat of arms. Visiting the museum in the 1920s, writer Aldous Huxley (1894–1963) described it affectionately as an "absurd museum, filled with mixed, rich rubbish." It still retains the air of an antique shop full of unexpected exhibits.

South of the square, residential streets lined with patrician houses of the 17th and 18th centuries give way to a series of inner harbors with warehouses whose names—Appelhaven, Bierkade, Korenmarkt—give an idea of the commodities once shipped and stored here, apple, beer, and corn (grain). The main harbor is marked by a leaning tower, known as the **Hoofdtoren,** which was built in 1532 as a defensive tower but is now topped by a pretty bell tower. Two ship boys cast in bronze and clambering up the sea wall commemorate Willem Ijsbrantszoon Bontekoe, who was born in one of the nearby houses, and who wrote a bestseller in 1646 in the form of a diary describing a voyage to the East Indies.

From the harbor, look for a route marked with arrows set in the sidewalk. The route takes you back to the main square round the eastern side of the town, past some fine 17th-century houses, several of which now house art galleries and antique shops. ■

Hoorn

🄰 Map p. 213 C4

Visitor information

✉ Veemarkt 4

☎ (0229) 231055

Westfries Museum, Hoorn

✉ Rode Steen 1

☎ (0229) 280028

🕐 Closed Sat. & Sun. a.m., 3rd Mon. in Aug., April. 30, Dec. 25, Jan. 1

💲 $

Peperhuis, an imposing Renaissance building dating from 1625 that was once used for storing spices from Indonesia. The interesting displays here cover the history of the whaling and herring fishing industries, and the constant struggle the Dutch have faced to control the water that surrounds them and threatens at all times to encroach upon them.

Haarlem is a city of art—and of great places for enjoying first-rate food.

Haarlem

HAARLEM MAY ONLY BE FIVE MINUTES AWAY FROM Amsterdam by train, but it's a world away in atmosphere. Unchanged in appearance since the 17th century, the delightful city center is a maze of traffic-free streets, lined with bookstores, antique shops, and old-fashioned cheese mongers. In this town of numerous artists, the Frans Hals Museum is a must.

Haarlem

⛰ Map p. 213 B3

Visitor information

✉ Stationsplein 1

☎ (0900) 616 1600

Grote Kerk

✉ Grote Markt

☎ (023) 532 4399

🕐 Closed Sun.

💲 Free

The 12-mile (20 km) journey from Centraal Station to Haarlem is covered before you have time to settle into your seat. Haarlem's station is a model of art nouveau architecture, with decorative timber and wrought-iron details and colorful tile pictures. The tourist office (ideal for maps) is in the same building, and the town center is a ten-minute stroll to the south.

GROTE MARKT

Follow signs for Grote Markt and you will find yourself stepping straight into a Golden Age painting. All that has been added since the 17th century is a mass of busy sidewalk cafés, turning this leafy square into one large open-air dining room. The **statue** in the middle of

the square depicts Laurens Coster, whose reputation as the true inventor of printing (in 1423) has been eclipsed by the fame of Johannes Gutenberg (1400–1468), whose moveable type press followed 16 years later.

To the west of the square is the **Stadhuis** (Town Hall), an elaborately gabled Renaissance building fronted by the statue of a rather comely figure of Justice. Southeast of the square is the **Grote Kerk** (also known as Sint-Bavokerk, after its patron saint). This enormous Gothic church (built between 1400 and 1550) is made more attractive by the jumble of old shops that cling to its skirts—built by the church wardens to provide income for maintaining the church. The gorgeous interior is a rich mix of woodwork and brass, and the flamboyant organ is the one that Handel played in 1738, and Mozart in 1766. Look for information about recitals and come and hear why it was that Mozart shouted for joy on trying it out.

Next to the church is the extravagantly decorated group of buildings known as **Verweij Hal** (The Halls), whose gabled dormer windows project from a roof bristling with pinnacles, baroque scrolls, and lion masks. Meat and fish markets were once held here, but they are now used for displays of contemporary art organized by the Frans Hals Museum.

FRANS HALS MUSEUM

Farther south again is the Frans Hals Museum, a major museum by any standards, housed in the almshouse of 1610 where the artist Frans Hals (1581–1666) lived out his final years. The museum has an excellent collection of Dutch art, from early Renaissance works to experimental works by members of the CoBrA group (see p. 210), but the astonishingly powerful paintings by Frans Hals are the real attraction.

Hals was born in Antwerp but moved to Haarlem in the 1580s. Despite being one of the greatest artists of his age, he died (as did Rembrandt) in poverty, his genius unrecognized. Van Gogh loved Hals's work and would sit gazing at it for hours, claiming to have counted no fewer than 27 different tones of black in Hals's depiction of the clothing favored by the puritanical Regents whose portraits he painted. Like Rembrandt, Hals was brilliant at expressing the personality of his subjects or at adding an unexpected twist to a conventional group portrait. His huge canvas depicting the "Civic Guard of St. Adrien" (1633) at their annual banquet is one example. The inebriated state of the diners is mirrored in the tipsy angles of beards, ruffs, sashes, and flags. Indeed, as you search the composition for a horizontal line to serve as an anchor, looking at the picture too long may make your head swim.

TEYLERS MUSEUM

Haarlem's other museum of note is the Teylers Museum, which bridges the worlds of science and art. Thanks to the legacy of the founder, cloth merchant Pieter Teyler van de Hulst (1702–1778), the museum has an outstanding collection of early scientific instruments, but also a rich collection of drawings, including very rare works by Dürer, Rembrandt, and Michelangelo. ∎

Verweij Hal
- ✉ Grote Markt 16
- ☎ (023) 511 5840
- ⏱ Closed Sun. a.m.
- 💲 $$$ (cheaper if you buy a combined ticket for this & the Frans Hals Museum)

Frans Hals Museum
- ✉ Grote Heiligland 62
- ☎ (023) 511 5775
- ⏱ Closed Sun a.m.
- 💲 $$$

Teylers Museum
- ✉ Spaarne 16
- ☎ (023) 531 9010
- ⏱ Closed Mon.
- 💲 $$$

Works by the subversive virtuoso Frans Hals are on display in the former home for the elderly where the artist spent his final years.

A drive through the bulb fields of Haarlem

From late January through late July, the fields south of Haarlem are striped with the bold colors of crocuses and tulips, gladioli and lilies, grown for the bulb market and the cut-flower trade. Driving through this region, you can admire the vivid patchwork of colors created by this industry, and visit the superb show gardens at Keukenhof.

A stunning field of tulips in countryside near the Keukehof gardens

From Amsterdam head out of the city center along Vijzelstraat, and follow signs for 's-Gravenhage, taking the S100 for 0.5 mile (1 km), the S106 for 2 miles (1.8 km), then the A10/E22 for 0.5 mile (1 km), and finally the A4/E19 road southward for 11 miles (18 km). At junction 4, take the N207 exit, toward Lisse. When you meet the N208, after 4 miles (6 km), turn left for Lisse.

Lisse ① is an attractive town in the middle of the Bloembollenstreek, the bulb-growing district, whose flat, multicolored fields stretch for nearly 20 miles (30 km) from Haarlem in the north to Leiden in the south. Within the town, the small **Museum de Zwarte Tulp** (*Grachtweg 2A, tel 0252 417900, closed Mon., $*) is devoted to the fascinating history of the tulip, introduced to the Netherlands from Turkey in the 1550s, and so highly prized that small fortunes were once paid for prize blooms, including that of the elusive and legendary Black Tulip—a pure black bloom desired by all collectors, though no one had ever produced one, despite fraudsters persuading gullible customers to pay large sums of money for bulbs they claimed were black.

Just to the north of the town is the entrance to **Keukenhof ②** (*Tel 0252 465555, spring garden open mid-March–mid-May,*

summer garden Aug., $$$), the 80-acre (32 h) park that serves as a showcase for the Dutch flower industry. Spectacular color effects (and heady scents) are the theme of this park, where the bulbs are planted in layers to ensure a continuous show of color from March to May, complemented by the blooms of cherry trees and numerous sculptures. Some of the gardens are themed—natural gardens, water gardens, secret gardens, historical gardens, and mazes. In addition, there are pavilions with displays of photographs, works of art, and specialist plants such as orchids. During the summer, when the bulbs are dormant, there is an equally vivid display of perennial and bedding plants and flowering shrubs.

If you don't have a car, you can visit Keukenhof gardens by organized tour or by public transportation. Information on a combined train, bus, and admission ticket package (called Keukenhof Rail Idea) is available at Centraal Station (*Tel 0900 9292*).

From Keukenhof, turn right to follow the N208 southward through the bulb fields to **Sassenheim ③**. On the western edge of the town is the pretty **Kasteel Teilingen,** an 11th-century castle. Follow the N208 as it bends westward to meet the N206 near **Noordwijk aan Zee ④,** a seaside town with miles of glorious sand backed by dunes and perfect conditions for windsurfing.

The N206 will take you north to Haarlem through some of the bulb districts' most intensively colored fields. As you approach Haarlem, you can go into the city to visit the Frans Hals Museum and Sint Bavokerk (see pp. 222–23), returning to Amsterdam on the A5; or you can stay on the N206 and N201 and visit Zandvoort, perhaps returning to Amsterdam on the N201 via Hoofddorp.

Zandvoort ⑤ is Amsterdam's nearest beach resort, and it receives thousands of visitors in summer. It is big enough to cope

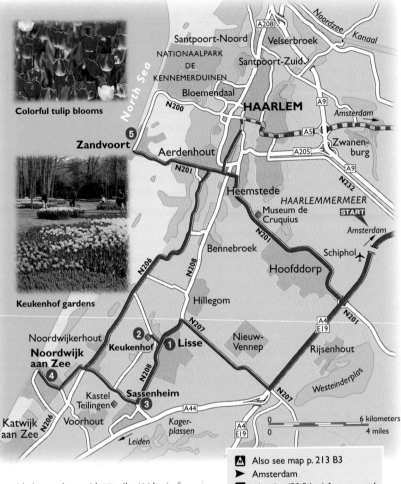

Colorful tulip blooms

Keukenhof gardens

(Map labels:) Noordzee Kanaal · A208 · Santpoort-Noord · Velserbroek · NATIONAALPARK DE KENNEMERDUINEN · Santpoort-Zuid · North Sea · Bloemendaal · N200 · HAARLEM · A9 · Amsterdam · A5 · Zwanenburg · **5** Zandvoort · Aerdenhout · A205 · N201 · A9 · N232 · Heemstede · HAARLEMMERMEER · Museum de Cruquius · START · N201 · Amsterdam · Bennebroek · Hoofddorp · Schiphol · N206 · N208 · Hillegom · Nieuw-Vennep · A4 E19 · N201 · **2** · **1** Lisse · Keukenhof · Rijsenhout · Noordwijkerhout · Noordwijk aan Zee · **4** · N208 · Westeinderplas · Kastel Teilingen · Sassenheim · **3** · N207 · Katwijk aan Zee · N206 · Voorhout · A44 · Kager-plassen · A4 E19 · Leiden · 0   6 kilometers · 0   4 miles

🇳 Also see map p. 213 B3
▶ Amsterdam
↔ 61 miles (98.5 km) from central Amsterdam
🕐 5 hours with sightseeing
▶ Amsterdam

NOT TO BE MISSED
- Keukenhof
- Noordwijk aan Zee

with the numbers, with 10 miles (16 km) of sand, part of which is given over to nude bathing. Behind the beach strip, the **Nationaal Park de Kennermerduinen** (Kennemer Dunes National Park) has varied habitats—lakes, woods, and heath, as well as extensive dune systems—that attract many rare and unusual birds, including black-tailed godwits, lapwings, and reed buntings.

If you return via Hoofddorp, you will pass the **Museum de Cruquius** (*Cruquiusdijk 27, tel 023 528 5704, closed Nov.–late Feb., $*) which shows how the bulb fields were created in the mid-19th century by draining the shallow Haarlemmermeer lake. The museum is housed in one of the pumping stations used

for the task, and it is named after Nicolas Cruquius (1678–1754), the engineer who devised the drainage scheme in 1750, though it was not implemented until 1852. One of the exhibits shows the waterways of the Netherlands, and the astonishing amount of land that has been reclaimed by drainage. ■

Art overboard!
A floating compo-
sition in the Hof
Vijver

Den Haag

A Map p. 213 B2
Visitor information
✉ Koningin
   Julianaplein 30
☎ (0900) 340 3505

Mauritshuis
www.mauritshuis.nl
✉ Korte Vijverberg 8
☎ (070) 302 3456
🕐 Closed Mon.
💲 $$$

Binnenhof
✉ Binnenhof 8
☎ (070) 364 6144
🕐 Closed Sun.
💲 $$$

**Haags Historisch
Museum**
www.bart.nl/~hhm
✉ Korte Vijverberg 7
☎ (070) 364 6940
🕐 Closed Mon.
💲 $$$

Panorama Mesdag
www.panorama-mesdag.nl
✉ Zeestraat 65
☎ (070) 310 6665
🕐 Closed Sun. a.m.
💲 $$$

**Haags
Gemeentemuseum**
www.museon.nl
✉ Stadhouderslaan 41
☎ (070) 338 1111
🕐 Closed Mon.
💲 $$$

Den Haag

DEN HAAG (THE HAGUE) IS THE POLITICAL CAPITAL OF THE
Netherlands, chosen as a neutral meeting point by the leaders of the
seven provinces that came together to form the Netherlands in 1586.
The city was then no more than a hunting lodge surrounded by a
park pale (enclosure) after which Den Haag (literally "The Hedge") is
named. Today it is an elegant city of palaces, public buildings, and
museums, with the seaside town of Scheveningen a short step away.

Den Haag Centraal Station is a 35-minute train ride from Amsterdam.
From the station (where you will also find the tourist office), it is a
short walk to Hof Vijver, the little lake that marks the historic center
of the city.

This tranquil stretch of water is all that remains of the medieval
moat that protected the early city. Reflected in its calm surface are the
noble facades of the parliament buildings and the beautiful
Mauritshuis, built in 1644 as a private mansion for Johann
Maurits when he retired, a very wealthy man, from his post as
governor of Brazil. The house was bequeathed to the state on his death
and now makes an elegant home

for the small but choice collection
of paintings making up the royal
collection. On just three floors you
will find some of the finest works
ever produced by Carel Fabritius
("The Goldfinch," 1654), Vermeer
("Girl with a Turban," 1660), and
Rembrandt ("The Anatomy Lesson
of Dr. Nicolaes Tulp," 1632).

From the Mauritshuis you can
wander freely around the court-
yards of the **Binnenhof,** home to
the Dutch parliament. When the
parliament is not in session, you
can visit the turreted **Ridderzaal**
(Knights' Hall), the fairy-tale castle
at the heart of the complex. Dating
from the 13th century, this was the
dining hall of the original hunting
lodge around which The Hague has

grown. You can trace the story of the city's development in old paintings, furnished rooms, and period dolls' houses in the adjacent **Haags Historisch Museum.**

FARTHER AFIELD

Where you go next depends on your interests. Shoppers should head for the tangle of pedestrian-only streets west of the Binnenhof, including **De Passage,** an elegant covered arcade. Antique shops and art galleries abound in a city of diplomats, politicians, and senior civil servants, as do upscale restaurants serving fine French-influenced cuisine.

Noordeinde, the main shopping street, takes you northward to a circular building housing the **Panorama Mesdag,** an astonishingly realistic circular painting of the North Sea coast on the inside wall, created in 1881 by various members of the Dutch Impressionist School, led by H.W. Mesdag (1831–1915). This painting lies adjacent to the **Vredespaleis,** the Peace Palace, a building donated by the Scottish-American

philanthropist Andrew Carnegie (1835–1918) and now home to the United Nations International Court of Justice, established in 1946.

Farther afield are attractions that will appeal to children as well as to adults. The **Haags Gemeentemuseum** contains the world's largest collection of works by Piet Mondrian (1872–1944), who is famous for his abstract study called "Composition in Red, Black, Blue, Yellow and Grey" (1920). The museum's Fashion Gallery is a reminder of the bewildering pace of change in 20th-century fashion in clothing and jewelry. Budding young scientists are well catered for at the **Museon,** next door, which is linked to the **Omniversum IMAX Theater and Planetarium,** showing three-dimensional images of the universe and spectacular volcanic eruptions.

Younger children will probably prefer **Madurodam,** a fictitious Dutch city that includes many of the Netherlands' finest monuments, modeled with astonishing accuracy at a scale of 1:25. Alternatively, the seaside town of **Scheveningen** is a short tram ride away (*Tram: 1, 7, 8, 9*). A stroll along the seafront promenade will introduce you to the golden sands and seafood restaurants of this 19th-century resort, built around the palatial **Kurhaus,** which was used for spa cures and now houses a luxury hotel and casino. Other attractions include **Sea Life Scheveningen** and the **Zeemuseum,** separate attractions both offering a glimpse of life beneath the ocean; the **Museum Scheveningen,** telling the story of the town's evolution from fishing port to elegant spa; and the **Museum Beelden aan Zee** (Sculptures by the Sea), a unique museum of 700 sculptures by various artists. ■

Museon

- ✉ Stadhouderslaan 41
- ☎ (070) 338 1338
- 🕐 Closed Mon.
- 💲 $$$ (combined ticket available with Omniversum)

Omniversum

www.omniversum.nl

- ✉ President Kennedylaan 5
- ☎ (070) 354 5454
- 🕐 Closed Mon.
- 💲 $$$ (combined ticket available with Museon)

Madurodam

www.madurodam.nl

- ✉ George Maduroplein 1
- ☎ (070) 355 3900
- 💲 $$$$$

Sea Life Scheveningen

- ✉ Strandweg 13
- ☎ (070) 354 2100
- 💲 $$$

Zeemuseum

- ✉ Dr Lelykade 39
- ☎ (070) 350 2528
- 🕐 Closed Sun. a.m.
- 💲 $$$

Museum Scheveningen

- ✉ Neptunusstraat 92
- ☎ (070) 350 0830
- 🕐 Closed Mon.
- 💲 $

Museum Beelden aan Zee

www.beeldenaanzee.nl

- ✉ Harteveltstraat 1
- ☎ (070) 358 5857
- 🕐 Closed Mon.
- 💲 $$$

Leiden

Leiden

▲ Map p. 213 B2

Visitor information

✉ Stationsweg 2d

☎ (0900) 222 2333

🕐 Closed Sun.

Molenmuseum de Valk

✉ 2e Binnenvestgracht 1

☎ (071) 516 5353

🕐 Closed Mon. & Sun. a.m.

💲 $

Rijksmuseum voor Volkenkunde

www.rmv.nl

✉ Steenstraat 1

☎ (071) 516 8800

🕐 Closed Mon. & Oct. 3

💲 $$$

Visit Leiden's last windmill.

LEIDEN IS A UNIVERSITY TOWN WITH A LONG AND honorable history and a lively student life. Rembrandt (born in Leiden in 1606) was a student at the law faculty before abandoning his degree to take up art. Highlights of the city include the excellent museums of antiquities and anthropology, the botanical gardens, and the many friendly cafés and antiquarian bookstores.

Leiden is 30 minutes from Amsterdam by train, and the station (home to the tourist office) stands just outside the historic city defenses. Three attractions lie close to the station, before you enter the city itself. One is the magnificent seven-story **Molenmuseum de Valk** (Falcon Mill), to the left as you exit the station. Built in 1743, it was home to ten generations of millers—and is now the city's last surviving mill. To the right of the station is the **Rijksmuseum voor Volkenkunde** (National Anthropological Museum), a place of color, noise, and vitality where exhibits cover life in diverse environments, from the tropics of Indonesia to the snows of the Arctic.

A little farther into the city, on the left, is the **Stedlijk Museum de Lakenhal** (Cloth Hall Municipal Museum), housing two treasures. One is a three-part altar painting by Lucas van Leyden (1494–1533) depicting "The Last Judgment" (1526–27); the other a humbler object—a vast bronze cauldron. The starving people of Leiden acquired it in 1574, after the defeat of the Spanish soldiers who had held their city to a year-long siege during the Revolt of the Netherlands (see p. 25). The paprika-spiced *hutspot*, or stew, found in the caldron is now cooked every year (on October 3) to commemorate the siege.

COURAGE & LEARNING

The brave citizens of Leiden withstood starvation and disease long enough for William of Orange, leader of the Dutch army, to inflict a decisive blow against the enemy. As a reward for this heroism, William founded the first university in the Netherlands here in 1575, and you will pass several noble classical buildings bearing the names of university faculties as you walk into the city, down Rapenburg.

Leiden was one of the first universities in Europe to have a Botanical Garden, planted in 1587. The entrance to the **Hortus Botanicus** lies halfway down Rapenburg, and you can see the original walled garden, named

after Carolus Clusius, Leiden's first professor of botany, and the man who introduced the tulip to the Netherlands.

Opposite the garden entrance, the alley called Kloksteeg leads to 15th-century **Pieterskerk,** a beautiful Gothic church of rose-pink brick, where John Robinson (1575–1625), leader of the Pilgrims, lies buried. Robinson was one of many Protestant refugees who found asylum in Leiden in the 17th century, and his preaching inspired the Pilgrims to set sail for the New World with their dream of building a new Jerusalem. Robinson was too ill to join the Pilgrims when they departed in 1620, and he never recovered his health, dying here in 1625.

Cobbled lanes and antiquarian bookstores surround the church, while two blocks north is the **Rijksmuseum van Oudheden** (National Museum of Antiquities), fronted by the 1st-century A.D. Temple of Taffeh, ancient Egyptian goddess of fertility. The temple was dismantled in 1960 and given to the Netherlands when it was threatened by the construction of the Aswan dam. The temple sets the theme for a museum rich in Egyptian artifacts, but which also has an informative exhibition devoted to the archaeology of the Netherlands.

SHOPS & CAFÉS

Leiden's commercial heart lies farther to the east, at the confluence of two Rhine channels—the Oude Rijn and the Nieuwe Rijn. The Nieuwe Rijn is crossed by the elegant **Korenbeursbrug** (Corn Market Bridge), a covered timber bridge dating from 1825 when it was built to provide shelter for the grain traders' stands. Off Hoogstraat, at the point where the river divides, you can watch students and visitors messing about in boats while enjoying a meal or drink at one of several floating cafés and riverside restaurants. ■

Stedlijk Museum de Lakenhal
www.lakenhal.demon.nl
✉ Oude Singel 28–32
☎ (071) 516 5360
🕐 Closed Mon., Sat. & Sun. a.m.
💲 $

Hortus Botanicus Leiden
✉ Rapenburg 73
☎ 071) 527 7249
🕐 Closed Oct. 3
💲 $

Rijksmuseum van Oudheden
www.rmo.nl
✉ Rapenburg 28
☎ (071) 516 3163
🕐 Closed Mon., Sat. & Sun. a.m., Oct. 3
💲 $

After seeing the sights, relax on a canalside terrace.

The art of painting pottery using techniques that have changed little in 350 years lives on at Delft potteries.

Delft

WHEN DUTCH EAST INDIA SHIPS RETURNED FROM THE other side of the world bearing Chinese porcelain, the potters of Delft were quick to copy the exotic new style. Thus the Delftware industry was born in the 17th century, and soon no Dutch home was without its blue-and-white painted tiles, jugs, and tulip jars. Today, the town is still full of shops selling new and antique pottery, but there is much more to see, including the last resting place of Prince William of Orange (1533–1584), one of the most important figures in Dutch history.

Delft

www.vvvdelft.nl

🅰 Map p. 213 B2

Visitor information

✉ Markt 83–5

☎ 0900 335 3888

🕐 Closed Sun. Oct.–mid-April

Stedelijk Museum Het Prinsenhof

✉ St. Agathaplein 1

☎ (015) 260 2358

🕐 Closed Mon.

💲 $

Legermuseum

✉ Korte Geer 1

☎ (015) 215 0500

💲 $

Delft is an hour's journey by train from Amsterdam (some routes involve a change at Den Haag). The historic center lies a few minutes' walk from the train station. Head as straight as you can until you reach the leafy banks of the long canal called Oude Delft. Shaded by lime trees and crossed by a series of hump-backed bridges, this is everyone's idea of the perfect Dutch canal. Its banks are lined with venerable old buildings, including **Oostindische Huis** at No. 39, the 17th-century Delft headquarters of the Dutch East India Company.

PRINSENHOF

Turning left along Oudeschans you come to **Stedelijk Museum Het Prinsenhof,** a cluster of old buildings in the shadow of the Oude Kerk tower. Originally the Convent of St. Agatha, the Prinsenhof was renamed in honor of Prince William of Orange, who met his untimely death here at the hands of a fanatical Dutch assassin in 1584. The prince used the convent as his campaign base during the Dutch Revolt. Fighting a long drawn out war of attrition against the Spanish Catholic rulers, he led the Dutch army to victory. Desperate to break Dutch morale, the Spanish trained one Balthazar Geraerts to carry out the assassination. In the morbidly named **Moordzaal** (Death Hall), you can see the holes in the wall made by the bullets that killed William. The museum also provides an atmospheric backdrop to displays of Delftware, paintings, tapestries, and other decorative arts.

Crossing Oude Delft to the lovely Gothic **Oude Kerk,** you can see the tombs of two more heroic Dutch military leaders: Admiral Maartin Tromp (1598–1653), who defeated the English fleet in 1652, and Admiral Piet Heyn (1577–1629), who captured the Spanish silver fleet in 1628. William of Orange was buried in nearby **Nieuwe Kerk,** which lies farther east, at the head of Delft's main square, with its massive 320-foot-high (100 m) tower, added in 1872. Here, in the otherwise relatively plain church, lies his richly decorated mausoleum. Designed in 1614 by Hendrick de Keyser (1565–1621), the leading architect of the Dutch Renaissance, the tomb is carved from black and white marble and depicts William in battle dress, with his dog. Four bronze Virtues stand at each corner, with Fame, depicted as a trumpeting angel, at his feet.

Also by Hendrick de Keyser is the Renaissance-style **Stadhuis** (Town Hall) on the opposite side of the long market square as you leave the church. Completed in 1618, it was one of the few buildings to survive an explosion that devastated much of Delft in October 1645, when the National Arsenal caught fire. The rebuilt arsenal in the south of the town now houses the **Legermuseum** (Army Museum), which takes in the whole sweep of military history in the Netherlands, including the founding of NATO and postwar conflicts

in the former Dutch colonies of Indonesia and Surinam.

IN PURSUIT OF PORCELAIN

Delft's streets are lined with shops selling new and antique Delftware, and several local factories offer tours. Of these, the name of **De Porceleyne Fles** (The Porcelain Flask) stands out because it was one of the first to be founded (in 1653). Still going strong, the factory provides a chance to see skilled ceramic artists at work. ■

Mellow tones make for that Delft touch.

De Porceleyne Fles
✉ Rotterdamseweg 196
☎ (015) 256 9214
🕐 Closed Sun. & Nov.–March
💲 $

Expansive proposition: Delft's main square

Rotterdam's red
Willemsbrug links
the north of the
river with **Nord Is-
land** in Rotterdam.

Rotterdam
www.vvv.rotterdam.nl
- Map p. 213 B1
Visitor information
- Coolsingel 67
- (0900) 403 4065
- Closed Sun.
  Oct.–end March

**Museum Boijmans
van Beuningen**
www.boijmans.rotterdam.nl
- Museumpark 18–20
- (010) 441 9400
- Closed Mon.
- $$$

Kunsthal
www.kunsthal.nl
- Westzeedijk 341
- (010) 440 0300
- Closed Mon.
- $$$

Natuurmuseum
www.nmr.nl
- Westzeedijk 345
- (010) 436 4222
- Closed Mon.
- $

Rotterdam

THE LUFTWAFFE FLATTENED ROTTERDAM IN MAY 1940,
leaving 75 percent of the city in ruins. Sixty years on, it proudly wore
the title of European City of Culture 2001, in recognition of its
enormous international appeal—a blend of the traditional arts and
ultra-modern architecture.

Rotterdam Railroad Station, an
hour by train from Amsterdam, is
not a good advertisement for the
city. Its bleak 1960s architecture is
soon forgotten as you walk down
the avenue that leads from the station to the harbor to the **Museum
Boijmans van Beuningen.**
This huge and important gallery
contains something for everyone:
works by Pieter Brueghel, Dürer,
Jan van Eyck, and Rembrandt
among the old masters, but also a

large modern art collection, with
well-known works by surrealist
artists Dalí and Magritte. The museum forms part of a new cultural
complex, with landscaped gardens,
outdoor sculptures, and various
exhibition venues. Close by you
will find the **Kunsthal** (Hall of
Culture), used for temporary
exhibits; the fascinating **Natuurmuseum** (Nature Museum), ex-
hibiting fossils, skeletons, insects,
and stuffed birds and animals; the

Chabot Museum
- ✉ Museumpark 11
- ☎ (010) 436 3713
- 🕐 Closed Mon., & all of Aug

Nederlands Architectuurin-stituut
www.nai.nl
- ✉ Museumpark 25
- ☎ (010) 440 1200
- 🕐 Closed Mon.
- $ $$$

Wereld Museum
www.wereldmuseum.rotterdam.nl
- ✉ Willemskade 25
- ☎ (010) 270 7172
- 🕐 Closed Mon.
- $ $$$

Euromast
www.euromast.nl
- ✉ Parkhaven 20
- ☎ (010) 436 4811
- $ $$$

Historisch Museum Rotterdam
www.hmr.rotterdam.nl
- ✉ Voorhaven 12
- ☎ (010) 476 1533
- 🕐 Closed Mon.
- $ $$$

Chabot Museum, dedicated to the work of Expressionist artist Hendrik Chabot; and the **Nederlands Architectuurinstituut,** covering town planning, architecture, and interior design. Farther away, on the southeastern edge of the park, is the **Wereld Museum** (World Museum), the reborn Museum of Ethnology.

To get your bearings, try taking the high-speed elevator to the top of the **Euromast,** which lies on the southwestern edge of the park. Built in 1960, the tower has restaurants and a viewing gallery 328 feet (100 m) up, but you can get higher still by taking the glass elevator up the Space Tower, added in 1970 and taking the total height to 607 feet (185 m).

DELFSHAVEN

From the Euromast, there are extensive views of the **Europoort,** now the world's largest container port, which stretches for 20 miles (32 km) along the banks of the Maas and the Rhine ("Rijn" in Dutch) to the North Sea. Rotterdam's older harbors (of which there are several) now provide a tranquil berth for leisure craft. To the west of the city is **Delfshaven,** a picturesque waterway filled with houseboats. The **Oude Kerk** (known as the Pilgrim Fathers' Church) stands on the harborside, marking the spot where the Pilgrims embarked for the New World on board the *Speedwell* in 1620. (They were soon forced to abandon this unseaworthy ship, and later set sail again from Ply-

Kijk Kubus
- ✉ Overblaak 70
- ☎ (010) 414 2285
- 💲 $

Maritiem Museum Rotterdam
- www.mmph.nl
- ✉ Leuvehaven 1
- ☎ (010) 413 2680
- 🕐 Closed Mon. (except in July & Aug.)
- 💲 $$$

Historisch Museum Het Schielandshuis
- www.hmr.rotterdam.nl
- ✉ Korte Hoogstraat 31
- ☎ (010) 217 6767
- 🕐 Closed Mon.
- 💲 $$$

mouth, in southern England, aboard the *Mayflower*.)

Alongside, a gabled granary called De Dubbelde Palmboom (The Double Palm Tree) has been converted to form the **Historisch Museum Rotterdam** (Rotterdam Historical Museum), with exhibits on the city's archaeology, history, and working life.

OUDE HAVEN

Across the other side of the city, Oude Haven (Old Harbor) has some of the city's most innovative architecture, which remains fresh and challenging, even though some of these buildings are now approaching their half-century mark. Piet Blom's **Kijk Kubus,** one such complex, designed in 1956, has cube-shaped apartments, tipped at dizzying angles, forming a crys-

A different angle on life: Piet Blom's iconoclastic cube houses

talline structure standing on top of stalk-like towers, with shops and cafés below. To live in a cube house, you need specially designed furniture, as you will see if you visit Overblaak 70. Another avant garde building is the public library, the **Gemeentebibliotheek,** similar in concept to the work of British architect Richard Rogers, with service pipes exposed on the outside of

the building and painted in bold primary colors. Other areas of the docks are undergoing development and will no doubt produce equally radical designs.

MARITIME ROTTERDAM

Along Leuvehaven, there are no fewer than three different museums, indoor and out, devoted to maritime themes, including the history of Rotterdam as a port and the history of the Dutch Royal navy. The **Maritiem Museum Rotterdam** (Maritime Museum Rotterdam) uses impressive multimedia techniques to tell the story, but the best way to get a feel for the modern port is to take one of the **Spido harbor tours** (*Tel (010) 275 9988, $$$*) that depart from nearby Leuvehoofd, the headland opposite the IMAX Theater. Short tours (75 minutes) and longer ones (from 2 to 6 hours) are offered. Both bring home the sheer scale of the Europoort, which links the open seas with the world's busiest river—containers transshipped here are carried by barge along the Rhine and its tributaries deep into the heart of France, Germany, Switzerland, and beyond.

CITY CENTER

North of the port, the historic city center holds yet another museum, as well as all the shopping facilities you would expect of a modern city.

International fashion chains and small boutiques can be found in the **Beurstraverse** shopping center, opposite the Beurs (Stock Exchange) along Coolsingel. Fashions from the past are the theme of the nearby **Historisch Museum Het Schielandshuis,** a classical 17th-century town house displaying clothing and furnishings from the 18th century to the present day. ■

Travelwise

On a bicycle built for three

TRAVELWISE INFORMATION

PLANNING YOUR TRIP

CLIMATE

In Amsterdam they say that the weather only has three states: If it's not already raining, then it has either just stopped or is just about to start. In truth, it doesn't rain quite as much as this suggests, but the city's maritime climate does mean that the sky looks gray and overcast for much of the time. Those cloudy Dutch skies were a great inspiration to landscape painters of the Golden Age, but to modern travelers, they are a warning not to travel far without a light waterproof coat or an umbrella.

Spirits soar perceptibly during the blissful months of summer, from June to late August, when temperatures can rise to the 80s°F (high 20s°C). That is when Amsterdammers like to make the most of the fair weather by eating and drinking out of doors. Fall can also be delightful, with blue skies and fluffy clouds and the trees turning to gold. Winter can bring freezing sea fog that hangs over the city for days at a time. As soon as the wind changes to an easterly direction, the fog blows away and is replaced by cold blue skies. Snow and deep frost is now rare, because the city has such a warm microclimate, so you are unlikely to see skaters on the canals of Amsterdam.

Average temperatures:
Spring: mid-March to mid-May 54°F (12°C)
Summer: mid-May to end August 75°F (24°C)
Fall: September to mid-November 54°F (12°C)
Winter: mid-November to mid-March: 50°F (10°C)

Average rainfall is three inches a month, with most falling from August to December, and the least in the spring.

WHAT TO TAKE

If you are coming to Amsterdam to enjoy the city's architecture and historic monuments, bring comfortable footwear. The weather can be unpredictable, so even in summer bring clothing that will keep you warm and dry. When it does turn warm, the sun can be intense, so make sure you have hats and sunscreen—this is especially important if you plan to go cycling in the countryside, as there are very few trees to provide shade in the Dutch polder lands.

The Dutch are very informal, and you do not need to dress for dinner except in the grander hotel dining rooms. The same applies to business attire: A jacket and tie is all you need for most occasions—wearing a formal suit is not necessary.

Before leaving for the airport, check that you have your passport and any necessary visas, airline ticket and hotel confirmation, insurance documents, money, travelers' checks, and credit cards, and, if you plan to rent a car, your driver's license. Don't forget any prescription medicines that you might need for the duration of your trip.

INSURANCE

Be sure to arrange adequate cover for medical and travel emergencies, including the costs of hospital treatment, emergency surgery, and repatriation.

It's a good idea to take a photocopy of important documents, including your passport and driver's license, and make a note of credit card numbers, emergency telephone numbers, and travelers' check details. Keep these somewhere separate from the originals so that you can inform all the relevant authorities if they are stolen.

ENTRY FORMALITIES

VISAS

Visitors from the U.S., Canada, Australia, New Zealand, Israel, Japan, South Korea, the European Union, and most non-E.U. European countries can visit the Netherlands for up to three months without a visa. People visiting from other countries need to apply for a visa in advance from the Netherlands Embassy in their own country. To stay longer than three months, you should apply in advance to the Netherlands Embassy in your own country for a residents' permit, which is usually granted if you can prove that you have the means of supporting yourself and a legitimate reason for living in the city.

CUSTOMS

Arriving at Schiphol airport, you will find that Dutch customs officers are almost invisible. They are more concerned with the illegal importation of meat, fruit, plants, and endangered species than contraband goods—though smuggling of hard drugs will lead to prosecution, and there is still a limit to the amount of goods that you can legally import duty free, whether you are arriving from within the E.U. or from outside. These limits are: 200 cigarettes (or 50 cigars or 250 g [8.82 ounces] of tobacco); two liters of still wine and either one liter of spirits (over 22 percent alcohol) or two liters of fortified wine (less than 22 percent alcohol); 60 ml of perfume; other goods to the value of 170 euros (about US $175).

These limits can change so check at your departure airport. Visitors coming from within the E.U. can import an unlimited quantity of duty-paid goods providing they are intended for personal use, and not for commercial purposes.

CURRENCY

There are no currency restrictions in force in the Netherlands.

QUARANTINE

To protect the all-important Dutch horticultural and agricultural industries, strict rules apply to the importation of animals, plant material, and foodstuffs. Check with the Netherlands Embassy in your own country before your departure.

DRUGS & NARCOTICS

The Netherlands is one of the world's most liberal regimes when it comes to cannabis use, but the *quid pro quo* is that they do not tolerate the possession of hard drugs, such as cocaine, ecstasy, speed, LSD, and heroin or its derivatives. If you need to import pharmaceutical drugs for personal use, you can avoid potential problems by carrying a statement from your doctor explaining what they are being used for.

HOW TO GET TO AMSTERDAM

AIRLINES

Since Schiphol airport is one of the busiest hub airports in the world, you will have no difficulty in finding direct flights from most destinations. Major carriers offering the most frequent services include the Dutch national airline, KLM, and its U.S. partner, Northwest.

Airline offices in Amsterdam
British Airways tel 346 9559
bmi British Midland tel 346 9211
Delta tel 201 3536
EasyJet tel (023) 568 4880
KLM tel 474 7747
Northwest tel 555 9999
United tel 504 0555

AIRPORTS

Schiphol proudly boasts it is one of the world's most modern and efficient airports, and that is largely true, though the lack of baggage handling staff in recent years created the well-publicized and long-term problem of baggage delays. Through co-operation with the airlines and additional personnel, Schiphol management has attempted to solve this problem.

Delayed flights are not usually a problem, though freezing fog can create complications in winter, and this can have a follow-on effect if early flights are delayed. If you do happen to be stuck for an hour or so, consider visiting the **Nationaal Luchtvaartmuseum** (National Aerospace Museum), housed in the giant aluminum dome known as the Aviodome, at the center of the airport complex (*Westelijke Randweg 201, tel 406 8000; www.aviodome.nl*). On view are 30 historic aircraft, including the Fokker triplane of the Red Baron, the World War I German ace fighter pilot, as well as interesting displays on space exploration.

Schiphol is served by its own railroad station. The ticket office is immediately to the right of the arrivals area, and all staff speak English. Trains call at Schiphol every 15 minutes on their way to the city center. If you want Centraal Station, be sure to take trains indicated for Amsterdam CS, and not those indicated for Amsterdam RAI. The latter go to the congress and exhibition center in the southern suburbs of the city. Be sure to hold on to your belongings.

The train offers the fastest route in, but if you are staying at one of the major chain hotels, there is also a KLM Hotel Bus, which anyone can use, not just KLM passengers. The bus departs from the main entrance of the airport every 30 minutes

and stops at half a dozen of the main hotels—the exact route is posted by the bus stop. It is more expensive than the train, but saves you struggling from the station with your luggage.

Taxis are about four times more expensive than the bus, so it can be just as cheap to take a taxi if four people share. The stand is just outside the main exit. Allow 20 to 30 minutes from the airport to your hotel—more if you arrive in rush hour.

Airport inquiries tel 0900 0141; www.schiphol.nl

BOAT

The following companies offer car and foot passenger ferry services across the North Sea between England and the Netherlands.

Stenaline tel 08705 707070; www.stenaline.com. Day and night sailings (3.5 hours) between Harwich and the Hook of Holland.

P&O North Sea Ferries tel 01482 377177; www.ponsf.com. Overnight services (14 hours) between Hull and the Rotterdam Europoort.

DFDS Scandinavian Seaways tel 08705 333000; www.dfdsseaways.co.uk. Overnight services (14 hours) on even-numbered days from Newcastle to IJmuiden, and back again on odd-numbered days.

CAR

Amsterdam is at the hub of several trans-European motorways, and is easily reached by road from continental Europe. Drivers from the U.K. can bring their car using the ferry services (see above), or the Eurotunnel shuttle service linking Folkestone to the French terminus at Coquelles (*tel 0870 241 2938; www.eurotunnel.com*).

TRAIN

Amsterdam is easily reached by fast modern trains from all parts of continental Europe, with several trains a day from Paris, Brussels, Berlin, Cologne, Frankfurt, Luxembourg, and beyond (for details of international rail services see the website at www.ns.nl). From Britain, Eurostar services provide a seven-hour passenger service to Amsterdam via Brussels (tel 08705 186186; www.eurostar.com).

GETTING AROUND

BY CAR

If you drive to Amsterdam, you will need to find a parking lot on arrival. Fortunately Amsterdam has an excellent electronic system for signposting lots on all the main approach roads to the city. Not only do the signs tell you where to go, but also which ones have space and which are full. Parking is expensive, so it is worth checking whether your hotel offers free parking when you reserve. If not, then go for one of the following relatively inexpensive long-term parking lots:

ANWB Parking Prins Hendrikkade 20a, tel 638 5330; open 24 hours.
Europarking Marnixstraat 250, tel 623 6694; open 6.30 a.m.–1 a.m. Mon.–Thurs. and Sun.; to 2 a.m. Fri. and Sat.
De Kolk Parking Nieuwezijds Voorburgwal 12, tel 427 1449; open 24 hours.
Parking in the street is the most expensive option. Spaces are difficult to find and meters need feeding 9 a.m.–11 p.m. Traffic police are vigilant about booting vehicles that who overstay their allotted time, or towing away cars that are parked illegally. This is all part of a deliberate policy to discourage car use. If your car gets booted, the yellow sticker placed on your windshield will tell you where to call and how to pay the fine to secure the

release of your car. If your car is towed away, you will need to go to the fines office at Weesperstraat 105a (open 8:30 a.m.–4:30 p.m. Mon. to Sat.), taking your passport, driver's license, and a credit card, travelers' checks, or sufficient cash to pay the hefty fine—which escalates for every day that you delay collecting the car.

BY TRAM, BUS, & METRO

Amsterdam has a fully integrated transportation system, which means tickets are valid for all forms of transportation, all of which link up to provide a seamless transition from one to the next. The hub of the system is Centraal Station, from where buses and trams depart for all parts of the city. There is also a metro station here, and to the left (next to the VVV tourist office) of the metro entrance is the office of GVB, the authority that runs Amsterdam's public transportation, where you can buy tickets, travel cards, excursion packages, and route maps.

Of the three options, trams provide a comprehensive service within the city center, and buses are the best link to the suburbs. The metro is really intended for commuters and serves the big housing estates ringing the city. As a visitor, you may never need to use it, unless your hotel is a long way from the city center, or you go to the RAI Convention Center.

Tickets can be bought from machines at the entrance to the platform on metro stations, and on board as you enter buses and trams, but this is the most expensive option. The cheapest way is to buy a *strippenkaart* (strip card), a strip of tickets that you have to fold and stamp when you get on the bus or tram. The idea is to fold over one unit for each zone you will pass through, and one more,

then put the strip card into the slot on the yellow stamping machines located by the doors (and at the entrance to platforms on the metro). If this sounds complicated, be assured it is very simple in practice. The whole of the city center is in the Centrum zone, so you normally only need to fold over two units for a typical journey. If you are unsure how many strips to use, ask the driver to stamp your card; many buses and trams have a conductor at the rear who will do it for you. Because it is very easy, you will not be able to persuade a ticket inspector that you are a confused visitor if they undertake an inspection. Without a valid ticket you will be subject to a fine on the spot. Tickets are valid for one hour from the time you stamp them and you can change from one form of transportation to another as often as you wish within that time. If you are going to make regular use of the system, consider an **All Amsterdam Travel Pass,** valid for one day's unlimited travel on bus, tram, metro, and Canal Bus, or a travel card *(sterabonnement)* valid for a week, month, or year, for the metro, bus, and tram system. To buy a travel card, you need a passport photograph; there are photo booths in the entrance to Centraal Station.

BY WATER

Trams will take you to your destination fast, but if you want a more leisurely ride, you can take to the water. Canal boat services provide a more romantic way of getting around, but they are not part of the public transportation system and are relatively expensive—having said that, your tickets will give you discounted entry to a number of museums, and holders of All Amsterdam Travel Passes (see above) can use the Canal Bus system for free.

Canal Bus tel 623 9886; www.canal.nl. Operating similar

hours to the Museumboot, the Canal Bus offers a regular service along three different routes, with 11 stops located close to major sites and museums.

Museumboot tel 530 1090; www.lovers.nl. This service departs from opposite Centraal Station and circles the city counterclockwise, via Prinsengracht and Herengracht, stopping at six landing stages, each of which is close to a cluster of museums. The service departs every 45 minutes or so from 10 a.m. until 5 p.m., and the complete circuit takes 1 hour and 35 minutes, though the idea is to buy a day pass for unlimited travel and hop on and off the boat as you work your way around Amsterdam.

BY TAXI

Traveling by taxi really isn't necessary in Amsterdam, unless you happen to be carrying large amounts of luggage. You are not supposed to hail taxis in the street—stands can be found on or close to the main squares or at the train station. You can call a taxi using the central taxi control service by calling 677 7777.

BY BICYCLE

Renting a bicycle isn't cheap and it is quite a responsibility ensuring that the bike is secure at all times. You can take out insurance against the event of theft, but the policy only pays up if you can prove that the bike was securely fixed to an immovable object when it was stolen. You also have to get used to back pedaling in order to brake, and you need sharp wits to avoid a collision in the crowded streets of central Amsterdam. Renting on a quiet Sunday is a good way of gaining proficiency, and using the bike to get out of Amsterdam and into the Dutch countryside is definitely to be recommended (see pp. 214–17).

If you are nervous about heading off on your own, several companies offer guided bike tours of Amsterdam and the nearby countryside, including **Yellow Bike** (Nieuwezijds Kolk 29, tel 620 6940) and **Mike's Bikes** (tel 622 7970).

To rent a bike, you will be asked to leave a blank credit card slip, or your passport and a cash deposit. Reliable rental companies in the city center are:
Mac Bike Mr Visserplein 2, tel 620 0985 and Marnixstraat 220, tel 626 6964.
Rent-a-Bike Damstraat 20, tel 625 5029.
Take-a-Bike Stationsplein 12 (turn left as you exit Centraal Station; the store is at the end of the station building where it can be located in an underground store) tel 624 8391.

PRACTICAL ADVICE

COMMUNICATIONS

POST OFFICES
Amsterdam's main post office is at Singel 250 (tel 556 3311), to the rear of the Royal Palace, a short way down Raadhuisstraat. It provides all services and sells stationery and packaging materials (open 9 a.m.–6 p.m. Mon.–Wed. and Fri.; to 8 p.m. on Thurs.; 10 a.m.–1:30 p.m. on Sat; closed Sun).

Poste restante mail can be collected from this office provided you have some form of identity. The address is: Post Restante, Hoofdpostkantoor, Singel 250, 1016 AB Amsterdam, The Netherlands.

TELEPHONES
Green public phone booths are located on main streets all over Amsterdam. Most take phone cards rather than coins, but many also take credit cards— useful if you are making an international call, though the minimum charge means that you

shouldn't use this for local calls. Phone cards are sold at most tobacconists and newsstands. Off peak rates apply before 8 a.m., and after 8 p.m., and all weekend.

If you are phoning within Amsterdam, you don't need the Amsterdam code (020); phoning elsewhere you do. International calls are preceded by 00, then the country code (1 for the U.S.A., 44 for the U.K.), then the area code minus the initial 0, then the number. In the Netherlands, toll phone numbers are preceded by the code 0800; premium rate lines by the code 0900; and mobile phones by 06.

USEFUL TELEPHONE NUMBERS
International number inquiries 0900 8418
International operator 0800 0410
National number inquiries 0900 8008
National operator 0800 0101

ELECTRICITY

Dutch sockets are of the Continental two-pin type, so you need a converter to use equipment with U.S. or U.K. plugs. The voltage (220, 50-cyle AC) is fine for U.K. equipment, but to use lower-voltage U.S. equipment you need a transformer.

ETIQUETTE & LOCAL CUSTOMS

The Dutch are very informal, and you are unlikely to cause offense unless you behave in a drunken or loutish manner. Nobody dresses up to go out except for the most formal of restaurants. Business attire is smart casual. Shake hands on meeting and parting until you know someone well; thereafter, it is normal for men to kiss women and for women to kiss other women three times lightly on alternate cheeks.

PRACTICAL ADVICE

The Dutch don't like people to call around uninvited—always make an appointment, and be punctual. If you are invited to someone's house, take a gift of flowers, chocolates, or pastries.

Birthdays are very important—but it is expected that the person whose birthday it is should buy the presents! Children take candy to share with their close friends, and grown-ups take pastries or cookies to work to share with colleagues over coffee. Morning coffee is a much-loved daily ritual, but the Dutch style is to use evaporated milk in coffee rather than fresh milk or cream.

FESTIVALS & EVENTS

See also National holidays (p. 242)

JANUARY
New Year Celebrated by dressing up, drinking too much, and letting off fireworks.

MARCH
Stille Omgang (Silent Procession) On the first Sunday in March, devout Catholics celebrate the Miracle of Amsterdam with a silent candle-lit procession along Heiligeweg (Holy Way), the city center street where the miracle took place (see p. 24) and on through the Red Light District. Tel (023) 524 6229.

APRIL
National Museum Weekend On a weekend in mid-April, state-run museums throughout the Netherlands open their doors for free and mount special events, with extended opening hours. www.museumweekend.nl

Koninginnedag (The Queen's Birthday) The Queen's official birthday, on April 30, is an excuse for a huge city-wide street party. This has little to do with royalist sentiment (though the royal family is held in great affection

by the Dutch) and is really a means of letting off steam after the rigors of winter—where Catholic countries have carnival, the Calvinistic Dutch have come up with this instead.

MAY
Herdenkingsdag and Bevrijdingsdag (Remembrance Day and Liberation Day) The center of Amsterdam comes to a halt at 7:30 p.m. when the Queen emerges from the Royal Palace to cross Dam Square and lay a wreath at the foot of the Nationaal Monument, in honor of the war dead of the Netherlands and its dependencies. Two minutes silence is observed from 8 p.m. The following day is a national holiday celebrating the liberation of the Netherlands from Nazi rule on May 5, 1945. The gay community holds its own ceremony at the Homomonument to highlight the Nazi persecution of homosexuals.

JUNE
Holland Festival The popular annual month-long Holland Festival is a nationwide celebration of the very best in the international performing arts. The program features top names in dance, music, and theater, and there are plenty of free fringe events. Tel 530 7111, www.hollandfestival.nl

AUGUST
Grachtenfestival During mid-August there are free chamber concerts given by orchestras and choral groups at various locations around the canal circle, but principally from a floating pontoon moored in front of the Pulitzer Hotel (see p. 252). Tel 421 4542.

SEPTEMBER
Bloemen Corso (Flower Parade) Summer ends with another burst of color from this spectacular parade of floats, decorated with millions of

flower blooms. It starts from the international flower auction in Aalsmeer, in the southern suburbs, and makes its slow way via Leidseplein and Spuistraat to Dam, arriving at 4 p.m. for a reception in the Royal Palace, then returning by floodlight at 9 p.m. Tel (029) 732 5100.

Open Monumentendag (Open Monument Days)
Whether you are an architecture buff or just a busybody, you'll love this opportunity to see inside some of Amsterdam's finest historic monuments, from public buildings and Golden Bend mansions turned into offices to private houses. If there's a Monumenten flag flying outside, it's an invitation to knock on the door and go in. www.openmonumentendag.nl

DECEMBER
Sinterklaas Intocht (Feast of St. Nicholas) As well as being the avuncular, present-bearing figure of Christmas cards and street decorations, St. Nicholas was also the patron saint of seafarers, and so his feast day, on December 6, has always been as important a celebration in Amsterdam as Christmas Day itself. The somewhat commercialized Sinterklaas Intocht (Arrival of Santa Claus) is celebrated in mid-November, when St. Nicholas steps ashore in front of Centraal Station, with his retinue of black-faced helpers (called Zwaarte Pieten, Black Peter) to help him deliver presents, ostensibly having sailed from Moorish Spain. This signals the start of the build-up to Christmas, and on December 5, the eve of St. Nicholas Feast Day, the Zwaarte Pieten are kept busy climbing up and down chimneys to deliver presents to sleeping children. These gifts are opened the next day—the grown-ups join in the fun by exchanging small gifts (often practical jokes) and poems that poke fun at the recipient's habits and temperament.

FURTHER READING

Amsterdam, a brief life of the city, by Geert Mak. This entertaining and intelligent history of the city was written by one of Amsterdam's best-known journalists and commentators.

The Undutchables, by Colin White and Laurie Boucke. Written by Americans who lived and worked in Amsterdam for many years, this humorous account of the Dutch and their culture explains what they really think about Sex 'n Drugs and Rock 'n Roll, how to behave on your birthday (a very important celebration for them), and how to haggle in the flea markets.

The Holland Handbook, edited by Stephanie Dijkstra. Described as the indispensable reference book for the expatriate, this is full of practical information for anyone intending to live in the Netherlands, whether for a few weeks or several years. It covers everything from starting your own business to getting your children into a Dutch school.

Building Amsterdam, by Herman Janse. All you need to know to understand the architecture of Amsterdam, with meticulously hand-drawn sections to explain the different parts of a typical canalside house.

The Diary of Anne Frank: the critical edition, edited by David Barnouw and Gerrold van der Stroom. There are numerous editions of the famous wartime diary of Anne Frank, but this is the best because it provides the complete text of the diaries, including material that was cut from many editions because it was considered too personal.

The Embarassment of Riches, by Simon Schama. Some would say that Simon Schama's prose is itself embarrassingly prolix, but there are many who enjoy reading his speculative and highly subjective account of Dutch cultural history.

Rembrandt's Eyes, by Simon Schama. Another mammoth tome full of psychological speculation about the life and mind of the great Dutch artist and an insight into the wider meanings of his works.

Love in Amsterdam, by Nicolas Freeling. One of numerous detective stories set in Amsterdam in which detective Van der Valk probes a mystery and comes up with an unexpected result.

The Girl with a Pearl Earring, by Tracy Chevalier. This historical novel is set in the 1660s and concerns a 16-year-old girl called Griet who is hired as a servant in the household of the Dutch painter Johannes Vermeer. The story is full of information about the life and work of the artist.

Tulip Fever, by Deborah Moggach. Another historical novel set in 17th-century Amsterdam, this riotous book concerns the antics of painter Jan van Loos against the background of the speculative market for rare tulips.

LIQUOR & NARCOTICS LAWS

Individuals can legally buy and consume alcohol from the age of 16. Supermarkets and shops can only sell beer and wine or alcoholic beverages with an upper alcohol limit of 13 percent. Spirits are only sold from liquor stores.

Amsterdam takes a remarkably lenient view of drug consumption. Some years ago, the Dutch decided that soft drug use was no worse than alcohol consumption, and did not warrant being treated as a criminal activity. At first the authorities let it be known that they would turn a blind eye to so-called "coffee shops," where hash is sold and consumed. More recently, they have had to apply for a license, which means

meeting minimum standards of hygiene and medical knowledge.

MEDIA

NEWSPAPERS
You can buy the world's leading newspapers and magazines from the Athenaeum Nieuwscentrum on Spui, Waterstone's (Kalverstraat 152), or the American Book Center (Kalverstraat 185). The Dutch read *De Telegraaf* (establishment) and *De Volkskrant* (progressive).

TELEVISION
It is very likely that you will have access to satellite TV from your hotel room, and with it a bewildering choice of TV stations in all the main European languages. Dutch television is rather dull, so most people in Amsterdam watch the BBC or MTV.

RADIO
As you will hear if you take a taxi, most people listen to Radio 3, the commercial pop and chat channel (91.5 FM). More serious talk radio and news is broadcast (in Dutch) on Radio 5 (1008 AM).

INTERNET SITES
There are two official tourist office websites worth looking at: www.holland.com covers the whole of the Netherlands, and www.visitamsterdam.com focuses on the city. Both contain good up-to-date information on events and exhibitions, as well as general information and an on-line accommodations reservations service.

MONEY MATTERS
The euro is the official currency of the Netherlands. Euro banknotes and coins were introduced in January 2002. Banknotes are in denominations of 5, 10, 20, 50, 100, 200, and 500 euros, while coins are in denominations of 1 and 2 euros, as well as 1, 2, 5, 10, 20, and 50 cents. The Netherlands' former currency, the guilder, went out of circulation in early 2002.

Euro travelers' checks are widely accepted as are major credit cards, and you can use your debit card or credit card to draw euronotes from an ATM.

The GWK bank in Centraal Station is open 7 a.m.–midnight for foreign currency exchange, cashing Euro checks and travelers' checks, and drawing cash on debit or credit cards.

MUSEUM YEAR CARDS

Anyone who stays in Amsterdam for a week or so and visits the major museums will save money by buying a Museum Jaarkaart (Museum Year Card). These are available from museums or VVV tourist offices and admit you free to all state-run museums throughout the Netherlands, including Amsterdam's big three, the Rijksmuseum, the Van Gogh Museum, and the Stedelijk Museum. They do not, however, admit you to any special exhibitions, where a separate admission charge applies. To buy a year card you need a passport-sized photograph, available from photo booths in the entrance hall to Centraal Station.

NATIONAL HOLIDAYS

Very little closes in Amsterdam except on the three big occasions of New Year's Day, the Queen's Birthday (April 30), and Christmas Day. In addition, the following are also public holidays; some dates vary from year to year according to the liturgical calendar:
Good Friday
Easter Monday
Liberation Day (May 5)
Ascension Day (May or June)
Whitmonday (June)
St. Stephen (December 26)

OPENING TIMES

Banks Mon.–Fri. 9 a.m.–4 or 5 p.m.
Post offices Mon.–Fri. 9 a.m.

–5:30 p.m., Sat. 10 a.m.–1 p.m.
Stores Mon.–Fri. 9 a.m.–5:30 p.m, Sat. 10 a.m.–5 p.m. Thursday is late night shopping when many stores open until 9 p.m., and while some close on Monday mornings, many are now open on Sunday.
Pharmacies Open during shop hours, and on a rotation schedule to cover nights and weekends.

RELIGION

All religions are represented in Amsterdam, with Islamic mosques and prayer centers growing in number even as church-going among the Dutch declines. English-language services take place at 10:30 a.m. and 7:30 p.m. on Sunday at Christ Church (Anglican; Groenburgwal 42, tel 441 0355); and at 10:30 a.m. at the English Reformed Church (Church of Scotland/Presbyterian; Begijnhof 48, tel 624 9665). Catholic Mass is said in English at 10:30 a.m. and noon every Sunday at the Church of the Holy Family (Zaaiersweg 180, tel 465 2711) and in Latin at 9:30 a.m. on Sunday at De Krijtberg church (Singel 448, tel 623 1923). For information on Orthodox Jewish services, tel 646 0046, and for Liberal Jewish services, tel 644 2619. Details of prayer times and other activities in the Muslim community are available from the Islamic Cultural Center (tel 698 2526).

REST ROOMS

Men are reasonably well provided for, with olive green, Parisian-style pissoirs located all around the city center. These rather smelly, historic artifacts are being replaced by mobile plastic pissoirs which, instead of draining straight into the nearest canal, are lifted on to the back of a truck and carted away when they need emptying.

Streetside public conveniences are otherwise very rare—

traditionally people use café rest rooms, but these are only for customers, so you should buy a drink before using the facilities. Museums and public buildings all have clean modern facilities.

TIME DIFFERENCES

The Netherlands observes Central European Time, one hour ahead of Greenwich Mean Time in winter (end October to end March) and two hours ahead in summer.

TIPPING

Value added tax and service charges are included in hotel, restaurant, and shopping bills, and taxi fares. Tips for extra service are not necessary in cafés or bars unless you feel the service was outstanding, in which case give the tip directly to the server or bartender, rather than leaving it on the table. In restaurants, a tip of five to ten percent is always appreciated but not necessary: pay the waiter directly by rounding up the bill. Taxi fares are already high and Amsterdammers don't give tips on principle, especially if the driver behaves as if he or she is doing you a favor, or if they get you lost or give you a bad ride. If you get a good driver, tip up to about ten percent of the fare.

Some rest rooms have a notice posted stating the charge for using the toilet—if not, a tip of 50 cents is normal.

TOURIST OFFICES

Tourist information services are provided by the VVV (pronounced Fay Fay Fay in Dutch).
There are two branches in Centraal Station: one on Platform 2, and one on Stationsplein, the waterfront opposite the station entrance (see p. 49). Both open daily 9 a.m.–5 p.m.
As well as providing an on-the-

spot accommodations service, the VVV sells maps, listings magazines and guide books, and provides a ticket agency for concerts, plays, and guided tours. The VVV has become increasingly commerical and charges for all its services. Information can be obtained far more effectively by asking your hotel concierge or going to the official tourist office website (www.holland.com and www.visitamsterdam.com). There is also a telephone inquiry service (tel 0900 400 4040) but this charges a premium rate and it can take time to get through (and at present it only operates weekdays).

TRAVELERS WITH DISABILITIES

The Netherlands is one of the most progressive countries in the world when it comes to providing access and information for travelers with disabilities, and those hotels, museums and buildings that meet minimum standards promote themselves by using the international accessibility symbol. Tourist offices have full information on disabled facilities, and they include this information in their published literature. Mobility International Nederland (tel 0343 521795) gives advice on suitable accommodations in Amsterdam, and throughout the Netherlands.

VISITOR INFORMATION

Day by Day is the most comprehensive English-language listings magazine. It is published monthly by the Amsterdam Tourist Office and is available free in hotels, or for a small charge from tourist offices.

EMERGENCIES

CRIME & POLICE

The Amsterdam police speak English, and, as they say in their

guidance notes for visitors to the city, they have just seen just about every excess of human behavior, so don't be afraid of asking them for help. There are police stations in central Amsterdam at Beursstraat 33 (just off Damrak), at Nieuwezijds Voorburgwal 104, Marnixstraat 148, and also at Elandsgracht 117. These are the stations to visit if you have been robbed or need help for whatever reason. The police will take a statement, cancel your credit cards, provide telephone facilities, and help with contacting your embassy if necessary.

EMBASSIES/ CONSULATES

Canadian Embassy Sophialaan 7, The Hague (tel 070 311 1600)
American Consulate Museumplein 19, Amsterdam (tel 575 5309).
British Consulate Koningslaan 44, Amsterdam (tel 676 4343)

EMERGENCY PHONE NUMBERS

Police, fire or ambulance 112
24-hour pharmacy 694 8709
24-hour medical advice 592 3434
24-hour dental advice 570 9595

HEALTH

There are no health risks involved in visiting Amsterdam other than those that are self-created. HIV/AIDS is a real threat and if you are at all worried you can call the AIDS Helpline (tel 0900 20420 40, 24 hours). The Samaritans have a Helpline with English-speaking staff (tel 675 7575). For contraception advice, try the family planning center at Aletta Jacobshuis, Overtoom 323 (tel 616 6222 for an appointment). If you are worried about drugs, call the Jellinek Drugs Prevention Center on 626 7176. The nearest outpatients' department for medical emergencies is the

VU Ziekenhuis, De Boelelann 1117 (tel 444 4444).

LOST OR STOLEN CREDIT CARDS

American Express tel 504 8000, or 504 8666 after 6 p.m.
Diners Club tel 0800-0334 toll free or 654 5500
MasterCard tel 030 283 5555
Visa tel 660 0611

LOST PROPERTY

If you lose something on a train you can go to the lost property office at Stationsplein 15 (tel 030 235 3923, Mon.–Fri. 8 a.m.–8 p.m.; Sat. 9–5). Items lost on a bus, tram, or the metro are held at the GVB Lost Property Office, Prins Hendrikkade 108–114 (tel 460 5858). For property lost elsewhere, try the local police station first, then the lost and found office at Stephensonstraat 18 (some way out of town, near Amstel station), open weekdays only 9:30–3:30 (tel 559 3005).

WHAT TO DO IN A CAR ACCIDENT

If anyone is injured you must dial 112 and call the emergency services without delay. Otherwise, move the vehicles so they are not causing an obstruction and exchange names, addresses, telephone numbers, and registration numbers and ask to see the other party's driver's license to confirm these details. Try also to take the details of any independent witnesses. You should also make a note of the events leading to the collision, with sketch drawings, which you may need as part of your insurance claim. The Royal Dutch Touring Club (ANWB) offers an emergency breakdown service (tel 0800 0888) which you can join on the spot (you may already have reciprocal membership if you belong to a motoring organization in your home country).

HOTELS & RESTAURANTS

Amsterdam is one of Europe's most popular weekend break destinations, and this small city does not have enough hotel rooms to meet the demand. As a result, hoteliers are able to charge premium rates for what are often second-rate accommodations. The way to avoid the worst hotels is to give yourself maximum choice by making a reservation well ahead of your visit. This is true no matter what time of year you plan to travel. Even outside of the main holiday season, the city hosts trade fairs, events, and conferences that can easily take up all the budget- and mid-priced accommodations in the city.

HOTELS

Online reservations

Several websites offer on-line reservation services.
www.holland-hotels.com An excellent site representing budget to deluxe hotels, including apartments and houseboats. Details of availability, special offers, and tariffs. Pictures show rooms; maps show precise locations.
www.visitamsterdam.nl The official site of the Amsterdam Board of Tourism. This has a search engine and on-line reservation facility. Comprehensive, but not always up-to-date information on availability.
www.holland.com The official website of the Netherlands Board of Tourism. Click on "Where to stay" to inquire about accommodations by type and by destination.

Reservations

If you have to go to Amsterdam on short notice and all rooms are full, you can try reserving a room by calling at the tourist office at the airport. This office is often less busy than the ones in downtown Amsterdam. If all the hotels within your price bracket are fully reserved, consider staying in another nearby town or city like Haarlem or Utrecht, and commuting to Amsterdam by train. Hotel prices in Dutch provincial towns can be much cheaper than in Amsterdam.

Hotel facilities

Most hotels in Amsterdam do not have bars, business centers, health clubs, tennis courts, swimming pools, etc. Many are in historic buildings where planning laws prohibit structural changes and so don't have elevators, air-conditioning, or facilities for guests with disabilities.

Avoiding problems

Wise travelers always check the precise location of their hotel: Beware weekend-break packages that advertise their hotels as being in central Amsterdam when they are really located out in the southern suburbs. If the hotel is close to a tram or metro stop, there is no problem, but many people discover too late that "central Amsterdam hotel" does not always mean what it says. Use the www.visitamsterdam.nl website to find out exactly how close you are to the center and to public transportation.

Check the location of your room in the hotel. Many hotels overlook busy streets and not all of them have adequate sound-proofing or air-conditioning. Rooms at the rear may be preferable to a room with a view that overlooks a busy street.

RESTAURANTS

You can eat very well in Amsterdam, choosing from a great range of cuisines and at reasonable prices. With the exception of one or two large Chinese dim sum palaces, this is a city of small characterful restaurants, with a strong ethnic contribution from the former Dutch colonies of Indonesia and Surinam. The cooking in ethnic restaurants is likely to be authentic and traditional, not adapted to Western tastes, and all the more enjoyable for that. Vegetarians are also well catered to—almost every restaurant and café will have meat-free dishes on the menu.

The restaurant scene in Amsterdam is unlike that in New York or London, which has star chefs and signature dishes; it's mostly one level up from the café, serving basic food to customers who don't want frills.

If you have set your heart on a particular restaurant, always reserve earlier in the day (you should also double check if you want to pay by credit card—some restaurants insist on levying a surcharge). Most of the city's restaurants are small and intimate, with seating for no more than 40 or so customers. On Thursday (late-night shopping), Friday, and Saturday nights, tables fill fast. Once you have a table, nobody will hassle you to eat up and move on. The notion of turning tables over twice in an evening is alien to the Dutch temperament. You must remember to ask for the bill at the end of the meal: It is considered rude for the server to bring the bill before you are ready to go.

The flipside is that service can be slow. Nobody seems to mind

---

PRICES	

HOTELS
An indication of the cost of a double room without breakfast is given by **$** signs

$$$$$	Over $200
$$$$	$150–$200
$$$	$100–$150
$$	$75–$100
$	Under $75

RESTAURANTS
An indication of the cost of a three course dinner without drinks is given by $ signs

$$$$$	Over $75
$$$$	$50–$75
$$$	$35–$50
$$	$20–$35
$	Under $20

---

this, because eating out is seen as a social activity, with as much emphasis on drinking and chatting as on eating.

Only the grander restaurants have designated non-smoking areas—even where restaurants try to accommodate those who dislike tobacco smoke, the gesture is rendered futile by the lack of adequate air-conditioning. Hotels and restaurants listed are arranged alphabetically by price category in each district.
L = lunch D = dinner

NIEUWE ZIJDE

HOTELS

🏨 GOLDEN TULIP GRAND HOTEL 🍴 KRASNAPOLSKY
$$$$$
DAM 9, 1012 JS
TEL 554 9111
FAX 622 8607
E-MAIL book@krasnapolsky.nl
www.krasnapolsky.nl
This luxurious 19th-century hotel offers views of the copper-domed Royal Palace rooftop and the festive crowds in the central square from the rooms at the front of the hotel. It also has some 36 furnished apartments in restored historic houses, which are ideal for families. The belle epoque decor is stunning. Breakfast and lunch are served in the monumental glass-roofed Winter Garden, while dinner choices include the intimate and elegant Brasserie Reflet, the Shibli Bedouin restaurant, or one of two Japanese restaurants.
🛗 469 🍽 150 ⬛ ⬛
🍸 ⬛ All major cards

🏨 HOTEL DE L'EUROPE
🍴 $$$$$
NIEUWEZIJDS DOELENSTRAAT 2–8, 1012 CP
TEL 531 1777
FAX 531 1778
E-MAIL hotel@leurope.nl
www.leurope.nl
Built in the grand style in

1896 (renovated in 1995), the l'Europe stands on the site of a medieval bastion at the junction of several canals, so it is almost entirely surrounded by water. A water taxi will carry you here, if you wish, and the waterside setting can be enjoyed from many of the spacious balconied rooms. The Empire-style Excelsior Restaurant counts as one of the best in Amsterdam for haute cuisine.
🛗 100 🍽 50 ⬛ ⬛
⬛ 🍸 All major cards

🏨 CROWNE PLAZA 🍴 AMSTERDAM CITY CENTER
$$$$
NIEUWEZIJDS VOORBURGWAL 5, 1012 RC
TEL 521 1737
FAX 620 1173
E-MAIL info@crowneplaza.nl
www.crowneplaza.nl
This hotel in the heart of the city is popular with American visitors and business travelers. The elegant rooms have everything you could want, and if you splurge out on one of the 50 Club rooms, you enjoy exclusive use of the Club Lounge, with its roof terrace and views over central Amsterdam. The Dorrius Restaurant re-creates 17th-century ambience in a modern building, and the menu features Dutch delicacies, from Zeeland oysters to traditional "hotchpotch," updated for modern tastes.
🛗 270 🍽 45 ⬛ ⬛
⬛ 🍸 All major cards

🏨 DIE PORT VAN CLEVE 🍴 $$$
NIEUWEZIJDS VOORBURGWAL 176–180
TEL 624 4860
FAX 622 0240
E-MAIL dieportvancleve .amsterdam@wxs.nl
www.dieportvancleve.nl
Standing next to the Magna Plaza shopping center in the

heart of the city, Die Port van Cleve is popular with Dutch visitors as well as people from further afield because of its central location and reasonable prices. The Brasserie De Poort and the blue-tiled Bodega De Blauwe Parade serve traditional Dutch food; sample authentic *erwtensoep* (pea soup), delicious Zeeland mussels, or you could order steak and hope to be the lucky winner of the free bottle of wine that comes with every thousandth one ordered.
🛗 120 ⬛ 🍸 All major cards

🏨 NOVA
$$
NIEUWEZIJDS VOORBURGWAL 276–280, 1012 RS
TEL 623 0066
FAX 627 2026
E-MAIL novahotel@wxs.nl
www.bookings.nl/hotels/nova
This rambling hotel is very well placed for exploring the city center and canal circle. The bright rooms have modern furniture, and all have a refrigerator. It is popular at weekends, so you may have difficulty making a reservation at short notice for Friday through Sunday night, but weekdays are less busy. If you are traveling as a family, ask about the larger rooms, some of which have small kitchens.
🛗 59 ⬛ ⬛
⬛ 🍸 All major cards

🏨 FLYING PIG DOWNTOWN
$
NIEUWENDIJK 100, 1012 MR
TEL 420 6822
E-MAIL headoffice@flyingpig.nl
www.flyingpig.nl
This excellent two-hostel chain for young people offers single and twin rooms and dormitories sleeping four, six, or eight people. All rooms have showers and toilets, and there is a communal kitchen and a lively bar. The comfort and rock-bottom prices ensures a line of would-be

HOTELS & RESTAURANTS

guests. You can reserve on-line, and if the hotel is full, call on the morning of your intended visit and ask to be put on the standby list. Of the two hostels, the Downtown branch in Amsterdam's main shopping street is noisier but more popular. Lighter sleepers might prefer the Palace, at Vossuistraat 46, in the Museum Quarter (tel 421 0583).

🛏 150 💳 MC, V

RESTAURANTS

SOMETHING SPECIAL

🍴 LUCIUS

Deliberately frugal, Lucius is simply one of the best places to eat fish in Amsterdam. The white-tiled walls are bare except for the blackboards that tell you what is freshest and best that day—if in doubt, go for the gargantuan seafood platter and work your way through an exotic plateful of shellfish and crustaceans. Smart-suited business executives come here as well as families with children.

$$$$
SPUISTRAAT 247
TEL 624 1831
🍴 80 🚋 Tram 1, 2, 5
🕐 Closed L daily 🚭
💳 All major cards

🍴 SUPPER CLUB

$$$$
JONGE ROELENSTEEG 21
TEL 638 0513
www.supperclub.nl
Where else but in Amsterdam would a restaurant turn eating into a sensual experience? Instead of tables expect to dine Arabian style, seated on big white mattresses with plump cushions. Everyone eats the same international-style dishes created with flair by chefs who perform in the open kitchen. Dancers and magicians entertain, and there is a resident masseur. On theme nights, the decor and food are coordinated

and projectors throw images onto the walls—street scenes, works of art. Reservations are compulsory. Go as a group and don't take things too seriously!

🍴 150 🚋 Trams 1, 2, 5, 🚭
🚭 💳 All major cards

🍴 IE KLAS

CENTRAAL STATION,
STATIONSPLEIN 15
$–$$$
TEL 625 0131
Also known as Eersteklas, this atmospheric restaurant occupies the former first-class waiting room on Platform 2b of Amsterdam's Centraal Station. Aproned waiters serve everything from burgers (perfectly cooked from prime ingredients) to classic Dutch and French dishes beneath the high ceilings and frescoed walls of this fine building. In doing so they continue the European tradition of excellence in providing travelers, and anyone else who cares to drop by, with a very high standard of catering.

🍴 45 🚇 Centraal Station Metro, all buses and trams to Centraal Station
🚢 Museumboot & Canal Bus to Centraal Station
💳 All major cards

🍴 HET BEGIJNTJE

$$$
BEGIJNENSTEEG 6
TEL 624 0528
Called the "Little Nun," this French-style restaurant is located in a converted coach house looking into the cloistered Begijnhof, a lovely setting that is best appreciated in summer, when you can eat in the sheltered courtyard. The Begijntje serves a fixed-price daily menu, which includes one or two options for each course, but if you have particular preferences or dislikes, it is worth checking the menu at the time you make your reservation.

🍴 60 🚋 Trams 1, 2, 5
🕐 Closed Sun. 🚭 💳 No credit cards

🍴 HAESJE CLAES

$$
SPUISTRAAT 273–275
TEL 624 9998
With its old wood paneling and Delft tiles, the Haesje Claes is everyone's idea of the cozy old Amsterdam of an Old Master painting. Some people say it suffers from being too popular, and that the service doesn't always match the charm of the surroundings, but with an extensive menu of traditional Dutch and international dishes, it has something for everyone. Look out for the gerookte paling (smoked eel) and zalmssouffle (salmon soufflé).

🍴 150 🚋 Trams 1, 2, 5 🚭
🚭 💳 All major cards

🍴 LUXEMBOURG

$$
SPUISTRAAT 22–24
TEL 620 6264
Re-creating the atmosphere of the Parisian Left Bank, this very popular bar-cum-brasserie is the meeting place for Amsterdam university students and lecturers, arty types working in the worlds of publishing, advertising, and the media, and a broad cross-section of visitors to the city who come for the reading table, where you can browse magazines and newspapers from all over the world. If you want, you can simply linger over a coffee or sample snacks from a menu that is as eclectic as its clientele, ranging from Chinese dim sum to delicious patisseries.

🍴 80 🚋 Tram 1, 2, 5 💳 All major cards

🍴 PANINI

$$
VIJZELGRACHT 3–5
TEL 626 4939
Caffeine freaks should know that this small Italian café

came top in a local survey to find the city's best coffee. As the name suggests, Panini sells bread-based snacks—including delicious focaccia warm from the oven, pizzas, ciabatta, and filled rolls of various kinds. In the evening, you can also sit down to an informal and inexpensive bowl of pasta and a glass of good wine.

🛗 20　🚋 Trams 16, 24, 25
🚭 All major cards

OUDE ZIJDE

HOTELS

🏨 GOLDEN TULIP
🍴 BARBIZON PALACE
$$$$$
PRINS HENDRIKKADE 59–72, 1012 AD
TEL 556 4564
FAX 624 3353
E-MAIL
info@gtbpalace.goldentulip.nl
www.hotelbook.com/goldentulip
Opposite Centraal Station, this deluxe establishment is a blend of old and new, incorporating the facades of 19 gabled houses from the Golden Age, and hung with Dutch Master paintings. Split-level rooms with ancient oak beams contrast with the neoclassical splendor of the atrium, with its marble pillars and sail-shaped drapes. The distinctive Vermeer restaurant has been awarded a Michelin star for its classical French food, and it occasionally plays host to guest chefs offering a wide variety of cuisines.

🛏 274　🛗 50　🔁 🚭 🔆
🐧 🚭 All major cards

🏨 THE GRAND SOFITEL
🍴 DEMEURE
$$$$$
OUDEZIJDS VOORBURGWAL 197, 1012 EX
TEL 555 3111
FAX 626 6286
E-MAIL hotel@thegrand.nl
www.thegrand.nl
First a royal residence, then

the City Hall, and later the Admiralty from where Holland's powerful navy was controlled, this splendid historic building in the heart of the old city is now Amsterdam's most luxurious hotel, the favored haunt of visiting rock stars and pop royalty. History comes as standard in all the magnificent rooms, many with delightful views. Luxury and grandeur extend to the hotel's dining room, the Café Roux, a stylish restaurant serving classic French dishes, but with the added lightness of touch that characterizes the style of Albert Roux, the renowned Michelin-starred chef, who supervised the concept.

🛏 182　🛗 35　🔁 🚭 🔆
🐧 🐦 🚭 All major cards

🏨 WINSTON
$$
WARMOESSTRAAT 129, 1012 JA
TEL 623 1380
FAX 639 2308
E-MAIL winston@winston.nl
www.winston.nl
You would think that a location in the Red Light District close to all-night bars and sex shops would be a disadvantage, but plenty of people love the Winston Hotel because it is a pulsating place to stay, the antidote to too much lace, Delftware, and tulips. The hotel has a growing number of "art rooms," designed "to get art out of the frames and into your head." Various Dutch contemporary artists have been given free rein to decorate every available surface so that rooms have become works of art. Visit its excellent website to see exactly what that means. The hotel also has some very large rooms capable of sleeping up to six people—sharing the costs with friends can make this a very cheap hotel in which to stay.

🛏 67　🔁 🚭 🚭 All major cards

RESTAURANTS

SOMETHING SPECIAL

🍴 THE BALMORAL
Proof that Amsterdam has every kind of exotic cuisine is this romantic candlelit restaurant specializing in Scottish cuisine. For those unfamiliar with one of the world's up-and-coming food styles, this isn't all neeps (boiled turnips) and haggis (a savory mixture of lamb, oatmeal, onion, and herbs) though they feature on the list of starters. Instead it is based upon tender and tasty organic beef, wild salmon, seafood, venison, and game, in season. Scottish single malt whisky is the natural accompaniment, and there are more than 85 to choose from.

$$$
NIEUWE DOELENSTRAAT 24
TEL 554 0600
🛗 50　🚋 Trams 4, 9, 14, 16, 20, 24, 25　🕐 Closed L daily
🔆 🚭 AE, MC, V

🍴 CENTRA
$$$
LANGE NIEZEL 29
TEL 622 3050
Friendly Spanish tapas bar and café, where you cannot help but make friends as you sit at long communal wooden tables. You can point to dishes that you like the look of but don't know how to name, or you can ask the mostly Spanish regulars for a recommendation.

🛗 40　🚋 Trams 4, 9, 14, 16, 20, 24, 25　🚭 No credit cards

🍴 BIRD THAIS
$$
ZEEDIJK 72–74
TEL 620 1442
Originally just a snack bar, Bird proved so popular that the owners opened this restaurant across the street where you can enjoy generous portions of genuine Thai street food seated at wooden tables in

HOTELS & RESTAURANTS

one of several small rooms. Try the *tomyam* soup (shrimp and lemongrass) or *pad thai* (noodles with a choice of meat or vegetable garnishes).
🎟 50 🚋 Trams 4, 9, 16, 20, 24, 25 🕐 Closed L daily ⊘ ♿ ⬣ All major cards

🍴 DE BRAKKE GROND
$$
NES 43
TEL 626 0044
Tucked away down the alley that runs behind the Grand Hotel Krasnapolsky, De Brakke Grond is a cultural center specializing in the promotion of all things Flemish—the Belgian cousins of the Dutch. As well as an extensive wine list, the menu recommends various Belgian beers as accompaniments to each of the dishes, which range from truffle-flavored meat casseroles to the freshest of fish. Eat in the wood-paneled main dining room or on the tranquil patio.
🎟 50 🚋 Trams 4, 9, 16, 24, 25 ⊘ ♿ ⬣ All major cards

SOMETHING SPECIAL

🍴 HEMELSE MODDER
The fixed-price menu at this excellent restaurant is stylish and innovative, combining French and Italian influences. Each day there is a choice of meat and fish dishes, and the vegetarian menu features spicy Indonesian-style curries and stir fries. Originally set up by squatters, the restaurant is now professionally run, but still attracts a youthful clientele.
$$
OUDE WAAL 9
TEL 624 3203
🎟 50 🚋 22, 32, 33, 34, 35, 36, 39 🕐 Closed L daily & Mon. ⊘ ♿ ⬣ AE, MC, V

🍴 LA MARGARITA
$$
LANGEBRUGSTEEG 6
TEL 624 0529

Powerful margaritas and large portions are the secret of this friendly Mexican restaurant; head for the roof terrace for the best views, especially at sunset. Fish fans will enjoy the ceviche—raw fish marinated in zingy lime juice.
🎟 40 🚋 Trams 1, 2, 4, 9, 14, 16, 20, 24, 25 🕐 Closed L daily, and Mon. ⊘ ♿ ⬣ All major cards

🍴 NAM KEE
$$
ZEEDIJK 111 & GELDERSEKADE 117
TEL 624 3470 (ZEEDIJK);
TEL 639 2848 (GELDERSEKADE)
Nam Kee's Zeedijk branch is almost synonymous with Amsterdam's Chinatown—there is even a novel named after it (*The Oysters of Nam Kee* by Kees van Beijnum). The Geldersekade branch, around the corner, is less frenetic and slightly more upscale. The service can be brusque, but that doesn't stop people flocking for some of the best and cheapest food in town, including *ma pa tofu* (bean curd with black bean and garlic sauce) or sizzling scallops.
🎟 150 🚋 Trams 4, 9, 16, 24, 25 ⊗ No credit cards

🍴 ORIENTAL CITY
$$
OUDEZIJDS VOORBURGWAL 177
TEL 626 8352
The number of Chinese people who come here to eat shows that it is the genuine article. Specializing in dim sum (until 4:30 p.m.), there is also a long list of Cantonese dishes. Some rate it Amsterdam's best Chinese restaurant.
🎟 130 🚋 Trams 4, 9, 16, 24, 25 ⊘ ♿ ⬣ All major cards

🍴 PALMERS
$$
ZEEDIJK 4–8
TEL 427 0551
This old bar-cum-restaurant,

PRICES

HOTELS
An indication of the cost of a double room without breakfast is given by **$** signs
$$$$$	Over $200
$$$$	$150– $200
$$$	$100–$150
$$	$75–$100
$	Under $75

RESTAURANTS
An indication of the cost of a three course dinner without drinks is given by **$** signs
$$$$$	Over $75
$$$$	$50–$75
$$$	$35–$50
$$	$20–$35
$	Under $20

with its low-ceilinged rooms, has an atmosphere redolent of old maritime Amsterdam, and some of the customers are as colorful as the dishes, which range from steaks, fish, and tapas to the more unusual grilled kangaroo steak and chocolate soup.
🎟 40 🚋 Trams 1, 2, 4, 9, 14, 16, 20, 24, 25 🕐 Closed L daily

JODENBUURT, PLANTAGE, & OOSTERDOK

HOTELS

🏨 BARBACAN
$$
PLANTAGE MUIDERGRACHT 89, 1018 TN
TEL 623 6241
FAX 627 2041
E-MAIL Info@barbacan.nl
A no-frills, hideaway hotel with simply furnished rooms on a quiet back street near the zoo, with a surprising number of good inexpensive restaurants (Turkish, Greek, Italian, Chinese) in the vicinity and a late-night grocery a short stroll away.
🛏 15 🚋 Trams 9, 14 ⊘ ⬣ All major cards

IBIS AMSTERDAM STOPERA
$$
VALKENBURGERSTRAAT 68,
1011 LZ
TEL 531 9135
FAX 531 9145
E-MAIL H3044@accor-
hotels.com
www.ibishotel.com
Opened in 2000, this
purpose-built IBIS chain hotel
offers modern rooms and
Gallic charm at budget prices.
🛏 207   🚃 Trams 9, 14   ⬆
Ⓢ   ❄   🆂 All major cards

PARKLANE
$$
PLANTAGE PARKLAAN 16,
1018 ST.
TEL 622 4804
FAX 626 7827
Value-for-money, tourist-class
hotel in the leafy Plantage,
with views from the front
rooms across the treetops of
Wertheimpark, and a tram
terminus in the same street
ready to whisk you to all
corners of the city.
🛏 11   🚃 Trams 9, 14   ❄
🆂 All major cards

REMBRANDT
$$
PLANTAGE MIDDENLAAN 17,
1018 DA.
TEL 627 2714
FAX 638 0293
E-MAIL R.oplanic@chello.nl
Close to the Zoo and well
located for the
Tropenmuseum and the
Waterlooplein area. It has an
impressive breakfast room
with mock medieval wall
hangings, and some large and
airy family rooms, decorated
in colonial style, with bird
cages and bamboo and rattan
furniture. The largest rooms
are at the front where the
noise from passing trams will
disturb light sleepers—ask for
a back room overlooking the
garden. There is a parking lot
(spaces must be reserved).
🛏 16   🅿 5   🚃 Trams 7, 9,
14   🅿   ❄   🆂 All major
cards

ARENA
$$
'S-GRAVESANDESTRAAT 51,
1092 AA
TEL 694 7444
FAX 850 2415
E-MAIL info@hotelarena.nl
www.hotelarena.nl
The Arena, located in a
converted 19th-century
orphanage, is attractive to
young budget travelers, but
provides the facilities of a
hotel, including bathroom and
TVs in every room and crisp,
modern design. The hotel has
its own nightclub with reduced
admission for hotel guests.
Enjoy the sunshine on the
garden terrace of the hotel's
alfresco café.
🛏 207   🚃 Trams 7, 10
⬆   Ⓢ   ❄   🆂 All major
cards

AMSTEL BOTEL
$
OOSTERDOKSKADE 2–4,
1011 AE.
TEL 626 4247
FAX 639 1952
E-MAIL Info@amstelbotel.com
www.amstelbotel.com
For something entirely
different, how about a night or
two on board this floating
boat hotel, moored along a
quiet back street between
Centraal Station and the
spectacular NEMO museum?
For a three-star hotel the
prices are very reasonable,
which explains its popularity
with younger visitors. Cabins
come with shower cubicle,
toilet, telephone, TV, and
internal video channel, plus a
view over the water.
🛏 176   ❄   📺   🆂 All
major cards

RESTAURANTS

NAM TIN
$$$
JODENBREESTRAAT 11–13
TEL 428 8508
You can judge the authenticity
and quality of this Chinese
restaurant by the number of
Chinese families who come
here. Huge though it is, Nam
Tin doesn't feel at all canteen
like because of the skillful use
of screens to divide up the
rooms. Staff are efficient but
not pushy, and the menu is so
big that you will need plenty
of time just to read it. There
are many specialties here that
you won't find elsewhere—
braised eggplants, salt and
pepper squid with sea salt,
garlic and chili—be adventu-
rous and try something new.
The steamed oysters are
delicious.
🪑 400   🚃 Trams 9, 14, 20
Ⓢ   ❄   🆂 All major cards

LA SALA
$$$
PLANTAGE KERKLAAN 41
TEL 624 4846
Packed into a space no bigger
than the average living room,
this family-run restaurant
specializes in Spanish and
Portuguese food. As the
evening wears on, it can get
hot and noisy, but once you
have dined on grilled
prawns, swordfish, or tender
grilled steak, followed by
creamy egg pudding, you
won't mind one bit.
🪑 30   🚃 Trams 9, 14, 20
🕐 Closed L daily   🆂 All
major cards

SEA PALACE
$$$
OOSTERDOKSKADE
TEL 626 4777
This vast red-and-gold
floating restaurant, moored in
the sheltered harbor to the
east of Centraal Station, re-
creates the atmosphere of
Hong Kong harbor. Peking
duck and standard
Cantonese fare come with
great riverside views. If you
are looking for an alternative
to the less-than-inspiring
food at the nearby NEMO
museum, come here for the
excellent dim sum lunches,
served up to 3:30 p.m.
🪑 800   🚃 Any Centraal
Station tram   Ⓢ   ❄
🆂 All major cards

HOTELS & RESTAURANTS

🍴 DE MAGERE BRUG
$$
AMSTEL 81
TEL 622 6502

Come here for the views of that Amsterdam icon, the Magere Brug (Skinny Bridge), which looks especially charming as the sun goes down over the Amstel River, and the outline of the bridge is lit up with white lightbulbs. This bastion of Dutch culinary traditions serves smoked eel with mustard-and-dill sauce, as well as mussels and fresh fish, and such homey dishes as calves' liver and onions.

🍴 40 🚋 Trams 9, 14, 20 ⬛ AE, DC

🍴 KILIMANJARO
$–$$
RAPENBURGERPLEIN 6
TEL 622 3485

Inspired by the traditional meat and vegetarian dishes of North and East Africa (from Moroccan dishes cooked in tajine to antelope from Tanzania), Kilimanjaro is an affordable and relaxing restaurant, with a patio and waterside tables that make dining outside a pleasure in summer. Don't miss the refreshing fruit cocktails. Credit cards subject to a four percent surcharge.

🍴 40 🚋 Bus 22 ⊕ Closed L daily and Mon. ⬛ All major cards

🍴 JERUSALEM OF GOLD
$
JODENBREESTRAAT 148
TEL 625 0923

Apart from the café at the Jewish Historical Museum (see below), this is Amsterdam's only kosher restaurant, so it gets very busy, especially on Sunday. Simple and unpretentious, the menu features various lamb dishes, such as kheema (spiced lamb) and shwarma (Middle Eastern spit-roast lamb).

🍴 54 🚋 Trams 9, 14, 20 ⊕ Closed D Fri. & all Sat. ⬛ No credit cards

🍴 MUSEUM CAFÉ, JEWISH HISTORICAL MUSEUM
$
JONAS DANIEL MEIJERPLEIN 2–4
TEL 626 9945

One of two cafés in the city offering kosher food (see Jerusalem of Gold above). It serves such quintessentially Jewish dishes as gefilte fish (fish pate with horseradish), and knish (cheese-filled puff-pastry cigars). The café serves Jewish cakes, including almond bolus and ginger bolus, unique to the Amsterdam Jewish community.

🍴 20 🚋 Trams 9, 14, 20 ⊕ Closed D daily ⬛ No credit cards

THE NORTHERN CANALS

HOTELS

🏨 RENAISSANCE
🍴 $$$$
KATTENGAT 1, 1012 SZ
TEL 621 2223
FAX 627 5245
E-MAIL renaissance.amsterdam@renaissancehotels.com
www.renaissancehotels.com

A short step from the station and the buzzing commercial center, the Renaissance enjoys a quiet and scenic location at the start of the canal circle. Many rooms have views across gabled rooftops, or to the domed roof of the Lutheran church next door, which the hotel uses for conferences and events. The hotel's Splash fitness club is one of the best in the city.

🛏 405 🍴 45 🚋 Trams 1, 2, 5 ⬛ 🗔 🗔 🗔 ⬛ All major cards

🏨 CANAL HOUSE
$$$
KEIZERSGRACHT 148, 1015 CX
TEL 622 5182
FAX 624 1317
E-MAIL canalhouse@compuserve.com
www.canalhouse.nl

Entering the Canal House hotel you almost feel you should dress in period costume, for this lovely old pair of canalside houses is entirely furnished in antiques. Even your bed is likely to be a stately period piece, which is why the hotel proudly advertises the opportunity to "sleep in the 17th century." In keeping with the period charm, there are no TVs and the fragility of many of the furnishings means that children under 12 are not allowed. Mirrors and chandeliers set the scene for breakfast in a room that overlooks the garden. The price is reasonable for such luxury, and with only 35 rooms, reserve early.

🛏 35 🗔 🗔 ⬛ All major cards

🏨 WIECHMANN HOTEL
$$$
PRINSENGRACHT 328–332, 1016 HX.
TEL 626 3321
FAX 626 8962
E-MAIL Info@hotelwiechmann.nl
www.hotelwiechmann.nl

The Wiechmann attracts discerning visitors who appreciate the hotel's old-fashioned charm. The hotel was converted from a pair of canalside houses and furnished with the antiques and family heirlooms of the Dutch-American Wiechmann family, who opened their doors to guests in 1947 and continue to extend a warm welcome. The front rooms enjoy leafy views over Prinsengracht to the Jordaan district. There are also larger rooms ideal for families.

🛏 40 🗔 ⬛ All major cards

RESTAURANTS

🍴 CHRISTOPHE
$$$$$
LELIEGRACHT 46
TEL 625 0807
www.christophe.nl

Christophe won his first Michelin star in 1989 and has kept it ever since. Having trained at the Ritz in Paris and in the U.S., his style is Mediterranean with world influences: Eggplant fondant with cumin is a Middle Eastern classic, while scallops flavored with orange and saffron reflects the sunny style of California. Whether you choose from the daily fixed-price menu, the shorter and less expensive Petit Menu or from the à la carte, quality and innovation are guaranteed. Reservations advised.

🛏 40 🚊 Trams 13, 14, 17, 20 🕐 Closed L daily, Sun. & Mon. 🚭 🃏 All major cards

SOMETHING SPECIAL

🍴 DE GOUDEN REAEL

The best way to find this enchanting hideaway restaurant is to take a tram or taxi to Haarlemmerplein and then walk through the traffic-free Western Islands, across pretty bridges with enchanting views. The restaurant occupies the last in a row of distinctive gabled buildings along Zandhoek, built in 1623, and takes its name from a novel by Dutch author Jan Mens (1897–1967). With this background you might expect food that harks back to the Dutch Golden Age, but the chef specializes in French regional cooking, always reflecting the dishes and wines characteristic of the chosen region of France. Not only does the menu change regularly, but so does the wine list. Food lovers flock, as do the many artists, photographers, and designers who live in nearby warehouse conversions, so be sure to reserve well ahead.

🍴 $$$$
ZANDHOEK 14
TEL 623 3883
🛏 50 🚊 18, 22 🕐 Closed L Sat. & all Sun. 🚭 🃏 🃏 DC, MC, V

SOMETHING SPECIAL

🍴 GROENE LANTEERNE

Not to be confused with the similarly named fondue restaurant (see this page), this intimate and romantic place serves top-quality French cuisine, with a menu that changes daily, depending on what is best in the market, and an impressive list of wines to complement the inspired food. Reservations advised.

🍴 $$$$
HAARLEMMERSTRAAT 43
TEL 624 1952
🛏 20 🚊 Trams 18, 22 🕐 Closed L daily & Sun. 🃏 All major cards

🍴 BORDEWIJK

$$$
NOORDERMARKT 7
TEL 624 3899
The Bordewijk consistently tops the list of Amsterdammers' favorite restaurants, combining a beautiful location in the quiet square beside the Noorderkerk, with a menu that will please everyone by its sheer range of choice, combining French, Asian, and Italian. For dessert, however, there is no choice—everyone agrees that Bordewijk creates the best *tarte tatin* in town.
🛏 48 🚊 Tram 3 🕐 Closed L daily & Mon. 🚭 🃏 🃏 All major cards

🍴 ALBATROS SEAFOODHOUSE

$$
WESTERSTRAAT 264
TEL 627 9932
The jaunty blue-and-white nautical decor tells you that this Jordaan restaurant is dedicated to fish. Sole, plaice, salmon, and tuna are all cooked to your taste and served fresh by friendly staff. Mussels are very popular and much easier to eat than a bowl of winkles (small snail-like marine creatures with spiral shells).

🛏 55 🚊 Trams 3, 10 🕐 Closed L daily & Wed. 🚭 🃏 All major cards

🍴 ALCANTARA

$$
WESTERSTRAAT 184–186
TEL 420 3959
Spanish and Portuguese dishes are on offer in this spacious white-tiled Iberian tapas bar and café, converted from a former movie house. Chilled white port or *vino verde* (literally meaning "green wine") makes a refreshing accompaniment to great grilled meat and fish dishes.
🛏 60 🚊 Tram 3, 10 🚭 No credit cards

🍴 DRAGON CORNER

$$
NIEUWEZIJDS VOORBURGWAL 4–10
TEL 622 3800
This smart Chinese restaurant sets new standards of quality in a part of town that is slowly coming up in the world. You will need time to make your choice from an extensive menu, but the staff are friendly and don't rush guests, as can happen in the more functional Chinese restaurants of Chinatown. The Peking duck is delicious. Once your order is placed, dishes come swiftly, and are presented with flair.
🛏 155 🚊 Trams 1, 2, 5, 13, 17, 20 🚭 🃏 🃏 All major cards

🍴 GROENE LANTAARN

$$
BLOEMGRACHT 47
TEL 620 2088
As a nation of cheese lovers, it is not surprising that fondue has become almost as much a national dish for the Dutch as it is for the Swiss. Here, as well as traditional fondue, you may find fish fondue and even an oriental dim sum version. Follow up with a delicious dessert.
🛏 40 🚊 Trams 10, 13, 17, 20 🕐 Closed L daily & Mon.–Wed. 🚭 🃏 AE

HOTELS & RESTAURANTS

🍴 HIMALAYA
$$
HAARLEMMERSTRAAT 11
TEL 622 3776
This unpretentious and friendly Indian restaurant will fill you with delicious *balti* (mildly spiced Indian casseroles cooked and served in an iron skillet called a balti) or tandoori dishes at very reasonable prices, and the chef will tailor the spiciness to suit your palate.
🪑 50 🚋 Trams 1, 2, 5, 13, 17, 20 🕐 Closed L daily
💳 All major cards

🍴 RUM RUNNERS
$$
PRINSENGRACHT 277
TEL 627 4079
The perfect place to flop after a visit to the Anne Frank House. A Caribbean restaurant set around a sheltered courtyard in the lee of the Westerkerk. Sip fruity cocktails while enjoying the colorful decor, complete with turtles, fishponds, and screeching parakeets. The service is laid back and the menu ranges from large and flavorsome steaks to Caribbean-style casseroles.
🪑 140 🚋 Trams 13, 14, 17 🕐 Closed L daily 💳 All major cards

SOUTHERN CANALS

HOTELS

🏨 AMSTEL 🍴 INTERCONTINENTAL
$$$$$
PROFESSOR TULPPLEIN 1, 1018 GX
TEL 622 6060; FAX 622 5808
E-MAIL amstel@interconti.com
www.interconti.com
If you can afford to stay at this grand-luxe hotel, it probably doesn't matter that it's located on the edge of the city. The cost of the taxi ride to the city center will be small change by comparison with the room bill. In return

for your money, you can count on polished service (the staff to room ratio is two to one), and palatial rooms. The riverside setting provides romantic views from the bar, lounge, or brasserie, and from the Restaurant La Rive, the elegant Michelin-starred restaurant where the quality of the food is matched by a distinguished wine list.
🛏 90 🪑 60 ▪ ◻ ◻ ☎ ▾ 💳 All major cards

SOMETHING SPECIAL

🏨 🍴 BLAKES
Theatrical style combined with every luxury is the trademark of this trendy boutique hotel, part of the ultra-chic Anouska Hempel empire. Every individual room looks as if it comes straight from the pages of an interior design magazine, whether it be the bold minimalism of the Japanese-style bedroom—black bamboo furniture and natural silks combined with white walls—or more classic color schemes of lavender and rose. The restaurant menu combines French, Italian, Thai, and Japanese influences, and the service is as stylish as the food.
$$$$$
KEIZERSGRACHT 384, 1016 GZ
TEL 530 2010
FAX 530 2030
E-MAIL hotel@blakes.nl
www.slh.com/blakesam
🛏 26 ◻ ◻ 💳 All major cards

🏨 PULITZER 🍴 $$$$$
PRINSENGRACHT 315–331, 1016 GZ
TEL 523 5235
FAX 627 6753
E-MAIL Res100-amsterdam@luxurycollection.com
www.luxurycollection.com/pulitzer
The Pulitzer combines every modern luxury with all the charm and romance of the

PRICES

HOTELS
An indication of the cost of a double room without breakfast is given by $ signs
$$$$$ Over $200
$$$$ $150– $200
$$$ $100–$150
$$ $75–$100
$ Under $75

RESTAURANTS
An indication of the cost of a three course dinner without drinks is given by $ signs
$$$$$ Over $75
$$$$ $50–$75
$$$ $35–$50
$$ $20–$35
$ Under $20

17th-century canalside residences that were joined together in 1968 to create the hotel. It was the brainchild of art-loving Peter Pulitzer, grandson of the newspaper publisher who founded the annual Pulitzer prizes for journalism, literature, music, and drama. The rooms are all uniquely furnished and feature original works of art, as do the reception areas and the inner courtyard, with its light-filled Garden Room. Top-quality international cuisine and faultless service are the hallmarks of the Pulitzer Restaurant. In summer the hotel hosts an arts festival with musicians performing on barges moored in the Prinsengracht.
🛏 226 ◻ ◻ 💳 All major cards

🏨 AMERICAN CROWNE 🍴 PLAZA AMSTERDAM
$$$$
LEIDSEKADE 97, 1017 PN
TEL 556 3000
FAX 556 3001
E-MAIL american@interconti.com
www.amsterdam-american.crowneplaza.com
The perfect hotel for culture vultures, with the Rijks-musuem across the road, and

for night owls, with the city's best nightspots on the doorstep, the American occupies a prime position on the city's busiest square. The hotel's many art deco features make this an atmospheric place to stay, whether breakfasting beneath Tiffany lamps in the celebrated Café Americain or sipping late-night drinks in the popular Night Watch bar.

ⓘ 188 🔲 🔲 🔲 🍸 🔲 All major cards

AMBASSADE
$$$
HERENGRACHT 225-353
TEL 555 0222
FAX 555 0277
E-MAIL info@ambassade-hotel.nl
www.ambassade-hotel.nl
Set in a quiet but central part of Amsterdam, this hotel is a sensitive conversion of ten 17th-century canalside residences, beautifully furnished with antiques to retain all the period charm. Despite the lack of a restaurant and the steepness of the stairs, the hotel has a loyal and regular clientele, so reserve well in advance.

ⓘ 124 🔲 🔲 All major cards

AMSTERDAM HOUSE
$$$
AMSTEL 176A, 1017 AE
TEL 626 2577 (FROM THE U.S. 800 618 1008)
FAX 626 2987 (FROM THE U.S. 904 672 6659)
E-MAIL info@amsterdamhouse.nl
www.amsterdamhouse.com
Amsterdam House is an agency specializing in the rental of hotel rooms, apartments, and houseboats all over Amsterdam, available on short or long rental—from a few days to several months or more—and accommodating from two to ten people. Some apartments and boats are equipped as offices with fax, photocopier, and answering machine, as well as telephone and Internet

facilities. Linens and cleaning are included in the price.

🔲 All major cards

SEVEN BRIDGES HOTEL
$$$
REGULIERSGRACHT 31, 1017 LK
TEL 623 1329
The Seven Bridges feels like a family house—and you are treated like a family member—rather than a hotel, and you are just far enough from the buzzing nightlife of Rembrandtplein to enjoy the tranquility of the canals, without having too far to walk in search of adventure. With luck you will end up in a room that looks out onto one of Amsterdam's most photogenic sights, the famous group of seven bridges marking the junction of four canals.

ⓘ 40 🔲 🔲 AE, MC, V

GASTHUISMOLEN-APARTMENTS
$$
GASTHUISMOLENSTEEG 10, 1016 AN
TEL 624 0736
FAX 420 9991
E-MAIL gasthuismolen@ flash.a2000.nl
These self-catering apartments, in an excellent location, in a quiet street four blocks west of Dam Square, can accommodate up to four people, and are ideal for families or groups. Apartments consist of bedroom, kitchen, bathroom, and living room with a sofa bed; the linens and cleaning are included in the room price.

ⓘ 15 🔲 🔲 MC, V

HANS BRINKER
$
KERKSTRAAT 136-138 1017 GR
TEL 622 0687
FAX 638 2060
www.hansbrinker.com
A budget hotel offering rock-bottom prices aimed at students, backpackers, and

impoverished young travelers. Huge but friendly, well run, and clean. A bed in a dorm will cost as little as $20, but prices are three times higher if you want the greater privacy of a single, double, or triple room.

ⓘ 260 🔲 All major cards

RESTAURANTS

DE OESTERBAR
$$$–$$$$$
LEIDSEPLEIN 10
TEL 626 3463
There is something deliciously ironic about eating something so unashamedly upscale as oysters in a part of Amsterdam renowned more for fries and mayonnaise, a typical Dutch dish. This old established oyster bar still manages to preserve a certain timeless hauteur, while also being thoroughly modern. As you tuck into seafood or a mixed seafood plate of turbot, halibut, and salmon, you can expect to be watched by the very fresh and decidedly alive fish that are delivered twice daily and kept in aquaria until the fateful moment when someone places an order.

🍴 50 🚋 Trams 1, 2, 5 🔲 🔲 All major cards

D'VIJFF VLIEGHEN
$$$$
SPUISTRAAT 294-302
TEL 624 8369
You may hear locals scoff and dismiss the Five Flies as a tourist trap, but tourists love it for a reason: History comes with every mouthful of delicious food as you sit on genuine antique benches and admire authentic Rembrandt drawings and old tiles in this heavily timbered, 16th-century house. The old fruit market (which perhaps gave rise to the amusing Five Flies name) has long gone, but the restaurant proudly serves homegrown (and often organic) ingredients in its mix of Dutch and international

HOTELS & RESTAURANTS

dishes. Game (pigeon, venison, wild boar) features on the menu, along with hearty dishes such as sweetmeats and lamb's tongue, but you can also enjoy grilled fish or a simple salad. Though not cheap, the indulgent service combined with the quality of the food and the cozy ambience all contribute to a memorable evening.
🛏 150 🚋 Trams 1, 2, 5 🕐 Closed L daily 🚫 🚫 🚫 All major cards

🍴 LES QUATRE CANETONS
$$$$
PRINSENGRACHT 1111
TEL 624 6307
Bankers, consulate staff, and media tycoons can all be found lunching at this highly regarded restaurant, set in a converted 17th-century warehouse, with a delightful garden to the rear. The name is a pun on the address— "four ducks" and "four ones" both sound similar in Dutch. As well as duck, treat yourself to the signature dish of roasted whole lobster with lobster risotto and small vegetables in a foamy lobster gravy—extravagant but well worth the expense for a special occasion. Alternatively, put yourself in the hands of the chef: The Surprise Menu includes a range of fine wines, carefully selected to complement the food.
🛏 60 🚋 Tram 4 🕐 Closed Sun. 🚫 🚫 🚫 All major cards

🍴 'T SWARTE SCHAEP
$$$$
KORTE LEIDSEDWARSSTRAAT 24
TEL 622 3021
Another bastion of quality in the otherwise fast-food desert of Leidseplein, the Black Sheep manages to remain aloof from the nightlife bustle outside its antique-decorated walls. The darkened beams of this

17th-century home have seen famous actors, movie stars, and even royalty dining on classic French and Dutch cuisine, with a strong emphasis on fish.
🛏 50 🚋 Trams 1, 2, 5 🚫 🚫 🚫 All major cards

🍴 TEPPAN YAKI HOSOKAWA
$$$$
MAX EUWEPLEIN 22
TEL 638 8086
The high prices charged here are justified by the excellent quality and freshness of the imported ingredients. As in a traditional Japanese *teppan-yaki* house, diners sit around a hotplate while the chef performs his magic; the delicious cooking smells guarantee your taste buds will be well and truly whetted by the time the food lands on your plate.
🛏 90 🚋 Trams 1, 2, 5 🕐 Closed L daily 🚫 All major cards

🍴 CASA DI DAVID
$$$
SINGEL 426
TEL 624 5093
The House of David is a genuine Italian restaurant with handsome and flamboyant waiters, serving traditional pizza cooked in a wood-fired oven, as well as a full range of classic Italian meat and pasta dishes.
🛏 50 🚋 Trams 1, 2, 5 🕐 Closed L daily 🚫 🚫 🚫 All major cards

🍴 CILUBANG
$$$
RUNSTRAAT 10
TEL 626 9755
Elegantly decorated in contemporary style, Cilubang serves authentic Indonesian cuisine in a quiet and civilized atmosphere. The menu makes rewarding reading, with plenty of information on the many dishes that go to make up the *rijsttafel*—a banquet consisting of anything up to 35 separate

small dishes, and an ideal way to sample the range of different foods.
🛏 30 🚋 Trams 1, 2, 5 🕐 Closed L daily 🚫 🚫 🚫 All major cards

🍴 DYNASTY

Over ten years ago Dynasty broke out of the straitjacket of being classified as just another Chinese restaurant by combining the culinary traditions of Canton, Thailand, Indonesia, and even Japan into a pan-Oriental style. Since then it has never looked back. Smart and fashionable, Dynasty is the favored haunt of Ajax soccer stars and anyone else who wants to see and be seen. Typical dishes include Vietnamese spring rolls, bursting with the flavor of mint, and shaking beef (spicy beef cubes on a bed of Chinese lettuce). Palms and potted orchids, silks, and watercolor paintings create a modern Oriental ambience, and in summer you can dine beneath paper parasols in the courtyard garden.
$$$
REGULIERSDWARSSTRAAT 30
TEL 626 8400
🛏 50 🚋 Tram 1, 2, 5 🕐 Closed L daily & Tues. 🚫 🚫 🚫 DC, MC, V

🍴 INDABA
$$$
UTRECHTSESTRAAT 96
TEL 421 3852
Enthusiasts of exotic cuisines can notch up the tastes of South Africa at this unusual restaurant, where the menu is all in Afrikaans (ask your waiter for an explanation). Most of the dishes consist of charcoal broiled meats, though crocodile hotpot is also on the menu, and you may find *snoek*—a firm barracuda-like fish.
🛏 45 🚋 Tram 4 🕐 Closed L Sun. & Mon. 🚫 🚫 🚫 All major cards

KORT
$$$
AMSTELVELD 12
TEL 626 1199
Kort is the perfect choice for a sunny day, and is one of the most relaxing places to eat out of doors in central Amsterdam. The café terrace basks in the warmth of its south-facing terrace, in the shelter of the Amstelkerk, with no-through traffic and only the sounds of children playing in the adjacent playground to disturb the tranquility. Service can be slow if the café is busy, but nobody minds—the food is surprisingly adventurous, with Middle Eastern and African influences evident in the spiced fish (the house special) and Moroccan fish *tajine*.
🍴 45 🚊 Tram 4 🕐 Closed Tues. in winter 🚭 ❄
🏦 All major cards

SLUIZER
$$$
UTRECHTSESTRAAT 43–45
TEL 622 6376
The long-established Sluizer has achieved classic status, with its fish, steaks and game, and such dishes as duck's breast in bilberry sauce, or fillet of sole wrapped around smoked salmon. With its wood-paneled decor and business clientele, this is a safe bet for seekers of Dutch tradition.
🍴 60 🚊 Tram 4 🚭 ❄
🏦 All major cards

SLUIZER VISRESTAURANT
$$$
UTRECHTSESTRAAT 45
TEL 622 6557
Sister restaurant to the above, this is a much more modern and boisterous establishment, with marble-topped tables and friendly waiters serving first-rate fish dishes to an appreciative clientele. Try scallops, octopus, the fresh catch of the day, or *waterzooï*, the traditional Dutch fish stew.
🍴 100 🚊 Tram 4 🚭 ❄
🏦 All major cards

TEMPOE DOELOE
$$$
UTRECHTSESTRAAT 75
TEL 625 6718
Ask any Amsterdammer which restaurant serves the best Indonesian food and the name Tempoe Doeloe is very likely to crop up. Going strong now for 20 years, it combines truly authentic dishes with polished service—everyone is made to feel like royalty when served with one of the restaurant's legendary *rijsttafel* banquets, consisting of 12 or 24 little dishes, contrasting in taste and texture (they also serve a vegetarian version). Reservations advised.
🍴 50 🚊 Tram 4 🚭 ❄
🏦 All major cards

HARD ROCK CAFÉ
$$
MAX EUWEPLEIN 59–61
TEL 523 7625
Yes, Amsterdam has got one, too—in fact this branch was the 100th to open, and it repeats the successful formula of all the others by serving American "home" cooking against a backdrop of rock and roll memorabilia, with T-shirts and merchandise to prove that you've survived the line. The menu has something to please everyone, from the All-American hamburger, to ribs, barbecued chicken, pasta, and pizza.
🍴 150 🚊 Trams 1, 2, 5
🏦 All major cards

PORTUGALIA
$$
KERKSTRAAT 35
TEL 625 6490
Exactly what you would get in Portugal. The laid-back service and homey cooking—*presunto* (mountain-cured ham), grilled sardines, swordfish and tuna steaks, *bacalhau* (salt cod cooked with olives, garlic, and boiled eggs), and chicken *piri piri* (flavored with chili sauce)—are popular with students, families, and local Portuguese.

🍴 40 🚊 Trams 1, 2, 5
🏦 All major cards

ROSE'S CANTINA
$$
REGULIERSDWARSSTRAAT 38–40
TEL 625 9797
Famed well beyond the bounds of Amsterdam, Rose's Cantina is a huge and rambling restaurant with a party atmosphere—helped no doubt by the quality of the margaritas, which connoisseurs claim to be the best outside of Mexico. Large portions of Mexican classics such as guacamole, refried beans, burritos, and tacos, combined with low prices and a busy atmosphere, make this a must for a fun night out.
🍴 80 🚊 Trams 1, 2, 5
🕐 Closed L daily 🚭 ❄
🏦 All major cards

DE BLAUWE HOLLANDER
$
LEIDSEKRUISSTRAAT 28
TEL 623 3014
Dutch restaurants are hard to find because the Dutch, understandably, want something different when they eat out. This restaurant is one of the very few places in Amsterdam to serve genuine Dutch fare—and it is a place where you can fill up on excellent food at rock-bottom prices. Meals are served, farmhouse style, at one of four big communal tables. For a really earthy Dutch experience, try *erwtensoep* (a thick soup of split peas flavored with bacon), *stampot* (mashed potatoes and root vegetables flavored with sausage), and *flaflip* (semolina pudding with red currant sauce). If that doesn't appeal, there are plenty more wholesome dishes, including salads and vegetarian choices.
🍴 40 🚊 Trams 1, 2, 5, 6, 7, 10, 20 🕐 Closed L daily
🏦 No credit cards

🍴 DANNEKOEKEN PAVILJOEN DE CARROUSEL

$

2E WETERINGPLANTSOEN

TEL 625 8002

If you have children, head for this fun pancake house, with its carousel theme, located in a small park opposite the Heineken Experience. As well as traditional Dutch pancakes, which are small and thick, it also serves Breton-style crêpes with savory fillings as well as sweet.

🍴 40 🚃 Trams 6, 7, 10, 24, 25 🕐 Closes 9 p.m. 🚫 No credit cards

🍴 FALAFEL MAOZ

$

REGULIERSBREESTRAAT 45

Wherever you are in Amsterdam, you are never very far from one of the city's numerous falafel takeouts. This one, close to Rembrandtplein, is typical: For well under $5, you get a pita bread stuffed with spicy deep-fried chickpea balls, and then you help yourself to a range of salads and sauces—some fiery hot, some pickled, some crisp and cool. These salads provide contrasting tastes and textures to the rather stodgy but filling chickpeas. There is simply no better bargain in Amsterdam, and certainly no fast-food snack that is healthier.

🚃 Trams 4, 9, 14, 16, 20, 24, 25 🚫 No credit cards

🍴 HET PANNEKOEKHUIS

$

PRINSENGRACHT 358

TEL 620 8448

The genuine Dutch pancakes served here are substantial and filling without being too thick. There's a choice of 70 fillings, any one of which will serve as an excellent lunch, or as a hearty snack for hungry children.

🍴 40 🚃 Trams 13, 14, 17, 20 🕐 Closes 8:30 p.m. 🚫 No credit cards

---

MUSEUM DISTRICT & THE NEW SOUTH

HOTELS

🏨 BILDERBERG GARDEN 🍴 HOTEL

$$$$$

DIJSSELHOFPLANTSOEN, 1077 BJ

TEL 664 2121

FAX 679 9356

E-MAIL garden@bilderberg.nl

www.bilderberg.nl

The charm of the Bilderberg derives from its setting in the gracious garden suburb of the New South. Taking its cue from its leafy surroundings, the modern hotel is set around a mature garden and many of the rooms look out onto trees and flowering shrubs. Jacuzzis are standard in all rooms and welcoming touches include fresh fruit and free newspapers. The Kersentuin (Cherry Stone) restaurant is one of the city's most prestigious eating places, serving French-style food with oriental influences.

🛏 98 🚪 🚫 🚫 📺 🚫 All major cards

🍴 HILTON AMSTERDAM 🍴

$$$$$

APOLLOLAAN 138, 1077 BG

TEL 710 6005

FAX 710 9000

E-MAIL amshitw@hilton.com

www.hilton.com

Beatles' fans will already be familiar with the interior of this hotel because it featured on the television news night after night in March 1969. That was when the newly married John Lennon and Yoko Ono invited the cameras into their bedroom as they turned their honeymoon into a "bed-in" protest for peace. Lennon chose what was then the best and most modern hotel in Amsterdam for his idiosyncratic protest. Comprehensive refurbishment has kept the hotel as luxurious now as it was then. Special features include bicycle rental,

---

PRICES

HOTELS

An indication of the cost of a double room without breakfast is given by **$** signs

$$$$$	Over $200
$$$$	$150–$200
$$$	$100–$150
$$	$75–$100
$	Under $75

RESTAURANTS

An indication of the cost of a three course dinner without drinks is given by **$** signs

$$$$$	Over $75
$$$$	$50–$75
$$$	$35–$50
$$	$20–$35
$	Under $20

---

boat rental from the hotel's own marina for a private and romantic canal tour, and a relaxing garden alongside the marina, perfect for drinks on sunny summer evenings.

🛏 271 🍴 125 🚃 Trams 5, 24 🚪 🚫 🚫 📺 🚫 All major cards

🏨 OKURA 🍴

$$$$$

FERDINAND BOLSTRAAT 333, 1072 LH

TEL 678 7111

FAX 671 2344

E-MAIL sales@okura.nl

www.okura.nl

The Okura is the business traveler's favorite because of its location, close to Amsterdam's main highways, the airport, and the RAI Conference Center. Though it looks like a suburban tower block from the outside, the rooms are elegantly decorated and come with extras such as fax machines, video tapes and a video player, and internet access via the television. Even if you are not staying here, the hotel's restaurants make ideal venues for business entertaining as well as relaxation. The top-floor Ciel Bleu restaurant is one of Amsterdam's top French restaurants (jacket and

---

tie recommended), serving faultless food with a stunning view over the city. Also very highly rated are the Japanese restaurants, Yamazato and Sazanka.

☎ 370 ⚑ 145 🚭 🛉 💆 🛢 ⚐ 💳 All major cards

🏨 ATLAS HOTEL
$$$
VAN EEGHENSTRAAT 64, 1071 GK
TEL 676 6336
FAX 671 7633
E-MAIL info@atlashotel.nl
www.atlashotel.nl

Rooms in this fine art deco hotel are a lot less expensive than its official four-star rating would suggest. That's the reward for staying in a hotel that is perceived to be a little off the beaten track. In reality, the luxury shops of P.C. Hooftstraat are just ten minutes away, as is the Concertgebouw concert hall, and the Rijksmuseum is a mere ten-minute stroll through Vondelpark. Most rooms have a view over the hotel's own garden or over Vondelpark.

☎ 24 🚭 💳 All major cards

🏨 ACRO HOTEL
$$
JAN LUIKENSTRAAT 44, 1071 CR
TEL 662 5538
FAX 675 0811

Perfect for the museums, this simple, tourist-class hotel offers clean modern rooms at reasonable prices, including family rooms, and three apartments for people planning to stay longer than a weekend. Bar and lounge.

☎ 51 🚭 💳 All major cards

🏨 DE FILOSOOF
$$
ANNA VAN DEN VONDELSTRAAT 6, 1054 GZ
TEL 683 3013
FAX 685 3750
E-MAIL

reservations@hotelfilosoof.nl
www.xs4all.nl/~filosoof

De Filosoof (The Philosopher) is the thinking person's hotel, especially if you are on a tight budget (the rooms are very good value) and interested in art (it is located close to all the major art museums). It is run by Ida Jongsma (who really is a philosopher) and the rooms feature motifs inspired by philosophical ideas. Guests enjoy the use of a library, garden, and bar, and the breakfast-time table mats feature texts from stimulating philosophical works.

☎ 25 🚋 Trams 1, 6 🚭 💳 All major cards

RESTAURANTS

SOMETHING SPECIAL

🍴 LE GARAGE
Le Garage, perhaps Amsterdam's trendiest restaurant, attracts media types, publishers, movers and shakers of the Internet world, actors, and TV personalities—as well as ordinary people willing to act the part and dress up for an evening of glamour. The extensive menu ranges from brasserie fare with world influences to more experimental dishes, such as cubed tuna tartare with curry.

$$$$$
RUYSDAELSTRAAT 54–56
TEL 679 7176
☎ 50 🚋 Tram 3, 5, 12 🕐 Closed L Sat. & Sun. 💳 All cards

🍴 BODEGA KEYZER
$$$
VAN BAERLESTRAAT 96
TEL 671 1441

The patina of respectable old age darkens the beams and walls of this classic restaurant, situated right next door to the Concertgebouw, and therefore the natural choice of concert-goers and musicians alike. Founded in

1905, service remains old-fashioned in the best sense, and the specialty (Dover sole meunière) has been around almost as long as the restaurant itself.

☎ 50 🚋 Trams 2, 3, 5, 12, 16, 20 💳 All major cards

🍴 DE KNIJP
$$$
VAN BAERLESTRAAT 134
TEL 671 4248

De Knijp is popular with post-concert music-lovers discussing the pieces they have just heard at the Concertgebouw. This classic brasserie with a split-level dining area, serves Dutch, French, and Italian food, from breast of goose to beef carpaccio.

☎ 50 🚋 Trams 3, 5, 12, 16 💳 All major cards

🍴 SAMA SEBO
$$$
P.C. HOOFTSTRAAT 27
TEL 662 8146

Smart Indonesian restaurant set in the trendiest street in Amsterdam. Traditional *rijsttaffel*, a 20-dish banquet, is so deservedly popular and so reasonably priced that the restaurant gets very busy, especially at lunchtime.

☎ 40 🚋 Trams 2, 3, 5, 20 🕐 Closed Sun. 💳 All major cards

🍴 CAMBODJA CITY
$$
ALBERT CUYPSTRAAT 58–60
TEL 671 4930

Kitsch surroundings and a busy atmosphere shouldn't put you off looking for this gem of an oriental restaurant in the area famous for its street market. As well as Vietnamese dishes (try the ginger chicken for an inexpensive treat), the menu also features Thai and Cambodian food. The carrots are exquisitely carved into peacocks and other birds, turning each dish into a work of art.

40 **Trams 16, 24, 25**
Closed Mon. **MC, V**

TOTÓ
$$
EERSTE CONSTANTIJN
HUYGENSSTRAAT 112
TEL 683 0028
In a town where many "Italian" restaurants are actually Turkish, this is an authentic trattoria, named after the Italian comic of the 1930s and serving good home-cooked food, from salads and pasta liberally bathed in the restaurant's own brand of olive oil to terrific tiramisu.
40 **Trams 1, 3, 6, 12**
Closed L daily **All major cards**

ZABAR'S
$$
VAN BAERLESTRAAT 49
TEL 679 8888
Convenient for the Concertgebouw (and therefore busy with concert-goers before and after performances), this gay-friendly Mediterranean restaurant is decorated with tiles, murals, and strikingly sunny colors. The decor compliments its robust seafood and vegetarian dishes, strong on garlic and olive oil. If you order house wine by the glass, you will be given a bottle and charged only for what you drink. Reservations advised. No cell phones.
32 **Tram 3, 5, 12, 20**
Closed Sat. & Mon. L, & all day Sun. **MC**

EXCURSIONS

DELFT

HOTEL

HOTEL DE PLATAAN
$$$
DOELENPLEIN 10–11, 2611 BP,
DELFT
TEL (015) 212 6046
FAX (015) 215 7327

E-MAIL info@hoteldeplataan.nl
www.hoteldeplataan.nl
This town house hotel is situated in the heart of the old historic center of Delft, close to the museum and marketplace. The bright airy rooms have modern Scandinavian-style furnishings, and include a stereo system, refrigerator, small kitchen area, and cups, plates, and cutlery. Snacks and drinks are available from the hotel café, which has an outdoor terrace.
48 **15** ****
All major cards

RESTAURANT

KLIJWEGS KOFFIEHUIS
$
OUDE DELFT 133
TEL (015) 212 4625
This canalside café is a popular choice for lunch because of its location alongside the city's principal waterway, and for its delicious *broodjes* (filled rolls) and pancakes.
30 **Closed Sun.**
No credit cards

HAARLEM

HOTEL

GOLDEN TULIP LION D'OR
$$$
KRUISWEG 34–36, 2011 LC
HAARLEM
TEL (023) 532 1750
FAX (023) 532 9543
E-MAIL
reservations@hotelliondor.nl
www.goldentulip.com
Established in 1810, this elegant hotel in the center of Haarlem makes a great base for soaking up the city's special atmosphere. The rooms are elegantly decorated with floral fabrics and colonial-style rattan furniture, and feature modern dataports, as well as cable TV. There's an à la carte restaurant for lunch and dinner.
34 **14** **** ** **
All major cards

RESTAURANT

SOMETHING SPECIAL

APPLAUSE
A young chef with a flair for Italian cuisine presides over this stylish and intimate restaurant on Haarlem's celebrated main square, the Grote Markt. Sample the Sicilian-style rib-eye steak with citron and pesto butter, or the delicious Mediterranean-style fish soup.
$$$
Grote Markt 23a
TEL (023) 531 1425
40 ** ** **All major cards**

DEN HAAG (THE HAGUE)

HOTEL

PETIT
$$
GROOT HERTOGINNELAAN
42, 2517 EH DEN HAAG
TEL (070) 346 5500
FAX (070) 346 3257
E-MAIL petit@worldonline.nl
The Petit is a friendly and comfortable hotel located in the smart embassy quarter of The Hague and within walking distance of the city's major museums.
20 **20** **** ** **
**** **All major cards**

RESTAURANTS

SAUR
$$$$
LANGE VOORHOUT 47
TEL (070) 346 2565
The emphasis here is on seafood, in all its most delicious forms: Six different kinds of oysters, lobster served five different ways, and a wide range of fish. The copper-topped seafood bar downstairs is a less expensive alternative to the club-like restaurant.
80 ** ** **All major cards**

Hotel **Restaurant** **No. of bedrooms** **No. of seats** **Trams** **Water transport** **Closed**

🍴 ZEBEDEUS
$$$
ROND DE GROTE KERK 10
TEL (070) 346 8393
Located in the shadow of Den Haag's medieval Grote Kerk (Great Church), Zebedeus is a friendly *eetcafé* serving snacks (ask for the Kleine Kaart, or Little Menu) up to 9:30 p.m. and more substantial meals at lunch and dinner. Salads include delicious and healthy apple-and-walnut, gorgonzola and avocado, or mozzarella, basil, and tomato, while the main menu features *kangoerobiefstuk* (kangaroo steak with port and pepper sauce), as well as more conventional salmon, lamb, and, for vegetarians, couscous dishes.
🛏 20 🚭 🌀 💳 All major cards

LEIDEN

HOTEL

🏨 GOLDEN TULIP LEIDEN
$$$
SCHIPOLWEG 3, 2316 XB LEIDEN
TEL (071) 522 1121
FAX (071) 522 6675
www.goldentulip.com
The reliable Golden Tulip chain is your best bet for conveniently located accommodations in Leiden. Though the steel and tinted glass building itself is very modern in design, the contrasting interior is decorated with handpainted copies of famous Dutch works of art, and the rooms are furnished in Indonesian colonial style with bamboo furniture. Modern amenities include minibars, in-room movies, modem dataports, and direct dial telephones. Meals are served in the Rubens Restaurant.
🛏 54 🛏 35 🚪 🚭 🌀 💤 💳 All major cards

RESTAURANT

🍴 SURAKARTA
$$$
NOORDEINDE 51–53
TEL (071) 512 3524
Javanese specialties are the order of the day at this smart Indonesian restaurant, and if you can't manage a whole 18-dish *rijsttafel*, go for the 12-dish *kleine rijsttafel*, or mini-version, or try the Javanese satay special with eight different varieties of barbecued meat, vegetables, and fish served with salad.
🛏 40 🚭 🌀 💳 All major cards

ROTTERDAM

HOTEL

🏨 BREITNER
$$
BREITNERSTRAAT 23, 3015 XA, ROTTERDAM
TEL (010) 436 0262
FAX (010) 436 4091
E-MAIL Hotelbreitner@hetnet.nl
www.hotelbreitner.nl
This comfortable and friendly central hotel is close to the station, Euromast, museums, and the Delfshaven harbor, making it a good base for exploring Rotterdam's many attractions. The building dates from after the war, but the interior creates the atmosphere of a bygone age, with its open fire, and cozy wood-paneled bar and café. The rooms are furnished in a more modern style, and there is a terrace garden for enjoying drinks in the open air in summer.
🛏 31 🛏 20 🚪 🚭 🌀 💤 💳 All major cards

RESTAURANTS

🍴 PARKHEUVEL
$$$$
HEUVELLAAN 21
TEL (010) 436 0766
Rotterdam's premier restaurant has two Michelin stars, and a fine location on the edge of Het Park, overlooking the Nieuwe Maas River so that wealthy captains of industry can lunch with a view of their cargo ships going in and out of the port. The "heuvel" is no mere hovel, but a round Bauhaus structure with glass walls and a clublike interior. Here you will be thoroughly spoiled for choice as you survey several fixed-price menus and an à la carte menu that includes such extravagant creations as ravioli of quail with cherries and asparagus, or fillet of beef with ragout of marrow and oxtail.
🛏 70 🚭 🌀 💳 All major cards

🍴 ROOS SALI
$$
KRABBENDIJKESTRAAT 95
TEL (010) 210 3362
Roos Sali is a friendly restaurant in a converted shop, where there are no appetizers or main courses, just a long list of Mediterranean-style salads, baked dishes (eggplant with parmesan cheese, tomatoes, and stuffed peppers), tapas and dips.
🛏 30 💳 All major cards.

🍴 ZILT
$$
CARGADOORSKADE 107
TEL (010) 290 9091
When in a port town like Rotterdam, what else should you eat but fish? Zilt, which means "salty," is located in the up-and-coming Docklands area, opposite an old bonded warehouse called the Entrepot-building. It serves a phenomenal number of different varieties of fish and seafood, and they come with great big French fries (*frites*), as well as plenty of home-made mayonnaise to dip them in—a Dutch tradition.
🛏 70 🚭 🌀 💳 All major cards

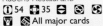
🚪 Elevator 🚭 Non-smoking 🌀 Air-conditioning 🏊 Swimming pool 💤 Health club 💳 Credit cards   KE

SHOPPING IN AMSTERDAM

Shopping in its most concentrated form is to be found along the three-quarter-mile (1.2 km) strip from Centraal Station south to Muntplein, via Nieuwendijk, Dam Square, and Kalverstraat. These traffic-free streets are lined by shops of all kinds: department stores and specialist boutiques, brash commercial outlets and old-fashioned shops of character, homegrown names and international brands. True specialist shops are found along Damstraat (where ethnic art shops and clothing boutiques selling original designs alternate with shops geared to marijuana smokers) and on the short radial streets of the canal circle. Here you will find florists and art dealers, specialists in Australian aboriginal art, Belgian beers, 1930s and '50s antiques, antiquarian books, books for gay and lesbian readers—a true potpourri of small shops with compelling window displays, staffed by knowledgable enthusiasts. P.C. Hooftstraat, in the Museum Quarter, is the place for designer fashion and all that is stylish in home interiors, while the nearby Spiegelkwartier has expensive art and antique shops selling museum-quality works. At the other end of the scale, there are plenty of bargains to be found at Amsterdam's numerous markets, and in the young and friendly boutiques of the Jordaan, whose main shopping street runs from Tichelstraat to Eerste Leliedwarsstraat.

OPENING HOURS

While most stores are open Monday to Friday from 9 a.m. to 6 p.m., (to 9 p.m. on Thursday) and from 10 a.m. to 5 p.m. on Saturday, smaller specialist shops tend to open later (around 11 a.m.) and close later (6 p.m.), while those in popular commercial areas will stay open on Sunday as well.

ART & ANTIQUES

Kunst & Antiekcentrum
de Looier Elandsgracht 109.
The Dutch love of a bargain is nowhere more apparent than at this covered market, with some 80 or so makeshift stands. Ostensibly an "art and antiques" market, some of the "collectibles" on sale here are really just other people's throwaways, but if you are into retro-chic, you can have fun looking for secondhand clothes, cocktail shakers or a 1950s-style clock—just be sure not to pay a lot for what can be little more than a glorified jumble sale.

Spiegelkwartier
Just across the bridge from the Rijksmueum, you will find more than 70 art and antique dealers trading from premises along Spiegelgracht, Nieuwe Spiegelstraat, and the adjacent streets. It is a pleasure just to walk down these streets and look at the window displays; the quality of much of the material on sale here—from Greek, Roman, and pre-Columbian antiquities to contemporary art—is as good as anything you will see in a musuem. The range of antiques and collectibles on sale is very wide, from Amazonian and Aboriginal art to toys, watches, and scientific instruments.

Thorbeckeplein Art Market
Local artists show and sell their work every Sunday (10:30–6) at this open-air market in Thorbeckeplein, a leafy square north of Rembrandtplein.

BOOKS

The triangular plaza opposite the Amsterdam Historical Museum, on Nieuwezijds Voorburgwal, has a coin, postcard, and postage stamp market on Wednesday and Sunday, and the narrow side streets (particularly towards the Spui end) have numerous small shops selling antiquarian books and prints, as well as stamps and coins. Another concentration of antiquarian booksellers is found in the Oudemanhuispoort covered passageway at the southern end of Kloveniersburgwal and Oudezijds Achterburgwal. In both cases, the stock is mainly Dutch, but you will find beautifully made books with attractive pictorial bindings.

American Book Center
Kalverstraat 185, tel 625 5537; www.abc.nl
The first floor is packed with people catching a free read of newspapers and magazines from around the world. This is also where you will find the heaps of bargain books and best-sellers with screaming discount labels, which might make you think the store is just a bit tacky. In fact, there are two floors above and one below packed with books on every subject.

Athenaeum Spui 14–16, tel 622 6248
Around the corner from its Kalverstraat rivals, the Athenaeum serves the university, and so has a good stock of academic books in many languages, as well as a news center selling most international newspapers and magazines.

The Book Exchange
Kloveniersburgwal 58, tel 626 6266
Unload your unwanted books here either for cash or in part exchange for secondhand novels, travel guides or classic literature.

Galerie Lambiek Kerkstraat 78, tel 626 7543; www.lambiek.nl
If you are into comics, you'll already be aware of this famous store selling new and secondhand comics from Europe, Canada, and the U.S., plus related toys.

Jacob van Wijngaarden
(Geografische Boekhandel) Overtoom 97, tel 612 1901
It's well worth the trek to this specialist shop near Vondelpark if you want maps or guides to just about anywhere in the world—including route maps that are essential for anyone heading off to explore the Netherlands on foot or by bike.

Vrolijk Gay and Lesbian Bookshop Paleisstraat 135, tel 623 5142
Comprehensive stock of literature—from classic to erotic—plus travel guides, postcards, and posters, and a useful notice board for finding out what's on where.

Waterstones Kalverstraat 152, tel 638 3821
A stone's throw from the American Book Center, Waterstones has a vast stock over several floors, and is the place to come if you prefer the higher production values (and, admittedly, higher prices) of U.K.-published books. There is a good travel section with a comprehensive range of books on Amsterdam and the Netherlands.

DEPARTMENT STORES & MALLS

De Bijenkorf Dam 1, tel 621 8080; www.bijenkorf.nl
Upscale and trendy at the same time, De Bijenkorf maintains its position as Amsterdam's leading department store by stocking a comprehensive range of clothing, cosmetics and accessories, furniture, works of art, household goods, toys, and children's wear.

Magna Plaza Nieuwezijds Voorburgwal
Four floors of shopping and cafés in this stunning conversion of the city's palatial former main post office, worth a look for the architectural grandiloquence and all the latest in branded European and U.S. fashion. Open seven days a week.

Maison de Bonneterie Rokin 140–142, tel 531 3400
As old-fashioned as the name suggests, this sumptuous establishment enjoys royal patronage and sells top-end designer label clothing and accessories—as well as sportswear, golf accessories, household goods, bed linens, and luxurious towels and bathrobes.

If you want a relaxing pause, visit the café-restaurant.

Metz & Co. Leidsestraat 34–36, tel 520 7020
No longer quite the home of cutting-edge design that it once was, Metz & Co. continues to be the place where wealthy and fashion-conscious Amsterdammers go to shop for designer clothes and furnishings.

DESIGN & INTERIORS

Binnenhuis Huidenstraat 3–5, tel 638 2957
Binnenhuis (meaning "Interior") stocks beautiful furnishing fabrics, but the main reason for paying a visit is for the one-of-a-kind decorative accessories, from masks and African statuettes to sleek enamel bowls or flower vases that you are unlikely to see in any other home.

Capsicum Oude Hoogstraat 1, tel 623 1016
Dutch colonial history is encapsulated in this fabric shop, which not only sells Belgian linen and lace, but also takes you to the hot and colorful world of the tropics with its Indonesian ikats, its gorgeous natural silks from Thailand, and its Indian printed cottons.

Kasstoor Rozengracht 202–210, tel 521 8112
You've been to the museums and seen the revolutionary furniture designs of Le Corbusier, Gerrit Rietveld, and the de Stijl movement, so this is where you come to buy copies of their now-classic designs, or new work by the radical young furniture designers of today.

FASHION

Clubwear House Herengracht 265, tel 622 8766
Warehouse clubwear and tickets for events and parties all under one roof.

DKNY P.C. Hooftstraat 60, tel 671 0554
Smart and colorful Donna Karan

classics, from jeans to evening wear, for men, women, and kids.

Esprit Spui 10, tel 626 3624
Shop for youthful fashions at affordable prices in a fine Empire-style building, plus popular café with summer terrace.

Housewives on Fire Spuistraat 102, tel 422 1067
If you need party gear and want to look wild, come to this amusingly named clubwear shop selling new and secondhand clothes and accessories. Hair on Fire, the in-house salon, will fix your hair and makeup or pierce your body parts.

Hugo Boss P.C. Hooftstraat 49–51, tel 364 0412
Classic lines for men and women for business and casual wear from the German designer.

Lady Day Hartenstraat 9, tel 623 5820
Well-established shop selling very upscale vintage clothes and accessories—haute couture rather than off the rack.

Laura Dols Wolvenstrat 7, tel 624 9066
Ever set your heart on a Dior number but shrank at the cost? Your luck might be in at this boutique packed with vintage clothes with the emphasis on sparkly, lacy, and little black things from the cocktail party era.

Sissy Boy Kalverstraat 199–210, tel 638 9305
Homegrown label selling basics for both sexes, plus other lines such as French Connection.

Stilett Damstraat 14, tel 625 2854
T-shirt emporium with witty and arresting slogans; wear one and watch peoples' heads turn.

FLOWERS

Bloemenmarkt Singel.
The Bloemenmarkt (Flower Market) consists of some 15 stands operating from floating

pontoons moored in the Singel Canal between Koningsplein and Vijzelstraat. The florists here sell cut flowers, pot plants, bulbs, seeds, and garden plants (from flowering shrubs to clipped topiary). They are knowledgeable about export laws, so they will be able to advise you on suitable plants, bulbs, or flowers to take home, and will package them to withstand handling during the journey.

FOOD

Albert Heijn Various branches, including Nieuwezijds Voorburgwal 226, Vijzelstraat 113 and Jodenbreestraat 21 www.ah.nl
If you are self-catering in Amsterdam, looking for picnic food, or a cheap alternative to eating in a café or restaurant, this supermarket chain is worth getting to know. The Nieuwezijds Voorburgwal branch (behind the Royal Palace, on the opposite side of the road to the Magna Plaza shopping center), is fronted by a food court selling all sorts of takeout goodies, from seafood platters to barbecue ribs and sausages. The stores have a good range of deli-style foods, bread, fruit and veggies, plus juices, wines, beer, and mineral water—though you will have to go to a liquor store if you want to buy your drinks ready chilled.

Boerenmarkt Nordermarkt Amsterdam's farmers' market takes place every Monday in front of the Noorderkerk in the Jordaan and, like such markets everywhere, the standholders vigorously promote their quality home-produced organic food. You can sample their cheeses, honey, fruit juices, breads, olives, and oils before you buy, and many Amsterdammers would not dream of getting their fruit and veg anywhere else.

Chocolaterie Pompadour Huidenstraat 12, tel 623 9554 Transported from the streets of Paris to the canals of Amsterdam,

this popular pastry shop also sells exquisite hand-crafted chocolates, and the tiny tea room allows you to taste on the spot and then buy some for later.

De Kaaskamer (The Cheese Room) Runstraat 7, tel 623 3483 This specialist shop in the canal circle is the place to come for cheese. A good aged Gouda travels well, and is deliciously nutty—a different cheese from the flavorless slabs served up as standard breakfast fare in many hotels. The knowledgeable staff here will tell you anything you want to know about the 200 or so cheeses they have in stock, including which wines to drink with them.

Geels & Co. Warmoesstraat 67, tel 624 0683 Left over from the days when Warmoesstraat was the trading hub of Amsterdam, this splendidly old-fashioned tea and coffee shop now looks out of place amid the sex shops of the Red Light District, but once inside you step into the gentler world of tea and coffee conoisseurship. Come here for all sorts of accessories, and for the mini museum upstairs (open Tues., Fri. & Sat. afternoons) tracing the history of tea- and coffee-drinking in Amsterdam.

JEWELRY

Amsterdam has long been the undisputed center of the European diamond cutting and polishing industry since Jewish refugees fled to the city from Antwerp in the 16th century. Diamonds are no cheaper here than anywhere else, but there is a very wide choice, and the rival diamond companies compete to offer free factory tours that are informative and entertaining even if you do not intend to buy.

Coster Diamonds Paulus Potterstraat 2–8, tel 305 5555 Showrooms are conveniently sited at the back of the Rijksmuseum.

Gassan Diamonds Nieuwe Uilenbergertstraat 173–175, tel 622 5333 Huge factory premises in the former Jewish Quarter.

Van Moppes Diamonds Albert Cuypstraat 2–6, tel 676 1242; www.moppesdiamonds.com Discover the characteristics that make diamonds so valuable.

MARKETS

Albert Cuypstraat The biggest of them all (some claim it's the biggest in Europe, though there must be some serious rivals), Albert Cuypstraat market is a colorful and multi-ethnic feast for the senses, selling everything from food to sexy lingerie. The store is open daily except for Sunday.

Noordermarkt Every Monday bargain hunters flock to this makeshift market where traders sell their wares from blankets placed on the ground and shoppers sift through the assorted junk trying to think of a reason to buy. A must for market addicts, and an amusing insight into the Dutch love of browsing in the hope of finding the ultimate bargain.

Waterlooplein This permanent flea market (daily, except Sunday) has a long history, as revealed by the vintage photographs in the nearby Jewish Historical Museum. Now a popular tourist attraction, it has gone upscale and is a great place to shop for clothes, shoes, leatherwear, crafts, gifts, and CDs. As well as the open-air stands, there are various warehouse outlets selling new and vintage clothes and bric-a-brac. The clothes are often of the highest quality—just temporarily out of fashion.

MISCELLANEOUS

Condomerie het Gulden Vlies Warmoesstraat 141, tel 627 4174 Raising the display and packaging of condoms to an art form, this shop on the fringes of the Red Light District is a far-from-salacious outlet for prophylactics in every imaginable shape, size, color, and flavor, including novelty options.

De Knopenwinkel
Wolvenstraat 14, tel 624 0479
The humble button gets a shop to itself, and if you are looking to match a long-lost button—no matter how ornate, elaborate, or old, you are as likely to find it here as anywhere.

De Witte Tandenwinkel
Runstraat 5, tel 623 3443
This being Amsterdam it is no surprise to find a shop devoted entirely to matters dental—everything you need for keeping your teeth white and healthy, including unusual items that might just persuade children to brush their teeth, to strange inventions such as glow-in-the-dark toothbrushes.

Female & Partners Spuistraat
100, tel 620 9152
Let's face it, people do come to Amsterdam for its sex shops, and this is one shop where women can indulge their curiosity without feeling threatened by a male-dominated clientele. Expect the usual range of items—magazines, videos, vibrators, and sexy clothing—but presented with more style than is the norm for this kind of shop.

Forever Rozengracht 51, tel
423 3388
This shop sells all sorts of objects preserved for posterity in see-through acrylic, from watch workings and beetles with gorgeously colored wings to toilet seats and paperweights.

Holland Gallery de Munt
Munttoren, Muntplein 12, tel 623 2271
If Delftware is on your list, this shop in the historic Mint Tower is an attractive place in which to view affordable small objects

such as hand-painted tiles, jewelry boxes, and thimbles.

Jacob Hooij Kloveniersburgwal
12, tel 624 3041
Culinary herbs and spices, health foods, medicinal compounds, and homeopathic remedies are the stock-in-trade of this ancient pharmacist, but Amsterdammers know it best as the home of *dropjes*, the nation's favorite candy. They are made of licorice and come in all sorts of shapes (see p. 95). So popular are they (especially as a preventative against colds) that 165,000 pounds (75,000 kg) are consumed in the Netherlands every day.

Klompenboer (Wooden Shoe Factory) Sint
Antoniesbreestraat 39–51, tel 427 3862;
www.woodenshoefactory.nl
Well-made clogs are comfortable to wear and durable, so if you are looking for typical Dutch footwear (and yes, the Dutch really do wear clogs), it is better to buy from Bruno, this specialist shoemaker than from a gift shop selling mass-produced novelties. Museum on the premises.

PGC Hajenius Rokin 92–96,
tel 623 7494
Unreformed tobacco lovers should head for this old-fashioned shop selling a bewildering range of cigars, clay, wood, and stone pipes, and loose tobacco for hand rolling or pipe smoking. The club-like atmosphere is enhanced by the uniquely masculine odor.

World of Wonders KNSM-
Laan 293–299 129, tel 418 4067
Relocated to the trendy Oostelijke (eastern) islands (bus 32), this is worth a look for unusual gifts, from clocks and bags of beautifully polished stones to silk flowers and executive toys.

MUSIC

Concerto Utrechtsestraat
52–60, tel 624 5467

If you are still into vinyl, or want to find European tapes and CDs no longer available back home, you've a good chance of finding them here as anywhere. The stock includes classical and rock music, and both new and secondhand material.

Get Records Utrechtsestraat
105, tel 622 3441
And if you can't find it at Concerto, move on down the street a little and check out this store, which carries lots of alternative and small independent label recordings on CD.

Sound of the Fifties
Prinsengracht 669, tel 623 9745
Amsterdam has a big jazz- and blues-loving community, so it's no surprise to find a shop devoted to the music of the pre-pop era. New and original recordings on vinyl and CD are available here, and the secondhand records are in good condition but not cheap.

POSTERS & REPRODUCTIONS

Art Unlimited Keizersgracht
510, tel 624 8419;
www.artunlimited.nl
Posters, postcards, calendars, and T-shirts are the stock-in-trade of Art Unlimited: the huge and comprehensive choice includes reproductions from major international museums (sorted by artists and subject) and artists' photos to remind you of your visit to Amsterdam.

Van Gogh Museum Paulus
Potterstraat 7, tel 570 5200;
www.vangoghmuseum.nl
Nearly everyone who visits the Van Gogh Museum emerges clutching one of the museum's distinctive triangular poster boxes, as it has an excellent range of reproductions of works by the artist. Housed in the museum is a well-stocked bookshop covering major artists and art movements of the last 150 years.

ENTERTAINMENT & ACTIVITIES

You'll never be lost for something to do in Amsterdam. From the world-renowned Concertgebouw Orchestra and the mellow harmonies of the city's jazz clubs to the carnivalesque excesses of the gay clubs, there is something here for every age and taste. Keeping track of it all is not difficult. Posters all over the town tell you what's happening in the club scene (clubwear shops such as Clubwear House and Housewives on Fire (see p. 261), also serve as information networks and ticket agents). Mainstream cultural events are detailed in *Day by Day*, the listings magazine sold at tourist information centers and available free from many hotels. Tourist offices are also outlets for theater and concert tickets, though you have to call in person and line up (check out the Holland Tourist Information desk at Schiphol airport when you arrive; this can be quieter than city center tourist offices and provides the same ticketing services). Alternatively, visit the AUB Ticketshop at Leidseplein 26 (open 10–6 daily, to 9 p.m. on Thurs.).

ENTERTAINMENT

BALLET
National Ballet Muziektheater, Waterlooplein 22, tel: 551 8225 (information); 625 5455 (reservations); www.het-national-ballet.nl
The Netherlands National ballet company has a repertoire of 20 Balanchine-choreographed ballets, set to muisc by Stravinsky, Hindemith, and Bizet, among others, but it's not all contemporary ballet—you can also see glitzy crowd-pleasing versions of such classics as *Sleeping Beauty* and *The Nutcracker.*

CINEMA
Most movies are shown in their original language (usually American) unless the words *Nederlands gesproken* appear under the title which means that they are home-grown Dutch movies or dubbed.
  Advance reservation is advisable especially for first-run cinemas and on evening showings from Thursday through Sunday. The 0900 1458 telephone number used by most of the first-run cinemas is a premium-rate line offering a computerized ticketing system, but at present this is only in Dutch, so you will have to get help, or visit the cinema in person to reserve if you only speak English. Be aware that only art-house movie

theaters show movies without a "pause." Larger theaters stop the movie midway so clients can smoke or buy sodas.

The Movies Haarlemmerdijk 161, tel 624 5790; www.themovies.nl
This fine art deco cinema (opened in 1928), has retained its stylish fittings and is now used to show art-house movies that have made the breakthrough to commercial success. The cinema has its own highly regarded restaurant so you can eat out and see a show in one venue.

Nederlands Filmmuseum Vondelpark 3, tel 589 1400; www.nfm.nl
The Dutch national archive of film has 35,000 movies in its well-stocked library. Drawing on this cinematic wealth, it mounts a full program of screenings. In summer there are outdoor screenings on the terrace overlooking Vondelpark.

Pathé de Munt Vijzelstraat 15, tel 0900 1458 (reservations line) Comfortable new first-run multiplex with seven screens in the city center.

Tuschinski Theater Reguliersbreestraat 26–28, tel 623 1510
Six separate screens are housed within this glorious art deco

cinema complex, which opened in 1921 and is often used for movie premieres. You can share in the glamour by joining with friends to secure one of the eight-person boxes, then sit back and watch the movie while sipping champagne.

CLASSICAL MUSIC
Beurs van Berlage Damrak 213, tel 627 0466
The trading floors of Amsterdam's former commodities exchange have been converted into concert halls for the Netherlands Philharmonic Orchestra and the Netherlands Chamber Orchestra.

Concertgebouw Concertgebouwplien 2–6, tel 671 8345
The Concertgebouw is renowned for the quality of its acoustics, which are exploited to the full by Riccardo Chailly, the Milan-born conductor of the resident orchestra, the famous Royal Concertgebouw Orchestra. Hearing them perform the big works of Mahler or Strauss is an unforgettable experience, and tickets are understandably in great demand, so reserve well in advance.

Netherlands Ballet Orchestra Muziektheater, tel: 551 8823 (information); 625 5455 (reservations); www.balletorkest.nl
As well as accompanying performances of the National Ballet, the Netherlands Ballet Orchestra gives concerts in its own right, including free 30-minute-long chamber concerts at 12:30 p.m. every Tues.

MUSIC FESTIVALS
See Festivals & Events on p. 240

Amsterdam Blues Festival Meervaart, Meer en Vaart 300, tel: 410 7700 (information) 410 7777 (reservations); www.meervaart.nl
Two-day festival held in mid-March in west Amsterdam;

international cult legends and home-grown talent.

Amsterdam Roots Festival

Various venues throughout the city and at Oosterpark; ticket information on 0900 0191. One of Europe's best world music festivals, held over a week in mid-June. Check at VVV.

NIGHTLIFE

BIMHuis Oude Schans 73–77, tel 623 1361; www.bimhuis.nl Named after BIM, the Dutch Musician's Union, BIMHuis is known throughout the world as the home of the very best in jazz and improvised music. Some of the best gigs (Thurs. through Sun. nights) are reserved well in advance, but you could just turn up for the free sessions, held every Tues. from 10 p.m.

Escape Rembrandtplein 11, tel 622 1111; www.escape.nl Huge nightclub (capacity 2,000) with resident DJs and international guests.

iT Amstelstraat 24, tel 625 0111; www.it.nl If you want to know how to dress to get past the door staff at iT, just take your clues from the photos displayed in the showcases by the entrance. Those with bodies worth revealing wear next to nothing, while the rest dress in every imaginable style. Ibiza-style house music dominates. Saturday night is for gay men only; everyone is welcome (suitably dressed or undressed) on Thurs., Fri., and Sun.

Maloe Melo Lijnbaansgracht 160, tel 420 4592; www.maloemelo.nl Music café specializing in blues; also rock and country bands, and jam sessions Sun.. Mon., and Tues.

Mazzo Rozéngracht 114; tel 626 7500; www.mazzo.nl Small and friendly with a relaxed door policy, which means the club fills quite quickly once the doors open at 11 p.m. (closed Mon. and Tues.). Mazzo is known for progressive dance and techno.

Melkweg Lijnbaansgracht 234a, tel 531 8181; www.melkweg.nl Housed in the city's former dairy, Milkweg (Milky Way) stays true to its 1970s hippie origins by staging a very diverse program of events, from cutting-edge contemporary dance, video, and cinema and theater programs, to pop, reggae, dance, dub, and house. Women get the place to themselves one Sunday a month at the Planet Pussy event.

Odeon Singel 460, tel 624 9711 www.odeontheater.nl Open seven days a week. The place to go Mon.–Wed. when other clubs are shut, Odeon offers three styles—disco, house, and R&B—on three different floors, some with their original baroque ceiling decorations.

Paradiso Weteringschans 6–8, tel 626 4521; www.paradiso.nl Paradiso is a converted church offering an unusual and intimate space for live bands, disco, and DJ events.

OPERA

Netherlands Opera

Muziektheater, tel: 551 8922 (information); 625 5455 (reservations); www.dno.nl The Dutch national opera company performs classics and new works in the modern setting of the Muziektheater. Tickets go on sale a month before the premiere.

THEATER

Boom Chicago Leidseplein Theater, Leidseplein 12, tel 423 0202; www.boomchicago.nl Founded in 1993, this English-language comedy theater is certain to have you in fits. Shows are nightly, with two on Fri. and Sat., and the choice includes regular tickets or combined dinner and show.

Comedy Café Max Euweplein 43–45, tel 638 3971; www.comedycafé.nl Stand-up comedy in English and Dutch. Free on Wed. evenings when new acts and new material make for an unpredictable mix; improvisation on Sun. and established acts Thurs.–Sat.

ACTIVE SPORTS

HEALTH CLUB

The Garden, at Jodenbreestraat 158 (tel 626 8772) is an inexpensive and central health club specializing in aerobics and step classes.

INLINE SKATING

The big event of the week is known as FNS—the Friday Night Skate. Up to 2,000 skaters meet for an 8 p.m. start in front of the Filmmuseum in Vondelpark and stewards control the crowd to prevent accidents during the three-hour, high-speed roll around the city. Rent-a-Skate at Vondelpark 7, at the Amstelweenseweg entrance to the park (tel 06 5466 2262) can supply the necessary wheels.

SOCCER

The Dutch team that every sports fan has heard of is Ajax, from Amsterdam. The chances of getting tickets to a game (tel 311 1144) are minimal because anti-hooliganism measures restrict sales to holders of official Supporters Club membership cards. You can visit the World of Ajax Museum (Arena Stadium, Arena Boulevard 3, tel 311 1469; metro station: Bijlmer) and wallow in the nostalgia of 25 years of the club's rise to the top of European football.

SWIMMING

The Marnixbad 25-m indoor pool (Marnixplein 9, tel 625 4843) is the best for serious swimmers. Mirandabad (De Mirandalaan 9, tel: 622 8080; www.mirandabad.nl) has the full tropical works: pebble beach, wave machine, water slides, whirlpool, and restaurant.

ILLUSTRATIONS CREDITS

Cover (tl), Max Jourdan/AA Photo Library. (tr), ImageState. (bl), Powerstock/Zefa Ltd. (br), Max Jourdan/AA Photo Library. (Spine), ImageState.
1, Nicholas Devore III/Network Aspen. 2/3, David Johns/Powerstock Zefa Ltd. 4, Photononstop. 9, Rijksmuseum, Amsterdam/AKG - London. 11, Robert Harding Picture Library. 12/13, Stuart Black/Travel Library. 14/15, Barry Lewis/National Geographic Society. 16/17, BenU International Picture Service. 18, Jon Lister/Impact Photos. 20/21, Max Jourdan/AA Photo Library. 23, Stuart Black/Travel Library. 24, Mecky Fogeling. 25, Amsterdams Historisch Museum. 27, W. van de Velde de Yonge/Nederlands Scheepvaart Museum. 28/29, Jan Abrahamsz Beerstraten/Amsterdams Historisch Museum. 30, Barry Lewis/National Geographic Society. 31, A. Woolfitt/Robert Harding Picture Library. 32/33, Max Jourdan/AA Photo Library. 35, Koninklijk Paleis. 36/37, Inge Yspeert/National Geographic Society. 38l, Wolfgang Kaehler Photography. 38r, Wolfgang Kaehler Photography. 39l, Mecky Fogeling. 39r, Jamie Carstairs. 40l, Stuart Black/Travel Library. 40r, Rijksmuseum, Amsterdam/AKG - London. 41l, Rijksmuseum Amsterdam. 41r, Rijksmuseum Amsterdam. 42/43, Max Jourdan/AA Photo Library. 44, Jamie Carstairs. 45, Sergio Pitamitz Temp/Powerstock Zefa Ltd. 46, Jamie Carstairs. 47t, Jamie Carstairs. 47b, A. Gin/Powerstock Zefa Ltd. 48/49, Brad Walker/Powerstock Zefa Ltd. 49r, Robert Fried Photography . 50/51, Nicholas Devore III/Network Aspen. 52/53, Jamie Carstairs. 53r, BenU International Picture Service. 54/55, Stuart Black/Travel Library. 55r, Michael Short/Robert Harding Picture Library. 56/57, Jamie Carstairs. 57b, Mecky Fogeling. 58, Ken Paterson/AA Photo Library. 59, Elk Photo. 60, Max Jourdan/AA Photo Library. 61, Richard Glover/Travel Library. 62, Robert Harding Picture Library. 63, Mecky Fogeling. 64, Barry Lewis/National Geographic Society. 66, Amsterdams Historisch Museum. 67t, Ken Paterson/AA Photo Library. 67b, L. Schimmelpennick/Amsterdams Historisch Museum. 68, A. Woolfitt/Robert Harding Picture Library. 69t, Robert Harding Picture Library. 69b, John Lawrence/Travel Library. 70, Jamie Carstairs. 71, Ken Paterson/AA Photo Library. 72, Stuart Black/Travel Library. 73, Elk Photo. 74, Jenny Acheson/Axiom. 75, Eddy Posthuma de Boer. 76/77, Eddy Posthuma de Boer. 77r, Eddy Posthuma de Boer. 78/79, Allard

Pierson Museum. 79b, BenU International Picture Service. 80, Stuart Black/Travel Library. 81, Clive Sawyer/Pictures Colour Library. 82, Elk Photo. 83, Ken Paterson/AA Photo Library. 84, Stuart Black/Travel Library. 85t, BenU International Picture Service. 85b, Wolfgang Kaehler Photography. 86l, Ken Paterson/AA Photo Library. 86/87, Jamie Carstairs. 88, Jamie Carstairs. 89t, Ken Paterson/AA Photo Library. 89b, Ken Paterson/AA Photo Library. 90/91, BenU International Picture Service. 92/93, Max Jourdan/AA Photo Library. 93r, Paul Murphy. 94, Paul Murphy. 95t, Alex Kouprianoff/AA Photo Library. 95b, Paul Murphy. 96, Max Jourdan/AA Photo Library. 97, Ken Paterson/AA Photo Library. 98, Robert Harding Picture Library. 99, Max Jourdan/AA Photo Library. 100, BenU International Picture Service. 102, Robert Fried Photography . 103, Museum Het Rembrandthuis. 104, Rijksmuseum Amsterdam. 105t, Rijksmuseum, Amsterdam, The Netherlands/Bridgeman Art Library. 105b, Mauritshuis, The Hague, The Netherlands/Bridgeman Art Library. 106, Max Jourdan/AA Photo Library. 107, Ken Paterson/AA Photo Library. 108, BenU International Picture Service. 109, BenU International Picture Service. 110, Alex Kouprianoff/AA Photo Library. 111, Jamie Carstairs. 112, BenU International Picture Service. 113, Max Jourdan/AA Photo Library. 114, Eddy Posthuma de Boer. 115, Charles Breijer/The Netherlands Photo Archives. 116, Max Jourdan/AA Photo Library. 117, Alex Kouprianoff/AA Photo Library. 118, Stuart Black/Travel Library. 119, Ken Paterson/AA Photo Library. 120t, Ken Paterson/AA Photo Library. 120b, Paul Murphy. 121, Robert Harding Picture Library. 122/123, Max Jourdan/AA Photo Library. 123r, Jamie Carstairs. 125, Max Jourdan/AA Photo Library. 126, Max Jourdan/AA Photo Library. 127, Alex Kouprianoff/AA Photo Library. 128, Ken Paterson/AA Photo Library. 129, Jamie Carstairs. 130, Ronald Badkin/Travel Ink. 131, Eddy Posthuma de Boer. 132/133, ImageState. 133r, Jamie Carstairs. 134, Paul Murphy. 135t, Alex Kouprianoff/AA Photo Library. 135b, Jamie Carstairs. 137, Jamie Carstairs. 138, Alex Kouprianoff/AA Photo Library. 140/141, BenU International Picture Service. 142l, Mecky Fogeling. 142r, Max Jourdan/AA Photo Library. 143, Max Jourdan/AA Photo Library. 144, Jamie Carstairs. 145, Stuart Black/Travel Library. 146, AKG - London. 148/149, Jamie Carstairs. 151, Ken Paterson/AA Photo Library. 152/153, Ken Paterson/AA Photo Library. 154/155, Jamie Carstairs.

156, Simon Harris/Robert Harding Picture Library. 157, T. Bognar/Trip & Art Directors Photo Library. 159, Ken Paterson/AA Photo Library. 160, Mecky Fogeling. 161, BenU International Picture Service. 162/163, Ellen Rooney/Axiom. 163r, Robert Harding Picture Library. 164, BenU International Picture Service. 165, Jamie Carstairs. 167, Jamie Carstairs. 168, George Wright/Axiom. 169t, Jamie Carstairs. 169b, Nigel Hicks. 170/171, ImageState. 171b, Robert Fried Photography . 172, Stuart Black/Travel Library. 173, BenU International Picture Service. 175, Caroline Penn/Impact Photos. 176/177, R Powers/Trip & Art Directors Photo Library. 177r, Lee Foster. 178, BenU International Picture Service. 179, BenU International Picture Service. 180, BenU International Picture Service. 181, Eddy Posthuma de Boer. 182/183, Robert Harding Picture Library. 183t, Max Jourdan/AA Photo Library. 184/185, Max Jourdan/AA Photo Library. 185b, Max Jourdan/AA Photo Library. 186, Max Jourdan/AA Photo Library. 188, Eric Smith/Trip & Art Directors Photo Library. 189, Rijksmuseum, Amsterdam/Bridgeman Art Library. 191, Barry Lewis/National Geographic Society. 192, Rijksmuseum, Amsterdam/AKG - London. 195t, Rijksmuseum, Amsterdam/AKG - London. 195b, Rijksmuseum Amsterdam. 196, Rijksmuseum, Amsterdam/Bridgeman Art Library. 197, Stuart Franklin/Magnum Photos. 198/199, Sergio Pitamitz Temp/Powerstock Zefa Ltd. 200, Amsterdam, Van Gogh Museum (Vincent van Gogh Foundation). 201, Rijksmuseum Vincent Van Gogh, Amsterdam, The Netherlands./Bridgeman Art Library, London. 202, Courtauld Gallery, London/Bridgeman Art Library, London. 203t, Amsterdam, Van Gogh Museum (Vincent van Gogh Foundation). 203c, Rijksmuseum Vincent Van Gogh, Amsterdam/Bridgeman Art Library, London. 203b, Amsterdam, Van Gogh Museum (Vincent van Gogh Foundation). 204l, © DACS 2001: Stedelijk Museum, Amsterdam, The Netherlands. /Bridgeman Art Library, London. 204r, Ken Paterson/AA Photo Library. 205, Stedelijk Museum, Amsterdam, Netherlands/Bridgeman Art Library, London. 206, Paul Quale/Axiom. 208, Alex Kouprianoff/AA Photo Library. 209, Barry Lewis/National Geographic Society. 211, Gavin Hellier/Robert Harding Picture Library. 212, BenU International Picture Service. 214tl, Blaine Harrington III. 214tr, BenU International Picture Service. 214b,

One of the world's largest nonprofit scientific and educational organizations, the National Geographic Society was founded in 1888 "for the increase and diffusion of geographic knowledge." Fulfilling this mission, the Society educates and inspires millions every day through its magazines, books, television programs, videos, maps and atlases, research grants, the National Geographic Bee, teacher workshops, and innovative classroom materials. The Society is supported through membership dues, charitable gifts, and income from the sale of its educational products. This support is vital to National Geographic's mission to increase global understanding and promote conservation of our planet through exploration, research, and education.

For more information, please call 1-800-NGS LINE (647-5463) or write to the following address:

National Geographic Society
1145 17th Street N.W.
Washington, D.C. 20036-4688
U.S.A.

Visit the Society's Web site at
www.nationalgeographic.com.

Published by the National Geographic Society

John M. Fahey, Jr., *President and Chief Executive Officer*
Gilbert M. Grosvenor, *Chairman of the Board*
Nina D. Hoffman, *Executive Vice President,*
            President, Books and School Publishing
Kevin Mulroy, *Vice President and Editor-in-Chief*
Elizabeth L. Newhouse, *Director of Travel Publishing*
Barbara A. Noe, *Senior Editor and Project Manager*
Allan Fallow, *Senior Editor*
Cinda Rose, *Art Director*
Carl Mehler, *Director of Maps*
Joseph F. Ochlak, *Map Coordinator*
Gary Colbert, *Production Director*
Richard S. Wain, *Production Project Manager*
Elizabeth Erskine, *Editorial Consultant*
Lawrence Porges, *Editorial Coordinator*

Edited and designed by AA Publishing (a trading name of Automobile Association Developments Limited, whose registered office is Millstream, Maidenhead Road, Windsor, Berkshire, England SL4 5GD Registered number: 1878835).

Virginia Langer, *Project Manager*
David Austin, *Senior Art Editor*
Hilary Weston, *Editor*
Keith Brook, *Senior Cartographic Editor*
Cartography by AA Cartographic Production
Richard Firth, *Production Director*
Picture Research by Zooid Pictures Ltd.
Liz Allen, *Picture Research Manager*
Area maps drawn by Chris Orr Associates, Southampton, England
Cutaway illustrations drawn by Maltings Partnership, Derby, England

ISSN 1538–5507

Printed and bound by R. R. Donnelley & Sons, Willard, Ohio.
Color separations by Leo Reprographic Ltd., Hong Kong.
Cover separations by L. C. Repro, Aldermaston, U.K.
Cover printed by Miken Inc., Cheektowaga, New York.

Visit the society's Web site at http://www.nationalgeographic.com

NATIONAL GEOGRAPHIC
TRAVELER

A Century of Travel Expertise in Every Guide